PAST. THEO.

W9-AEF-524

THE
DEATH-OF-GOD
MOVEMENT

CARMELITE MONASTERY
LIBRARY
SARANAC LAKE, N Y

A STUDY OF . . .
GABRIEL VAHANIAN • WILLIAM HAMILTON
PAUL VAN BUREN • THOMAS J. J. ALTIZER

THE
DEATH-OF-GOD
MOVEMENT

by

Charles N. Bent, S.J.

PAULIST PRESS

Westminster, Md.   New York, N. Y.   Glen Rock, N. J.

Amsterdam   Toronto

Imprimi Potest:
John V. O'Connor, S.J.

*Provincial, New England
Prov.*

February 4, 1967

Nihil Obstat:
Philip J. Donnelly, S.J.

Diocesan Censor Deputatus

Imprimatur:
✠ Richard Cardinal Cushing

Archbishop of Boston

March 22, 1967

Copyright © 1967 by
The Missionary Society of
St. Paul the Apostle in
the State of New York

Library of Congress
Catalog Card Number: 67-23604

Cover Design: Emil Antonucci

Published by Paulist Press
Editorial Office: 304 W. 58th St., N. Y., N. Y. 10019
Business Office: Glen Rock, New Jersey 07452

Printed and bound in the
United States of America

ACKNOWLEDGMENTS

George Braziller, Inc.—*The Death of God* and *Wait Without Idols* by Gabriel Vahanian. Reprinted with permission of the publisher. © 1961 and 1964 by George Braziller, Inc.

The Macmillan Company: *The Secular Meaning of the Gospel* by Paul M. van Buren. Copyright © 1963 by Paul M. van Buren. Used with permission.

The Westminster Press: *The Gospel of Christian Atheism* by Thomas J. J. Altizer. Copyright © 1966, W. L. Jenkins. Used with permission.

The Centennial Review of Arts and Sciences: "Theology and the Death of God" (Spring, 1964) and "William Blake and the Role of Myth" (Fall, 1965) by Thomas J. J. Altizer. Reprinted with permission.

Christian Century Foundation: "Theology in the Context of Culture" by Paul M. van Buren, *The Christian Century* (April 7, 1965). Reprinted with permission.

Christianity and Crisis, Inc.: "American Theology, Radicalism and the Death of God" by William Hamilton, *Christianity and Crisis* (Dec. 13, 1965). Reprinted with permission.

The Christian Scholar: "The Death of God Theologies Today" (Spring, 1965) by William Hamilton. Reprinted with permission.

University of Chicago Press: "Banished from the Land of Unity" by William Hamilton, *The Journal of Religion* (Oct., 1959). Reprinted with permission.

Nation Associates, Inc.: "Dietrich Bonhoeffer" by William Hamilton, *The Nation* (April 19, 1965). Reprinted with permission.

Playboy: "The Death of God" (Aug., 1966) by William Hamilton. Copyright © 1966 by William Hamilton. Reprinted with permission.

Theology Today: "Thursday's Child" (Jan., 1964) and "The New Optimism" (Jan., 1966) by William Hamilton. "World and History" (Oct., 1965) by Thomas J. J. Altizer. Reprinted with permission.

CONTENTS

FOREWORD

The currently popular death-of-God motif is generally associated with four names: Gabriel Vahanian of Syracuse University, William Hamilton of Colgate-Rochester Divinity School, Paul van Buren of Temple University, and Thomas J. J. Altizer of Emory University in Atlanta. But it is very difficult to discover any systematic or chronological development of the so-called "death-of-God movement." This phrase, like the term "existentialism," actually covers a whole spectrum of different ideas and opinions. Moreover, commentators today do not universally agree which of these should properly be called "death-of-God theologians." Some commentators, for instance, would exclude Vahanian from such a grouping, while others would insist on excluding van Buren. Yet a consideration of the views of all four should provide us with a basic understanding of the main thrust of this new movement. Each man has his own point of reference, and each employs his own method in analyzing the contemporary situation. However, there are some similarities in the conclusions reached by each. Such similarities are all the more remarkable in the light of the divergence in approach.

This work is an attempt to present in an abbreviated form the central ideas of these four men. An effort has been made to paraphrase closely their original statements and to offer pertinent quotations when necessary. Thus many of the nuances and overtones of their thought should emerge with a minimal amount of distortion or misinterpretation. Although Vahanian is not a death-of-God advocate, he has been included in this study because he treats this subject at some length, and his ideas may shed some light on the topic. A treatment of the views of van Buren is also included, despite the fact that he has publicly disclaimed any connection with the movement.

Following the general approach of a cultural historian, *Gabriel Vahanian* concludes that man's present religio-cultural notion of God is dead. Man's concept of God today, he maintains, is culturally determined, and, within the context of contemporary Western culture, is idolatrous, irrelevant, and meaningless. God dies whenever the concept of God becomes an idol or a cultural accretion. The current cultural phenomenon of the death of God exists because the dominant thought-forms of Western culture are now characterized by a radical immanentism that is diametrically opposed to the Christian conception of a transcendent and sacramental dimension pervading human existence. Vahanian is primarily interested in uncovering the roots of the gradual transition from a Christian to a post-Christian era. He deeply regrets the death of God in the modern world, and he points out that modern man is now searching and groping for a new and more relevant conception of God. But man will not be successful until he reaches an understanding of God based upon the revelation of the transcendent God—an understanding of God which somehow reflects the biblical awareness that the reality of God is independent of the cultural framework within which it is grasped. Only a cultural revolution, Vahanian concludes, will make such an understanding possible.

William Hamilton has been referred to as a type of death-of-God Billy Graham, and he is probably the most readable of these four men. His primary concern is with ethical considerations within the context of radical, "religionless" Christianity. He has expressed and communicated his views through such varied media as college lectures, television programs, books, theological periodicals, and *Playboy* magazine. He prefers an unstructured, fragmentary approach to theology, with the example of Jesus as the only integrating factor. His main contention is that God is dead for modern man, in the sense that today's Christian can no longer believe or hope in the personal, transcendent, provident God of Judaeo-Christian tradition. The only virtue still available to the modern Christian is love. And so, during the time of the death of God, man is invited to follow Christ more closely than ever before. Man must learn to follow Christ's example of selfless love, freedom, and availability to others in time of need. Hamilton sees today's radical Christian as characterized by an optimistic attitude, reflecting man's confidence in his own ability to solve his problems without reference to God. The radical Christian also expects the darkness occasioned by the death of God to be soon dispelled. Then man will finally discover a new meaning of faith and hope.

Paul van Buren is convinced that modern man can no longer accept the idea of God as a personal, transcendent Being who is operative in the world of men. He therefore employs an empirically-grounded methodology provided by linguistic analysis as he tries to determine the secular or profane meaning of the Christian gospel. The empirical criteria of the present era, van Buren argues, compel one to reject both literal theism and all its qualified forms which try to talk about God in a roundabout way by using indirect, analogous, or oblique language. Van Buren does not use the term "death of God," and has publicly dissociated himself from the movement. Nevertheless, his ultimate conclusions seem to put him squarely in the death-of-God camp. He is primarily interested in finding an ethical, functional, and socially relevant form of contemporary Christianity acceptable to the immanentist-grounded and secular-oriented Christian of today. The precision of semantic analysis, he insists, should be brought to bear on all religious and theological statements so as to determine their meaning, if any. He contends that theological predication is valid and meaningful within a secular context, but that all references to a transcendent Being must be carefully excised.

Thomas J. J. Altizer is one of the leading proponents of Christian atheism. Drawing upon studies in comparative religion and Eastern and Western mysticism, he advocates a return to the forward-moving, eschatological thrust of original Christianity. Oriental mysticism, he says, attempts to reach the sacred by negating man's present consciousness and history. Religious or orthodox Christianity uses much the same method. But the unique hallmark of authentic Christianity is its dialectical assertion that the sacred is reached only through a strong affirmation of what is radically secular and profane. Thus, instead of searching for a primordial sacrality, man should look forward to new manifestations of the sacred in this world. Regarding the polar relation between the sacred and the profane, Altizer adopts a dialectical mode of thought. He argues that all previous forms of spirit must be negated so that new forms might appear. Through an irreversible dialectical process, the primordial, transcendent, oppressive, absolute, sovereign God has died in Jesus Christ; God has annihilated himself so that a new manifestation of Spirit may appear under a profane form. An acceptance of the death of God, Altizer claims, provides man's only entrance into the 20th century. The death of God should be welcomed by the Christian as a redemptive act freeing man from servile bondage to an oppressive deity. At the same time it provides an opening for the emergence of a new humanity. Having abandoned all nostalgic attachment to the transcendent, today's radical Christian resolutely follows a totally immanent and wholly incarnate Christ, a fully incarnate Word or Spirit operative in the world today. He expectantly awaits a new epiphany of Spirit in the world. Altizer's Christian atheism is based on an integration of the insights of Friedrich Nietzsche, G. W. F. Hegel, and William Blake. In his own synthesis of radical Christianity, Altizer follows Nietzsche in the death-of-God motif; he employs Hegelian dialectic to relate the sacred to the profane; he uses the mystical insights of Blake to determine the full significance of the death of God for man.

In the following chapters a fuller and more comprehensive treatment of the ideas of these men will be presented *via* a topical analysis. At the end of each chapter a brief evaluation of the ideas contained in that chapter will be offered. The work is primarily intended to be expository. It is designed to serve as an introduction to critical analysis of the death-of-God movement; in no sense does it pretend to be an exhaustive study of the movement. It is hoped that this study will help to dispel some of the confusion which has clouded the death-of-God controversy.

I
GABRIEL VAHANIAN

1. Introduction

Christianity was undeniably a major contributor to the evolutionary development of Western culture. The Christian spirit and the Christian understanding of man, world, and God were incorporated into the cultural aspirations and realizations of the West. So Christianity identified in some degree with both the achievements and failures of that culture. In fact, many features and aspects of modern Western culture would be unimaginable outside of their Christian matrix.

Many people today maintain that Western man has severed all allegiance to a Christian world view and has now entered a new cultural era, an era characterized by a radically immanentist world view. Modern man, they say, now lives in a post-Christian era. The present age is neither anti-Christian nor non-Christian; it is simply post-Christian.

Further, some claim that Christianity has effected its own self-invalidation. Our present culture is moving in a direction completely divergent from that of organized Christianity. The modern view of man, nature, and reality, currently dominant in the Western world, is diametrically opposed to the traditional Christian view. Yet, paradoxically, man's view of reality is itself a product of the Christian cultural heritage. The changed thought patterns and categories prevalent today originated in a Christian milieu. They are therefore to be included in the cultural legacy of Christianity. We find that a profound transformation has occurred within the Christian tradition. Views of man and the world that are radically immanentist, scientific, and secular have replaced outlooks that were transcendental, mythological, and sacral-sacramental. For modern, post-Christian man God is neither necessary nor unnecessary. He is irrelevant; he is dead.

The preceding observations furnish Gabriel Vahanian of Syracuse University with a starting point for his analysis of modern man's transition to a post-Christian culture. The death of God, he feels, highlights the fact that the hallmark of modern Western thought is absolute immanentism. Culture today is impervious to the transcendental dimensions of the Christian vision. In his book, *The Death of God,* Vahanian tries to discover historical antecedents of the gradual corrosion and self-invalidation of Christianity. He also tries to assess the future of Christianity in the post-Christian era.[1]

2. Modern Religiosity

One of the central themes in Vahanian's analysis of the roots of the present situation is the concept of religiosity, the shallow modern surrogate for authentic biblical belief. Today's religiosity, he says, is a diluted and distorted version of original biblical faith. Belief has become purely formal and innocuous. Faith has become an end in itself, and man has come to believe simply for the sake of believing. But idolatrous religiosity is not faith; it substitutes superstition for faith.

Modern religiosity is also an expression of sublimated loneliness. It reduces religion to "togetherness" and induces an inauthentic, counterfeit sense of community. Religiosity is synonymous with religious curiosity; it underlies today's lack of profound interest in religion. The so-called religious revival of the previous decade marks the transition from a Christian to a post-Christian era.

Man, says Vahanian, has a natural tendency toward some form of religiosity. Man's inclination toward religiosity seems to be unavoidable. Thus, the death of God in contemporary society is not something accidental. It is grounded and rooted in man's basic in-

[1] Gabriel Vahanian, *The Death of God* (New York: George Braziller, 1961).

clination toward idolatrous religiosity. The ersatz substitution of religiosity for authentic religious belief culminated in the modern cultural phenomenon of the death of God. Biblical faith is dead today because its view of God and man has become incomprehensible. The essence of Christianity is something very alien to modern man. And yet, paradoxically, Christianity was one of the regulative or normative forces which created, or at least greatly influenced, the tenor of modern thought. It is socially fashionable today to be religious, but there is no profound interest in religion. Man's present religiosity stems from a loss of faith in God.

Part of the present difficulty, says Vahanian, lies in this: When Christianity became institutionalized, it began to usurp areas of human existence which naturally belong to the cultural sphere. Organized Christianity gradually abrogated the reciprocal freedom which should always characterize the relationship between religion and culture. Thus it betrayed the true prophetic spirit. Such a spirit would not try to wed itself to world traditions or enslave them. It would simply make use of them, while recognizing and respecting their autonomy. Organized Christianity has transformed faith into a cultural pattern. Man's current problem, says Vahanian, is finding out how to integrate or correlate the truth of Christianity with the empirical truths men live by. Man cannot live by either one alone; he needs both.

The dissolution of Christianity, he adds, is caused partly by superannuated structures, but largely by the removal of doubt from faith. Faith today is too structured. It is too monolithic and doctrinaire. It entertains no doubt, yet it is only the unbeliever who can truly believe. Belief and unbelief, faith and doubt, are polar elements, and man must learn to recognize this. Hope and doubt are essential elements of true faith. Part of the present crisis of faith is attributable to the fact that faith is no longer contingent upon unbelief.

Modern man's self-understanding is completely divergent from the traditional Christian idea of man. Man's concept of God has become a cultural accessory. A real transformation of attitudes has taken place. Idolatrous and culturally determined concepts of God have replaced the biblical concept, and a technically-oriented and syncretistic form of religiosity has begun to succeed Christianity.

Religion today resembles magic and is becoming increasingly difficult to differentiate from superstition. Despite our advanced culture, says Vahanian, our religious feeling and language are less refined than the biblical expressions of religious belief. In fact, in many instances, modern man's attempts to objectify and demonstrate God do more harm to religious belief than Friedrich Nietzsche's impassioned affirmation that God is dead. Vahanian comments:

> We have domesticated God in such a way that, as *Waiting for Godot* seems to imply, he evaporates into a tragicomic, mythological atavism; or he has become so diminutive as not to be recognizable any longer.[2]

Modern man is presented with a technological or do-it-yourself religion in which the form of faith one adopts is of little account. At times religion becomes a civic or a social matter. It is mass-produced in standard forms—Protestant, Catholic, and Jewish. Moreover, a blanket of anonymity is descending upon religion. Religious belief becomes more nebulous and amorphous as all forms of religious belief become more and more syncretistic. This idolatrous syncretism is intensified by the mounting pressure to secure more congenial international relations. Recent decades have witnessed the loss of Christian hegemony in world affairs. Once considered the only religion, Christianity today is proposed by many as simply the "best."

3. The Dishabilitation of the Christian Tradition

The modern view of man, nature, and God is in direct opposition to the biblical conception of reality. An analysis of the development of American Protestantism can concretely and tangibly demonstrate the elimination of the biblical view. We have here a clear example of the substitution of an immanentist for a transcendentalist world view. Three levels of development within American Protestantism are particularly noticeable. These help

[2] *Ibid.*, p. 54.

delineate three stages in the transformation of religious belief—moving from a transcendental view of reality to a radically immanent view. There was the initial movement from the new Adam of faith to the Christic man of religiosity. Secondly, we find that millenarianism played a major role in this metamorphosis. Finally, the social gospel of Christianity contributed greatly to Christianity's acculturation.

As to the initial movement (from the new Adam of faith to the Christic man of religiosity), Vahanian points out that religion in America had the opportunity for a completely new beginning. Despite the fact that the pilgrim resembled biblical man in many ways and was therefore like the original Adam, his beginning in Christ made him a radically new Adam. The pilgrim began by repudiating past tradition to insure a more authentic allegiance to God. Gradually, however, this allegiance and fidelity came to be grounded in man himself and not in God. The result was a new myth of Adamic man. An absolutely new beginning was postulated; this was situated in man himself and not rooted in God. Confidence in progress and the natural goodness of man replaced biblical hope and faith. One of the dominant formative elements of this new myth was the insistence by literary men that America should separate herself from European traditions and rely on her own sources of inspiration and expression. Following this insistence, America isolated herself in literature, art, politics, and religion. In the final analysis, the severance from religious ties eventually brought about the formation of the new American Adamic myth. This new secularized Adam became the Christ-figure in the novel of the 20th century, and thus Adamic man was succeeded by Christic man. By arrogating to himself the attributes of Christ, man usurped Christ's redemptive role. The qualities of Christ were universalized and attributed to man, thus perverting the biblical conception of the new Adam.

The kingdom of God was always eschatological to Protestants. They understood the kingdom to be present here and now in an inchoative way, resolutely preventing any identification of God's kingdom with the secular accomplishments of man. But gradually the principles of cosmic evolution and radical immanentism caused God's sovereignty to be viewed as merely nominal or constitutional. Vahanian regards millenarianism, the utopian view of an earthly kingdom, as the great corruptor of the original Protestant conception of the kingdom of God. For the American pilgrim, God's sovereignty always stood in judgment over man's undertakings. Man's achievements were not viewed as God's progressive revelation, but as signs or symbols of God's real presence in man's world. But millenarianism institutionalized God's sovereignty and fostered an immanentist optimism which gradually perverted the notion of the kingdom of God. It culminated in a monistic, this-worldly sacramentarianism summed up by the secularized ideal of a divine kingdom on earth.

> Originally that sovereignty was experienced as a present reality underlying all human beings and their social as well as religious aspirations and obligations. In the second stage, God's sovereignty was, so to speak, sublimated, intellectualized, or even supernaturalized: the Kingdom of heaven was so construed that Christ himself took on the appearances of a judge who shall sift the elect from the reprobate. It needs to be said that this kind of dualism, which separates Christians from non-Christians, inevitably amounts to a fundamental admission that faith is losing its relevance to the present. The conversionist zeal which accompanies such radical otherworldliness is evidence enough that the transcendental hope which once was incarnate in earthly tasks and responsibilities (as it ought to be) has now evaporated into speculative visions of ethereal if celestial structures. When the third stage arrives, the immediacy of God's sovereignty here and now has already become a myth. At least it is no longer effectual. While the autonomy of the earlier communities and the freedom of man were predicated on the idea of God's direct governance, the dualistic remoteness of God's heaven now no longer guarantees any present purpose to man's destiny and to the communal dimension of his existence.[3]

For the American Puritan, man was a dependent creature, the ultimate cause of whose happiness lay outside himself. Man exercised dominion over the physical world, but he recognized God as creator both of himself and the physical universe. Man did not view himself as self-sufficient. An empirical faith in God's immediate

---

[3] *Ibid.*, pp. 25–26.

sovereignty characterized the relationship between man and God. With the advent of a radically immanent world view, however, all of this changed. Religion today, Vahanian says, is accommodated to the various exigencies of the social and economic situation of man. A mass-tailored religiosity has idolatrously replaced man's biblical faith in the sovereign presence of God in the world. The kingdom of God is no longer viewed as an eschatological reality.

There was a further aspect of the evolution of American Protestantism and the dishabilitation of the Christian tradition accompanying it. This was the emergence of the social gospel movement at the end of the 19th century. In America the social gospel took the form of theological adjustments to the liberal mind. Its boast was flexibility and the power to cope with all the problems that plagued previous generations, as well as its ability to meet new problems as they arose. The movement was supremely confident of its ability to adapt itself to change. Its proponents considered it the fourth major epoch of Christian history (after early Christianity, the Middle Ages, and the Reformation). The movement focused on the worth of the individual and the necessity of religious institutions to meet the needs of emerging situations. Josiah Strong, a leading proponent of the social gospel, tried to curb religious rugged-individualism, stressing communal participation and individual awareness of responsibility to the community. Only through organization, he felt, could Christianity adequately meet the challenge of the nascent century.

The social gospel of Christianity, Vahanian contends, entertained the self-satisfied delusion of trying to establish God's kingdom on earth. Fundamentally it was characterized by an unbounded confidence in science, a naive view of the relation between religion and culture, and a belief in the self-evident relevance of Christianity to the emerging social situation. The social gospel regarded culture as an improvement over man's natural state, and the proponents of the movement eagerly anticipated a steady amelioration of the human condition. Having jettisoned the realistic and radical utopianism of the Jewish prophets and the American Puritans, its adherents substituted an idealistic and speculative utopianism which dreamed of establishing God's kingdom on earth. In this process, self-realized goals were substituted for the idea of God as the actual beginning and end of man. A pragmatic concentration on calculable goals displaced faith in a transcendent God. A cultural and civic religiosity resulted. The emphasis was shifted from the conflict between man's capacity for justice and his unjust inclinations to an intense trust in his innate innocence and infinite potential for improvement.

Biblical radicalism and its realistic appraisal of the human condition gave way to secular humanism. Man's actions were no longer viewed as manifestations of his faith and trust in a transcendent, omnipotent, loving God. The intrinsic worth of human activity was emphasized, to the exclusion of any other value, an emphasis which ultimately led to idolatrous religiosity and the dishabilitation of religious faith.

Despite its characteristic individualism and anti-authoritarianism and its concern with sin and salvation, the American tradition is essentially secularistic. It has brought about the acculturation of Christianity, taking obvious pride in the immanent worth of its goods and civilization. The fundamentally activist nature of American Christianity and its basic congruence with the secular American tradition clearly indicate that Christianity has undergone a leveling process, a process which distinguishes our age from past ages as being post-Christian. In the course of time, there has been a radical shift from biblical authority and religious sanctions to scientific, factual authority and sanctions.

Therefore the present era is post-Christian for at least three reasons. First, organized Christianity has become synonymous with religiosity. Secondly, Christianity no longer impregnates the cultural ethos of modern man whose dominant world view is diametrically opposed to the biblical and Christian view of reality. Thirdly, Christianity has forfeited its international hegemony and is no longer universally respected. The world has witnessed the dishabilitation of the Christian tradition. Man has moved from a Christian to a post-Christian era, from a transcendental world view to a radically immanent world view, and from a religious to a secular world view.

4. Christianity, Secularity, and Secularism

Despite the many deplorable features of crude religiosity, the tendency toward it is symptomatic of an authentic and legitimate groping for ultimate meaning. It demonstrates that the meaning of human existence must be a part of the reality of this world. And conversely, the religious upsurge of the 1950's made it abundantly clear that the reality of the world is revealed in religious existence. In the final analysis, Vahanian concludes, faith for the Protestant is inseparable from secularity. This conviction regarding the value of true secularity is strengthened by reflection on the authentic biblical view of man in his relation with God. We find no sharp dichotomy in the Old Testament's description of man's responsibility to God and his simultaneous involvement with the world. Vahanian makes a clear distinction between the two areas of commitment, but encounters no radical split between the religious and the secular. The religious and the secular dimensions of human life complement one another. Man's responsibility to God and his involvement with the world around him are polar elements producing an equilibrium marked by creative tension. The only valid biblical distinction is between the holy and the not yet holy.

Secularity, therefore, refers to the sphere of man's involvement and activity in this world. Secularism, on the other hand, is a form of religiosity, an inverted religion, and an idolatrous deification of such secular values as sex, democracy, or the classless society. Modern religiosity, Vahanian says, is actually a combination of Christianity, secularity, and secularism, with secularism playing the predominant role. Secularism is religiosity in which the present and immanent dimensions of existence are invested with the attributes of the eternal and the transcendent. Religious faith, material success, and mental stability are often literally equated in modern religion.

By its very nature, Vahanian says, Protestantism demands secularity. Martin Luther's rejection of the doctrine of indulgences brought about an increased Protestant concern for the here and now, a renewed and valid interest in the present sphere of man's responsible activity in this world. Luther extended the traditional notion of "vocation" to cover the whole spectrum of human occupations and involvement with the world. He rejected the idea that the term should be applied solely to the religious or clerical state. John Calvin pushed the idea even further. For him, the Christian serves God not only in, but also through, his vocation in life.

Christianity has always viewed the world as an instrument of God's glory and insists on a real, qualitative difference between God and man. In this way it has continuously reflected biblical tradition. But today the relevance of Christianity is being questioned in all quarters. Present religious acceptance of the world and current attempts to cope with spiritual problems are shaped by a world view radically different from the Christian view. These new attitudes emanate from a quest for cosmic harmony which will terminate in *ataraxia* or tranquillity. Modern man's culturally determined world view is no longer grounded in the biblical view of the world as God's creation and the sphere of man's commitment to him, in spite of incoherence, evil, and adversity.

The religious revival of the last decade was really not religious in the proper sense of the term, says Vahanian, because it embodied neither faith nor commitment. It was simply another form of escapism. Vahanian feels that one justification for such a judgment was the non-denominational popularity of various leaders of the movement. The movement was essentially anonymous; it did not even try to insert itself into the Judaeo-Christian tradition. A second piece of evidence that the movement was not really religious is the fact that religiosity, not authentic religion, profited from the revival. At the present time, a climate of *religionem et circences* seems to have replaced the old Roman *panem et circences*. Christianity has been swallowed up by the very riches it produced. The root difference between religion and religiosity was clearly seen by Sören Kierkegaard. He prophetically recognized the existential problem of becoming a Christian in an age permeated by the spirit of religiosity. He saw clearly that the problem of becoming a Christian was not a question of adopting one particular set of beliefs or one philosophical system instead of another, but rather of entering into a singular mode of being in relation to God and to one's fellowmen—as well as to oneself. Religious existence is theonomous existence. In large measure, being a Christian depends upon one's conception of God. This brings us to the third piece of evidence that the religious revival of the 1950's was not truly religious. Various conceptions of God commonly accepted by many modern Christians frequently lead to a devaluation of God.

Some of these concepts are plainly weird. God is referred to as a "Co-pilot" or a "Porter." Sometimes he is conceived of as a Cosmic Pal. But all the time he is the nicest fellow one can ever dream of meeting. All those concepts have a common denominator: they all are anthropomorphic and they all originate in the inflationary imagination of sentimentalism. But whatever the theological or philosophical connotations may be, this anthropomorphism means that men worship the God they deserve. Men create God in their image. Their concepts of God represent but a hypertrophy of their self-understanding, and sometimes a pharisaic or moralistic sanction of their aspirations. Man's understanding of the deity is dependent on his highest values, and these are often created by his environment. God becomes no more than the ideal man.[4]

It might be asked why this new "God-talk," which is nothing more than an amalgam of man's self-understanding and aspirations, is more objectionable than concrete and crudely anthropomorphic conceptions of God found in the Old Testament. The ultimate and root difference, says Vahanian, lies in the understanding which supports and accompanies these conceptions. The biblical and the modern understanding of God are poles apart. The anthropocentrism of the modern view leads man to conceive of the deity as a global hypothesis, a link in man's unsuccessful attempt to grasp the meaning of himself and his world. Such an understanding is diametrically opposed to the original theocentrism of biblical writing, according to which the reality of God is completely independent of the cultural frame in which it is grasped.

5. Religion and Culture

A pressing question which must be honestly asked at the present time is: Can Christianity be relevantly correlated with modern secularity? It might likewise be asked whether modern secularity

[4] *Ibid.*, p. 75.

allows such a correlation. Vahanian says that today's Christianity is increasingly anxious to demonstrate its contemporaneity with the modern world. Contemporary theology, whether it is labeled neo-Thomism or neo-Protestantism, reveals an undeniable concern for a theology of immanence to deal with the affairs of the modern world. Christianity seems anxious to be a part of the modern world and to share its future destiny. But, he asks, is not this very need for contemporaneity an indication of obsolescence?

Religion and culture are not to be confused with one another. But it is equally erroneous to radically separate them. Any sharp cleavage between religion and culture or any dualistic approach to the problem of their relation injures the dynamism and relevance of Christian tradition. Yet this is the precise approach chosen by many contemporary Christian thinkers who contend that the real Christian era is just about to begin. These men argue that we are witnessing the dawn, not the twilight, of Christianity. They are confident that Christianity will be able to completely inform the future cultural development of Western man once it is fully adopted. Vahanian says that Jacques Maritain, in *True Humanism,* contends that an authentic humanism—i.e., one which recognizes both the existence of an absolute superior to the order of the universe itself, and also the supratemporal value of the soul—is needed to replace the false anthropocentric humanism of the present era. Maritain is not suggesting a return to medieval Christendom; rather, he is advocating the adoption of a new pluralistic form of Christianity.

But Vahanian is convinced that the religious and cultural pluralism which Maritain proposes is essentially based on a concealed dualism, despite Maritain's firm opposition to any kind of dualism and to any sharp dichotomy between religion and culture. He points out that the pluralism proposed by Maritain is a pluralism held together by the minimum ideal: Whoever is not against you is with you. Maritain wants to move away from the medieval conception of the relation between religion and culture. Therefore, he proposes his own pluralistic approach by advocating a practical concern for common action, regardless of the ideological goal involved, provided that this concrete action does not contradict the principle of an Absolute above and beyond man. The future of

Western civilization, he maintains, rests on man's choice between the current anthropocentric humanism which is so prevalent and a true theocentric humanism. Only a Christian brand of humanism can usher in a new age of Christian culture, an age which would have at least three distinguishing features. First, it would involve a redefinition of the concept of man, a conception grounded in the rehabilitation of the idea that man is a creature of God. Secondly, this age would be based on a reassessment of culture and society which would result in a transfiguration of the temporal order. Thirdly, this new cultural age would recognize the obligation to tolerate heresies, that is, to respect conflicting ideals, as long as these different ideals do not prohibit community of action. This new age, Maritain insists, must be founded upon the distinction between the spiritual and the temporal orders, between religion and culture. But in Vahanian's estimation, such a view conceals a re-admission of the classical error of positing dualistic principles as operative in the world—setting up a dualism between heaven and earth, body and soul, and so forth. Vahanian argues that for Maritain culture is merely concerned with terrestrial matters while religion's goals are super-terrestrial. Vahanian sees this kind of differentiation as essential to Maritain's understanding of Christianity. The intrinsic weakness in the Christianity Maritain presents is that it attempts to leaven the evolving spirit of the contemporary world, yet thwarts or belittles the intrinsic worth and needs of that spirit.

To underline the weakness he sees in Maritain's system, Vahanian turns to Maritain's ideas about art and morality. He points out that Maritain employs the familiar Aristotelian and Scholastic distinction between the speculative and practical orders in trying to convey his ideas on morality and art. In *Art and Scholasticism,* says Vahanian, Maritain restates two exercises of the practical reason: doing and making. On one level, the practical reason influences man's ethics, his politics and his moral actions. On another level, the practical reason operates in the realm of "poetics," i.e., in the area of the arts and creative action. Maritain then introduces a further distinction. He maintains that the aim or goal of morality is the perfection of the person, while the end of artistic creation is the perfection of the thing made. For Maritain, art and morality constitute two autonomous worlds. In another work, *The Responsibility of the Artist,* Maritain studies the relation between the two in greater depth. He analyzes the relation between artistic creativity and ethical action under two headings: the individual's moral responsibility, on the one hand, and the perfection of the artistic work in relation to the artist's personal perfection, on the other. While he maintains the respective autonomy of both art and morality and denies any direct subordination of one to the other, Maritain believes that art may be indirectly and extrinsically subordinated to morality. In other words, the two spheres are independent but concentric. Vahanian concludes that for Maritain morality fundamentally means charity, and that perfection signifies the point at which any being reaches its end. Ultimate perfection, in Maritain's system, lies in some type of union with God, and such a union can be achieved only through charity. But Vahanian objects to such a view on the grounds that love or charity is defined by Maritain in terms of a super-terrestrial reality, thereby depriving the earthly object of this charity of any intrinsic worth. Furthermore, to stress this otherworldly dimension is inopportune, especially when Christianity is seeking contemporaneity with the modern world. In addition, the subordination of art to morality, however indirect or extrinsic, still remains and is emphasized.

In the final analysis, therefore, Maritain has failed to present a viable form of Christianity for modern man. His basic mistake, Vahanian says, is not that he believes in a transcendent God, but that he does not dissociate this belief sufficiently from 13th-century supernaturalism. By asserting that the Transcendent Absolute manifests itself only in such immanence as is found within the Christian Church, he depreciates the intrinsic worth of all other areas of the temporal community. His religious philosophy of culture and his theory of aesthetics reassert the old depreciation of life on earth. One also discovers an underlying disparagement of the intrinsic worth of man's secular activities.

Vahanian suggests that the central problem facing today's world is the urgent question: What does it mean to be a man? Christianity, in his opinion, has tended to disregard this problem in favor of a supernatural concern, a concern which is essentially deleterious to human existence here on earth. Man's battle today is within himself; it is not waged in the spaces between heaven and hell. Maritain is guilty of completely glossing over the phenomenon of the death of God in this post-Christian era. Maritain's Absolute is not the God of Abraham, Isaac, Jacob, or Jesus Christ. His Absolute is extremely vague and nebulous and reminiscent of the God of the philosophers. He substitutes the concept of an Absolute for the concept of God and, in the final analysis, his conception of God does not differ essentially from William James' definition of God as the ideal of everything. In the end, Albert Camus is more honest than Maritain because he did not hesitate to draw out all the consequences of the death of God. He was willing to face the absurdity of human existence, even to the point of despair, until a new hope or a new ethic should become manifest. Maritain's Absolute is no more than an apparition.

Maritain wants a humanism that is profane, but not one that is anthropocentric. His humanism is not based on man's finitude and limitations, but on the renunciation of this life as not good enough. The culture proposed by Maritain does not relate to man in his present condition. Actually, his humanism is a form of anti-humanism or counter-humanism, for his dualism leads him to adopt an otherworldly conception of religion.

> Maritain's philosophy of religion and culture reveals the presence of an ineluctable dualism at its very base. This dualism permits Maritain to separate religion from the cultural framework and institutions of society; at the same time it permits him to fill the gap thus created with the insertion of an absolute principle in terms of which both man and society are explained transcendentally. The result of this dualism is an otherworldly conception of religion.[5]

It is foolish, Vahanian adds, to hope for a new Christian culture once Christianity has forsaken the temporal structures of this world. If any truth is to come from religion today, it must deal with the concrete present and man's immediately evident this-worldly condition. In other words, the primacy of the spiritual must be realized in this world.

[5] *Ibid.*, p. 102.

In a work entitled *Sort de l'homme,* Maritain makes a distinction between what he calls the political significance of religion and the evangelical significance of religion. He believes that its evangelical significance will eventually prevail and inform the structures of modern society, while still remaining distinct from them. But all available evidence, Vahanian says, militates against such a hope, and an extension of his own arguments negates his expectation that Christianity will play a dominant role in the shaping of man's future cultural development. Thus contemporary man must look elsewhere for a solution to his present dilemma.

6. Present Culture

While the Christian believes that God is, and therefore that all is grace, modern man believes that all is grace because God is dead. He firmly believes that there is an immanent grace in the world around him which provides a meaning for human life. He is firmly convinced that the ultimate meaning of human life is derivative from an immanent principle of grace. Vahanian observes:

> Modern man is the legatee of the Christian as well as of the atheist. He agrees with the Christian that all is grace. He agrees also with the atheist that God is dead. His argument is: All is grace; therefore God is dead. For if life is meaningless, then there must be no God. But, if it is meaningful—and it must be, or else it contradicts itself—it is meaningful by virtue of some kind of *immanent* grace; therefore God does not exist. If all is grace, then God is dead. Or: All is grace because God is dead.[6]

If Christianity hopes to survive, says Vahanian, it cannot oppose life itself. It must confront the world in its full actuality. Past history indicates that Christianity has brought about its own self-invalidation. Saint Paul's emphasis on the imminence of the *parousia* implied the abandoning of concern about life in this world. Later on, the medieval synthesis defined grace as the perfecting of nature which did not destroy or abolish nature. At the

---

[6] *Ibid.,* pp. 106–107. Italics in original.

same time it led to the subordination of nature to grace and the creation of a calibrated scale of values between them. In such a framework, grace is everything, but everything is not grace.

The writings of some contemporary novelists reflect the attempt on the part of many today to say that everything is grace. And if everything is grace, then the traditional Christian subordination of nature to grace is no longer viable. What these novelists are trying to do is to describe Christianity's alienation from itself. Vahanian sees Georges Bernanos, for example, as saying that religion itself is responsible for the decay and corruption within Christianity. In Bernanos' novel, *The Diary of a Country Priest,* we find the protagonist, the country priest, fighting Christianity itself rather than moral corruption or the decay of society. His sins and his failures are not only personal but they also symbolically describe the inner paralysis of the Christian faith. For Bernanos, today's struggle is not external, a conflict between Christianity and the world, but a contest which is internal and taking place within Christianity itself. He believes that it was the clergy itself which secularized Christianity, not secularism. The sophisticated priest, full of empty formulas, has alienated Christianity from Western culture. Bernanos' priest rejects the sterile and vacuous forms of Christianity around him, and gradually begins to discover that all is grace. For Bernanos, the most devastating critique of Christianity is to assert that all is grace. In the end, only one exit remains for those who realize the present agony of Christianity: they must honestly admit that Christianity has ceased to inform life, and that it does not seem likely to do so in the future. Bernanos' priest and modern man are searching for a more human and richer conception of existence. In Bernanos, God's absence from the world is evident, and Christianity is responsible for that absence. Thus, if one wants to believe in God, or wants to save Western culture from decay and disintegration, he must rebel against Christianity.

Vahanian finds a similar portrait of the inadequacy of Christianity today in Graham Greene's novel, *The Power and the Glory.* In addition to fighting a pagan or an anti-Christian society, Greene's priest is also concerned about the lack of resources within Christianity itself. His addiction to alcohol and his fathering of an illegitimate child are symbolic external manifestations of the inability of Christianity to provide the inner dynamism required for life in this world. The faith which the priest represents is on the verge of extinction because it has become wholly inadequate to meet contemporary demands. In the end, Greene's priest also discovers that all is grace after he ceases to wear the clerical garb.

In both of these novels, the priest is more prophetic than sacerdotal, more anti-clerical than clerical. Neither is conscious any longer of being a representative of the Church. What Bernanos and Greene are actually saying, Vahanian concludes, is that authentic existence no longer depends upon one's allegiance to Christianity. Today, Western culture is desperately trying to find itself after shaking off the crippling shackles of a superannuated Christianity.

Other forms of literature also treat of this theme, the irrelevance of Christianity at the present time. Samuel Beckett's *Waiting for Godot,* for example, presents us with a play constructed around the idea of the irrelevance of Christian concepts. It seriously questions the value of Christian existence, an existence based upon the belief that there is a God who takes an interest in man and is concerned enough to enter the world of men. In the play, God never quite manifests himself to the two characters, Gogo and Didi, who are waiting for his entrance into this world. Beckett's use of the diminutive form "Godot," with all of the accompanying nuances and connotations, is symbolic of man's vacuous and errant imagination. Christians, he says, have made their God into a Godot, a miniature caricature of God, and their conception of the deity contains all of the attributes of an idol. Man foolishly clings to this image in his mind as though he could not live without it, when, of course, he actually can. For many Christians, God has become nothing more than an emotional outlet. Beckett employs the model of Christianity in order to show how anachronistic Christianity has become. Christians do not behave better in relation to their God than do Gogo and Didi in relation to their Godot. In the end, Vahanian concludes that Beckett does not believe in God, and even less in Godot. Godot lives only in the imagination of man. Man, therefore, has everything to gain by severing his atavistic attachment to such a pseudo-god or surrogate deity. The humanism advocated by Beckett resembles very closely that of Camus.

It is likewise helpful, Vahanian suggests, to consider the ideas of Archibald MacLeish on this topic, as expressed in *J.B.*, where he seems to be saying that Godot is all there is of God. Reflecting a Sartrean humanism, MacLeish declares that if God existed, man could not bear *not* to be that God. While Beckett is content to psychologize God away, MacLeish deifies man. Vahanian writes:

> The distance between Biblical man and post-Christian man can be shown by comparing Job and J.B. Job's predicament is that, though he believes in God, he acts at times as if he doubted. But he cannot be convinced by his doubt. At the end, his tragedy comes to the point: Without God, man would be nothing. J.B.'s predicament is that he does not believe in God, but he acts as if he does or wishes he did. At the end of his tragic life he clearly states that without man there would be no God.[7]

One of the hallmarks of the wisdom literature of the East, of which the Book of Job is an example, is its existential concern about man and his destiny. For biblical man, human existence was authenticated by the antinomy between wisdom and folly. In this literature, wisdom is viewed as a concomitant of piety and grace, and grace is understood as another form of justice. Moreover, human wisdom is considered to be a reflection of divine wisdom. There is a strict correlation between God's wisdom and man's wisdom, between God's justice and man's justice. Thus, for biblical man, God's justice is revealed in the wisdom and piety of man, the graceful life. But divine justice is not simply viewed as the sum total of human justice, nor is divine wisdom considered to be the sum total of human wisdom. Further, human experience belies the fundamental correlation between God's justice and man's justice. In this world the just man suffers. Why? In the eyes of biblical man, God's justice is something more than retributive justice. The sufferings of the just in this world lead to a tragic view of life. But man's justice and injustice, wisdom and folly, invariably point to the *otherness* of God despite—or precisely because of—the underlying correlation between man's justice and God's justice. God, therefore, remains wholly other even when grasped by faith. It follows that the existence of God cannot be deduced from the

[7] *Ibid.*, p. 123.

amount of justice in the world, nor can it be denied because of the evil and suffering in the world. For biblical man, Vahanian says, the tragic element of life consists in this: Suffering (and human experience as a whole) separates man from *himself*. In theological terms, the presence of God is a mystery or an abyss, and human experience appears as the possibility of man's self-alienation. But beyond this threat of self-alienation lies the affirmation of God's faithfulness to man. In biblical terms, therefore, faith is the response of the wise man's vision that all is grace; such faith cannot be justified by any theory of reward and punishment, or by any reasons, good or bad, because it is grounded in a different kind of logic, a logic based on human experience.

For J.B., "God is *reasons*"; he is something useful, and he represents just about all of the good things that J.B. is. But in the end J.B. is faced with a dilemma: Since man's innocence and the existence of God are mutually exclusive, then God, if he is God, is not "good," and if he is "good," he is not God. Man's life in this world is not something of his own choosing. In the last analysis, man is the lonely and innocent proprietor of his own "dirty self."

At first, the thesis of *J.B.* seems to support the proposition that the meaning of existence is to justify God. In other words, man is; therefore God is. Thus God depends upon man for his existence, and God is created in the image of man. If man is innocent, then God is unthinkable, and man's guilt consists precisely in creating God. The more he tries to justify the God he has created, the more miserable he becomes. But the original thesis is then modified, and the question is raised: Why should man, like a Sisyphus, continually attempt to justify God, when all that he is looking for in life is some meaning? If all that man wants is love, why should he seek God? For J.B., and for post-Christian man, there is neither justice nor divine love; there is only human love. God is not love, as he was for biblical man. Vahanian writes:

> Job, in the Biblical myth, could not understand suffering and evil, because for him God's existence was not in question. But J.B., or post-Christian man, does not understand evil and suffering because God does not really exist, except theoretically. For him, only love "is," and it is when it is freely given in spite of suffering, of injustice, of death, and,

finally, of God. And yet, in the face of God's uselessness, this love paradoxically justifies Godot, any Godot. To the virility of love succeeds a sheer sentimentality.[8]

Actually, says Vahanian, it is not the question of God or of religious existence that preoccupies the contemporary mind, but a question of materialistic utility and success. Modern man is not bothered by his spiritual mediocrity because he is completely unaware of it. The recent revival of religion springs from the cult of searching for reassurance and success, and MacLeish is correct in describing the predicament of a modern Job in terms of the cult of religiosity.

Another characteristic which identifies *J.B.* as a post-Christian work is its modern conception of tragedy. The tragic element in today's literature bears absolutely no resemblance to the Greek or the Christian conception of tragedy. Despite the obvious differences between them, both the Greek and the Christian conceptions are essentially religious and supernatural. In other words, they both demand some type of absolute, or at least the existence of some principle other than the human. Yet such a view is foreign, alien, and irrelevant in the modern era. Thus, either there is no tragedy possible today, or modern man has developed a completely new conception of tragedy.

Modern man, Vahanian continues, is neither awed by the death of God nor perplexed by the problem of suicide, and therefore neither Nietzsche nor Camus is a representative for modern man. Nietzsche and Camus warned against the desperate effort of trying to overcome despair by seeking refuge in transcendence. J.B. is content to affirm life and go on living. Human existence, for him, is not a tragedy; he denies that it should be. He moves through life without either committing himself to others or alienating himself from others. His view of life may turn out to be illusory, an illusion which he uses to replace the Christian vision of life. But illusion or not, it has replaced the illusion of an afterlife.

Vahanian further contends that the religiosity manifested in *J.B.* is narcissistic. He writes:

[8] *Ibid.,* p. 128.

Though it deals with a god which is nothing other than love itself, this god, or this love, is a purely human phenomenon. It is not an absolute above and beyond man. It does not confront man with a transcendental reality wholly other than himself. Sinfulness, or anxiety before that which threatens man from the outside, is totally absent from J.B.'s moral struggle. In theological words, he does not have to choose between a relative and the absolute, between the transitory and the permanent, between God and "reasons." In *J.B.*, man may no longer afford the luxury of thinking himself the measure of all things; he may even turn his back on the sentimental and immanental theism of the nineteenth century, centered on the cult of God's fatherhood and the brotherhood of men. A certain god may have become the measure of J.B.'s existence, his affections and his struggles and his predicament; but it is a god who reflects the image of man all too faithfully. Besides, what else could this god be, since the contemporary framework of man's self-understanding is, as *J.B.* shows, no longer transcendental? [9]

7. Cultural Incapacity for God

Theologically speaking, every age is post-Christian in the sense that every man and every situation stand under God's judgment. But the present age, says Vahanian, is culturally post-Christian because the fundamental orientation of contemporary culture does not allow man to adopt a Christian outlook. Why? Because the Christian view is essentially transcendental, while the view of modern man is essentially immanentist. The modern world is the heir to cultural as well as theological transformations. One sees this, for example, in the reversal brought about by the French and the American revolutions. The French Revolution brought an end to the ecclesiastical control of culture, and the American Revolution put an end to a theological control of culture and established theological liberty (i.e., freedom from theology). In the course of time, secular institutes gradually arrogated to themselves a sacral aura. The rights of man disestablished God's redemptive covenant with man, and the attributes of God gradually came to be con-

ceived as simply the highest predicates of man. God became identified with the essence of man, and there gradually emerged a
deification of man, so that in the middle of the 19th century Feuerbach noted that theology had become anthropology. God, he
claimed, is nothing but a notion derived from the highest and
purest predicates of man.

A radical shift in the culturally determined thought patterns of
modern man can be discovered by contrasting the Christian conception of man with that generally held by the contemporary
world. Within the Christian framework, and following in particular
the teaching of Saint Paul, man is viewed as coming to know himself in proportion as he knows God. He is thought to find himself only if he seeks God. Man's involvement with the world about
him is always considered from a transcendental point of reference.
Turning to the currently popular view of man, we find that a radical transformation of ideas has taken place. Modern man has discovered that the reality of the world today, with its concrete
immediacy and consistent immanence, provides him with a promising new context for possible self-understanding. God has become
irrelevant to the process of attaining self-understanding. Modern
man, says Vahanian, no longer really questions the existence of
God. Actually, the question of God's existence does not even arise
because the very concept of God has become useless. Such a conception, it is asserted, offers no resolution to man's predicament,
and therefore today's slogan is: If you find yourself, you will not
need to find God. Thus, modern man is not hostile to religion; he
simply ignores it because he is totally unconcerned with religious
questions.

Modern categories of thought are impervious to the world view
of Christianity because, in the course of Western intellectual development, the fundamental Christian categories have become
devalued. A comparison of the medieval world view with the one
which currently predominates provides clear evidence that there
has been a marked shift in the concerns of men during the inter-
vening period. This transition might best be described as a shift in
concern from transcendence to immanence. The medieval and
modern eras reflect very disparate world views and the gap between them is continually growing wider.

Vahanian says that some individuals, like Karl Jaspers, are very pessimistic about the future of a culture which jettisons the categories of faith. Unless some underlying transcendental conviction is operative, they argue, the culture is doomed to failure and total disintegration. But others, like Pitirim Sorokin, are far more optimistic, and remain convinced that our culture is not about to disintegrate. They feel that the present crisis may simply indicate that we are witnessing the substitution of one fundamental idea of culture for another. Another form of optimism is expressed by those who say that all that is needed today is to prune away some cultural accretions of Christianity. For example, Arnold Toynbee, in his *Civilization on Trial,* states that the fundamental task today is to purge Christianity of its Western accretions and liberate it from its Western exclusivism. He is not suggesting that Christianity is the only religion, or the best religion, or a superior religion, but only that it can become the best if certain elements are excised from it, and if it is made more flexible. The fate of Christianity, in his estimation, does not hinge on the doom of Western culture because there is a latent tendency toward universality within Christianity. But Vahanian disagrees with this position and argues parenthetically that Western culture is not Christian enough for Christianity. At the same time, it is too Christian for Christians to disown now. So Christianity seems to stand or fall with Western culture.

Vahanian then points out that Christopher Dawson admits that Christianity is bound up with Western culture, but then goes on to argue that Christianity still has a chance of winning out over the Western way of life. Modern man, Dawson maintains, is offered the choice between Christianity and nothing. And another Christian thinker, T. S. Eliot, in *The Idea of a Christian Society,* expresses the belief that contemporary man is offered the choice between the formation of a new Christian culture and the acceptance of a pagan one. Vahanian contends that Dawson and Eliot both err in thinking that Christianity is the loftiest and most spiritual revelation we know, and in according the highest validity to the Christian expression of religious belief. He says that Ernst Troeltsch once held this same thesis. He later rejected it on the grounds that there are scientifically and historically observable reasons which indicate that, regardless of the forms assumed by a religion, it cannot exist or retain any validity without depending upon a given set of intellectual, social, and cultural conditions. In other words, a given religion has supreme validity only within a given cultural context. Troeltsch also objected to the equation of universality or superiority with relevancy. Relevance, Vahanian continues, depends upon neither universality nor superiority, and Christianity ceases to be universal when it is no longer relevant to a particular culture. Christianity has failed in Western culture, and therefore it can hardly claim to have universal value and relevance. It can scarcely claim to be more authentic than any other religion. It is a fact, says Vahanian, that Christianity is no longer the object of absolute confidence. In substituting a radical immanence for transcendence, the modern world has chosen a path which leads to complete rejection of Christian thought categories. The crisis of the modern age involves the substitution of essentially secular tenets for the Christian fundamentals of Western culture.

8. The Cultural Disavowal of God

The problem of authority is perennial, but the present age is characterized by a notable dissolution of authority, a dissolution which Vahanian feels is attributable to the rise of scientific humanism and the failure of Christianity. This crisis is relevant to his thesis because he views authority as a symbol of faith. Religious authority, he insists, is designed to impel man toward the acceptance of a common religious belief; it is not designed to compel assent. Neither does it intend to eradicate personal autonomy for the sake of a blind assent to a structured system of beliefs which claims the sanction of an absolute or divine authority. Rather, it symbolizes a synthesis of subjective truth and objective reality, so that, in assenting to the demands of religious authority, the individual disclaims absolute validity for his personal convictions.

The present crisis, says Vahanian, is not one of authority, but one of faith, an inflationary faith. And in an effort to distinguish authentic faith from inflationary faith, he offers his own views concerning the nature of authentic faith. Faith, he says, attempts to define man in polar terms.

Faith is an attempt to reconcile subject and object, subjective truth and objective reality, the self and the world,
without overwhelming either of the terms. Faith is an attempt to reconcile the two dimensions of existence—personal
and impersonal, internal and external—without unifying
them. It attempts to define man in terms of a synthesis or
as the locus of a polarity and a tension between the absolute and the relative, the universal and the particular, the
world and the self. It means that man does not live by
logical consistency. Authority is a symbol of the kind of
self-understanding man reaches through faith. By contrast,
what characterizes our so-called religious as well as our
irreligious contemporaries is their common quest for logical
consistency. That constitutes today the most vital opposition
to the Christian tradition, and it comes from science and
humanism, although both were formerly grounded in the
Christian tradition.[10]

In turning to a consideration of the Christian basis of science
and humanism, Vahanian begins by saying that, from the viewpoint of traditional Christianity, there is no real conflict between
science and religion. According to this view, science and religion are
complementary or supplementary viewpoints, and conflict between the two arises only when there is a misconception regarding
the true nature of either one or the other. The findings and the
achievements of science do not invalidate the truth of the Christian
message, but this is not the problem that confronts modern man.
The dilemma of modern man, says Vahanian, is that he spends
his whole life in a search for consistency and a principle of unifica-
tion. The Christian view of man, on the other hand, indicates that
man's experience moves on another level than that of sheer logical
consistency.

According to the Judaeo-Christian view of the universe, there
are only two basic realities: God and his creation. In biblical
thought, God's reality cannot be deduced, either by addition or
subtraction, from the reality of creation. God is not viewed as a
part of the physical universe; he is always understood as being
wholly other than his creation. And despite the very anthropomorphic conceptions of God which one encounters in the biblical

---

[10] *Ibid.*, p. 165.

narrative, there always remains a distinct qualitative difference between God and man. God is never viewed as the ideal man, and divine qualities are never attributed to man. For biblical man, although God is wholly other and transcendent, nevertheless, he is present to, and operative in, his creation. That creation as a whole is coherent because all of its parts are related to a central source of meaning. This provides an integrating factor, even though some of the parts might lack relative coherence among themselves. The biblical God is never viewed as a *deus ex machina,* or as the world soul, or as the zenith of non-rational introspection, or as an absentee landlord. In biblical thought, God is never reduced to either an intellectual or moral principle directly accessible to man. The outstanding primordial quality of God was considered to be his ability to reveal himself to man—the Creator God who revealed himself to men as the source and end of man's reality. Biblical man was firmly convinced of a divine purpose guiding the human and historical facts of coherence, as well as those of incoherence.

Following the phenomenal development of science and the evolution of ethical theory, particularly in the last century, man discovered that science and ethics can offer an explanation of man and the universe without having recourse to the concept of God. Scientific technology and anthropocentric humanism propose a coherent and consistent view of man and the universe which challenges the relevancy of the Christian view. This development is ironic, Vahanian observes, since Christianity liberated these fields from their supernaturalistic bondage and set them on an independent course of inquiry. The Christian conviction that the world could have been created along totally different lines without detracting from God's glory led to the belief that independent empirical analysis of creation would culminate in renewed affirmation of God's glory in creation.

Vahanian maintains that, while Christianity confined itself to the transcendental, it fostered science as a method of obtaining a descriptive understanding of the physical universe.

Frequently in the past, however, men confused the goals of science and those of religion, and empirical fact was confused with a transcendental interpretation of its meaning. Initially, theology was regarded as the queen of the sciences and physical science was accorded a subordinate and ancillary role. An ambiguous Christian conception of science manifests itself here, Vahanian contends, because science, in this context, is not viewed as completely autonomous, since its primary function is to fulfill itself in the glorification of God. Such a conception of science, he continues, contains an implicit affirmation that there can be no other view of the universe except a religious one. But science followed its own internal logic and development and gradually came to view its role as trying to understand the phenomenological world itself, rather than trying to decipher God's intelligibility in the world. The world came to be viewed as a self-contained reality, with no recourse to any outside principle needed to explain its operations and its meaning. Man's knowledge of the universe, although relative, was still more certain than his knowledge of the absolute. And it was not long before this newly emergent view of the universe became a valid alternative to the Christian conception. This new view is atheistic and humanistic. It represents a totally immanent world view.

The crucial transition from one world view to another was caused by the natural human desire to unify science and religion. During this period Christianity desired to be modern, and it gradually accommodated itself to the cultural exigencies of the times. Traditional, or classical, Christianity had understood the physical universe as a revelation of God, and it was strongly convinced that reason did not conflict with revelation. Reason and faith were viewed as two independent spheres which are joined without confusion, so that they remain distinct but not separate. The various theological constructs of the modern period, however, give one the impression, says Vahanian, that the physical universe is the entire revelation of any God there is, and that reason is a far more cogent and effective principle than faith for grasping truth. In the 19th century, Christianity was rendered less mysterious, less religious, less demanding, and more cultural in accordance with the predominating mood of that era. In the course of time, as more and more Christian thinkers and theologians embraced the concept of a self-reliant and self-consistent world, God came to be viewed more and more as an intruder.

The inauguration of a post-Christian universe is to be imputed to the delinquency of Christianity rather than wholly to the arrogance of science or any other movement, materialistic or ideological, that Christians would like to construe as secularistic. Even if it intended to grapple with actual and not theoretically abstract problems confronting the concrete man of the nineteenth century, Christianity had intellectually misconducted itself, and forfeited its relevance. For the sake of winning the world, it lost its soul. This constant dilemma of Christianity was never more desperately urgent than to those who faced it with the embalmed corpse of a dead body of beliefs.[11]

Christianity began to forfeit its relevance when it asked to see the meaning of the universe confirmed empirically. Traditionally, faith in God had provided the necessary confirmation of meaning in the universe. After the rise of science, many Christians began to assent to the seemingly evidential confirmation of the universe's intrinsic meaningfulness, simultaneously hoping that God would be discovered to be its ultimate explanation. In the process, God became only an appendix to the physical world, a *deus ex machina*. In the post-Christian era, man is the measure of all things. His responsibility to this world is the only commitment which he recognizes and can justify, since he finds no immediately evident responsibility to God. It is man himself who creates and redeems the world. Evil is to be eliminated, not explained by appealing to a coherent view of the universe. Since man alone exercises supreme dominion over the physical universe, he alone provides meaning for that universe.

But the death of God, Vahanian continues, does not make things any easier for modern man, for he is still helpless and disoriented. His drive toward logical consistency, which has been apparently successful in eliminating any transcendent God, has not achieved consistency where it matters most, for man still needs to find himself. He finds himself right back at the same starting point, the only difference being that this time his search for meaning must be conducted under the aegis of atheistic rather than theistic principles. The modern ethic is thoroughly anthropocentric. God, as a postulate authenticating moral action, has become superfluous. Contemporary man rejects the Christian ethic of man's solidarity in

[11] *Ibid.*, p. 180.

sin and guilt, an ethic of forgiveness. In place of this, he substitutes an ethic of complete innocence, an ethic constructed on the solidarity of man's innate innocence in the absurd world in which he finds himself. He therefore searches for the meaning of human existence within his own immediate context, and completely rejects any transcendent source of meaning.

The theocentric symbols of Christianity were once relevant to the culture and humanism which they fostered. In the present cultural milieu, so impregnated by an atheistic and anthropocentric humanism, they have become totally irrelevant. Hell, for example, has become a questionable reality, and man now appears to be his own creator and redeemer. The clear and obvious meaning of present-day anthropocentrism, says Vahanian, is that the improbability of God is a practical fact, an everyday reality readily available to the experience of all reflective beings. Today the death of God is directly experienced by many men; it is not simply a theoretical declaration. Contemporary anthropocentrism stresses the irrelevance of God—be he real or just an idea—to concrete human existence. From the point of view of man's concrete situation in this world, therefore, God is dead.

Such a state of affairs, Vahanian comments, may only be temporary, a transitional stage in man's religious and cultural development. New social and cultural forces may yet arise which will change the present trend toward immanence. Scientifically, culturally, and theologically, it is impossible to identify God as the prime mover or the universal sustainer of the world of phenomena. Even if things are not as the atheists and humanists say they are, today's Christian must see that the relevance of the Christian view is even more hypothetical. The modern Christian is forced to acknowledge the validity of such counter-choices and to admit that the post-Christian era has dawned.

9. The Self-Invalidation of Christianity and the Death of God

The radical immanence of the modern mentality has resulted in a cultural and a religious incapacity for God. The immanentist concern with the here-and-now is reflected in two attitudes: first, in the technological, or scientific, mentality which finds no religious or divine dimension in the world; and second, in modern man's plea of innocence with respect to evil and injustice. The religiosity which characterized the so-called religious revival of the 1950's centered around an immanentist view of reality. Religiosity idolatrizes such things as peace of mind, physical health, material success, and the many other things that it considers to be adequate substitutes for the classical benefits of salvation. It seems to have run out of reasons for believing in God. Religiosity is neither Christian nor secularistic; it is idolatrous. It is pseudo-religious and pseudo-scientific, and it finally results in a leveling down of Christianity to the common denominators of a civic religion.

For biblical man, the opposite of faith was not involvement with secular matters, but an idolatrous concern with secular matters. Modern man, instead of adopting the biblical conception of faith and community, has turned to the Baals of religiosity, to a packaged God, and to a form of togetherness. In doing so, Christianity has capitulated to the demands of modern man. Martin E. Marty suggests that only a return to the original sources, to biblical faith, and to classical Protestantism can resolve the present crisis, and that man must somehow find a way to clarify for the present world the biblical meaning of God, man, and community. But the present crisis, Vahanian objects, is not that easily resolved, because we are here faced with a unique situation. We live in a post-Christian world which is impervious to the Christian transcendental view of reality. The radical monotheism of the age of faith is continually giving way to the radical immanentism of the present culture. And an immanentist Christian is a pseudo-Christian, for as Kierkegaard pointed out, a god who can be pointed out is an idol.

In addition to considering the cultural dimensions of the current religious crisis, Vahanian also studies it theologically. There are, he says, basically two theological approaches: the kerygmatic and the apologetic. The kerygmatic approach has the nature of a proclamation, and is exemplified by the theological writings of men like Karl Barth. The apologetic approach, on the other hand, functions as a defense or vindication of a position; this approach is frequently found in the writings of a Paul Tillich. Each approach has its own advantages and disadvantages. In his own evaluation of the apologetic approach, Vahanian disagrees with the contention of many that existentialism provides apologetic theology with a singularly useful vehicle for conveying the truth of the Christian faith to the modern world, because, in his estimation, existentialism, like technology, ultimately flows into the stream of immanentism. Therefore, it opposes the basic orientation of Christianity.

Existentialism, he says, has its Christian beginnings in the writings of Sören Kierkegaard. Other writers, like Pascal or Augustine or Dostoevsky, could be cited as parents of the existentialist movement, but the opposition of Kierkegaard and Nietzsche to Christianity deserves special consideration here. Kierkegaard was concerned with how to be a Christian when Christianity is dead, and Nietzsche was concerned with how to be a man when God is dead. For Kierkegaard, there was an infinite qualitative difference between God and man, but he had no alternative except to acknowledge with Nietzsche the exclusion of God from the framework of a self-sufficient universe and a self-reliant humanism. This acknowledgment was necessary because the problem of human existence is independent of the problem of God.

> To say that God is dead or to assert an infinite qualitative difference between God and man means not only that no ladder leads from man to God; it also means that there is no identity of substance between man and God, and, accordingly, that the problem of human existence is independent of the problem of God. Even as science, whatever its hypothesis, makes it impossible to identify this hypothesis with God, so also existentialism makes it impossible to identify God and man. The reality of man does not, logically or essentially, preclude the latter. That is why Kierkegaard could remain a Christian— but on the basis of the ancient formula: *credo quia absurdum*.[12]

Faith, for Kierkegaard, is not a fact or a state, but a constant becoming; it resembles a leap. Since God is infinitely remote from man, and since Jesus is not the ideal man, there is no immediate standard by which the act of existence can be measured and automatically authenticated. One is left only with the exigencies of love

---

[12] *Ibid.*, pp. 210–211.

and faith. According to this view, faith is understood as a process of constant becoming, as something which is constantly exposed to doubt. In faith, the sinful man is justified; the self becomes what it is not—it becomes itself. The self is understood as the dialectical element which mediates between life and death, between finitude and infinitude. To exist means to make free and responsible choices, and therefore the self is essentially freedom. But this freedom is not self-authenticated or self-mediating; it is related to, and requires the presence of, another. This relatedness is a mode of being whereby the self either realizes itself or alienates itself. Kierkegaard tries to define man's freedom in terms of his relatedness to God, the infinitely other, but in the final analysis, Vahanian observes, Kierkegaard maintains that a man is what he wills himself to be. And it is at this point, Vahanian points out, that existentialism no longer needs any theistic apparatus, and it begins to move into the area of radical immanentism. If a man is what he wills himself to be, this means primarily that he has no justification of his own for what he becomes, even in a theistic context. In atheistic existentialism, although man cannot justify himself, yet he must assume full responsibility for his acts. As Sartre has indicated, since God is dead, man is sentenced to be free; he is condemned to assume full responsibility for his actions.

Martin Heidegger's word for existence is *Dasein,* a term which is used to signify a "being there," irrespective of who or what put one there. Man, says Heidegger, is catapulted into a situation wherein he must accept all of the conditions and responsibility of exploring both the finitude and the possibilities of his existence. Existentialism, as some have indicated, is a partial rediscovery of some of the fundamental aspects of biblical man's understanding of the human condition. Moreover, existentialism is related to Christianity in a special way, and both Bultmann and Tillich have been quick to discover the root affinities which exist between existentialism and Christianity. Existentialism and Christianity both share the same basic view of man, in the sense that existentialism's phenomenological analysis of the human condition can easily be put into a Christian framework. The existentialist view of man is at least sympathetic, if not homogeneous, with the New Testament view of man.

But the advantages of employing existentialism as a vehicle for conveying Christian truth to the contemporary world, says Vahanian, soon turn into disadvantages. This becomes clear if we examine Bultmann's existentialist theology. Bultmann's theology borrows freely from Heidegger's philosophy, because he is convinced that philosophy actually takes precedence over theology. And it is better to admit this at the outset, he says, and then choose the best system available, rather than be accused later on of being unconsciously dependent upon a philosophical system. Secondly, Bultmann is firmly convinced that theology must isolate the essential content of the Christian message from its past expressions, that is, from the cultural, temporal, and temporary characteristics of the New Testament formulations. Besides, even the core of that message is dependent on a world view which is for the most part obsolete and unintelligible, and therefore this essential core of truth must be rethought and reformulated within the context of man's present situation. Thirdly, Bultmann contends that the world view of the New Testament is mythological, as is the central core of the New Testament message which is dependent on it. For example, in the New Testament narrative we are presented with a three-decker universe in which angels, demons, Satan, and supernatural powers are considered to be operative. But authentic faith, Bultmann insists, is independent of this outmoded world view, and the truth of the Gospel message is independent of the now irrelevant mythological conceptions of the New Testament era. Myth, in Bultmann's analysis, is contrasted with scientific knowledge, and it can be defined as the attempt to explain human nature in terms of divine intervention, the temporal in terms of the eternal, and the immanent in terms of the transcendent; it speaks of the divine in human terms. Scientific thought, on the other hand, employs categories of thought based on radical immanence. The task facing modern man, therefore, is that of demythologizing the biblical narrative, of making the truth of Christianity relevant to the modern world.

Bultmann is fully convinced of the validity and intrinsic worth of the basic thrust of mythological thinking, and he feels that it must be retained, but he is also fully convinced of the value of scientific thinking, and he thinks that existentialism offers a delicate balance of the good qualities inherent in each. Vahanian, however, feels that Bultmann's method is inadequate. He notes that a radical transformation has taken place with respect to man's understanding of himself and the world around him. There has been a transition from a sacral basis of cultural values to a thoroughly secular foundation, from a theistic view of man and the universe to a fundamentally atheistic view, from a transcendent view of reality to an immanent view. In other words, the transition is more radical and more comprehensive than a simple transition from a mythological to a scientific world view. Thus, Bultmann's theory would be correct only in the framework of a culture that is impregnated by a sacral or a sacramental conception of nature.

Karl Barth disagrees with Bultmann's methodology and insists that, once the core of the Christian message has been distilled or isolated, it cannot be manipulated and made to fit some philosophical system, lest it become subservient to that system. Bultmann, however, is persuaded that the core of the Christian message does not deal with God as he is in himself, but only as he is significant for man, for man's responsibility, and for man's salvation. According to this interpretation, theology and anthropology are very closely related, since Christianity and philosophy are both concerned with the same problem: authentic existence. But the central question which must be raised here is: Does the transition from inauthentic existence to authentic existence depend on God's intervention? Bultmann seems to indicate that the place accorded to Christ in the New Testament is decisive and indispensable, constituting the only possible source of realizing authentic existence. But Vahanian accuses Bultmann of being ambiguous on this point, since it seems to follow that, because faith is not viewed as a supernatural addition to man's self-understanding, it should be the attitude naturally attained by every man.

Both Bultmann and Tillich agree that the correlation of Christian truth with the methodology of existentialism is opportune and advantageous, since they both deal with the problem of authentic human existence, and they both attempt to provide meaningful answers to man's questions about himself and the world around him. While the exponents of Christian existentialism assume that the question of human existence leads to, or implies, the question

of God, Vahanian objects that we must first ask ourselves whether
or not one can legitimately go from one to the other. The question
of man and the question of God can certainly be correlated, he
admits, but it does not necessarily follow that the principle of correlation is included in the question of existence. In other words,
the problem of man does not necessarily imply the problem of
God. Man has come to see that reason is wholly indifferent; it can
lead toward or away from God. In addition to this, Vahanian adds,
Christian existentialism is grounded in a conceptual framework
basically hostile to the mentality of modern man.

Paul Tillich admits the possibility that one might have to cease
being a Christian in order to reach authentic existence in Christ.
Sartre goes even further, arguing that both Christ and God must
be abandoned in man's search for authentic existence, insisting
that the realization of authentic human existence requires an
atheistic form of humanism.

> In sum, existentialism is possible only in a world where God
> is dead or a luxury, and where Christianity is dead. It origi-
> nates in the decay and death of Christianity. It presupposes
> the death of God, although in some of its aspects it may wish
> that God had not died. Or all of this can be seen differently:
> in existentialism Christianity meets, in Carlyle's phrase, "not
> a tortured death but a quiet euthanasia." Or again: existen-
> tialism transcribes in secular themes some aspects of man's
> sinful condition before God. It is, in a word, a transcription
> of the tragic condition of existence. But this tragedy is without
> heroes (as Sartre contends it should be) and without martyrs
> (as Kierkegaard complained it was). It is a tragedy without
> the tragic element.[13]

10. Beyond the Death of God

Therefore, Vahanian concludes that our age is certainly post-
Christian. It is post-Christian because Christianity has degener-
ated into religiosity and moralism, and it is no longer defined in
terms of biblical faith. It is post-Christian because our modern culture is gradually losing the marks of that Christian spirit which

[13] *Ibid.*, p. 227.

formed and shaped it. It is post-Christian because tolerance has developed into religious syncretism, into an amalgam of beliefs and attitudes with no solid foundation or coherence. Every age, theologically speaking, is post-Christian, but the present era is also culturally post-Christian. Christianity has ceased to be one of the formative elements of contemporary society.

Vahanian maintains that, on both the popular and the intellectual levels, Christianity has reached the point of no return. God dies when he becomes an idol, a cultural accessory, or a human ideal. Today, our religio-cultural notion of God is dead, and it is the religiosity of the present era, an era which is neither pagan nor Christian, that has killed God. The irony of the legacy of the Christian tradition is that, through the mediation of religiosity, it has bequeathed us the death of God. Furthermore, the radical immanence of religiosity has deified man in the process of killing God, and this leads, in Vahanian's estimation, to the ultimate absurdity. For once God is dead and man is deified, man finds himself even more alone and more estranged from himself than he ever was before. At this point, man is now confronted by a new dilemma.

> The dilemma of radical immanentism is that it offers no resolution to man's predicament because, although it attempts to define man in terms of his relatedness to others, it can only project man as a god or a wolf to his fellow man. In biblical thought, too, man is defined by his relatedness to others— "Thou shalt love thy neighbor as [though he were] thyself." But man, a finite being, neither defines nor comprehends— he is defined and comprehended by God the Infinite, the Wholly Other.[14]

Vahanian's same basic thesis is echoed in an article entitled "Beyond the Death of God," where he says that the death of God is a cultural event by which modern man recognizes and acknowledges the transition from a Christian to a post-Christian era.[15] Culturally speaking, there was a Christian era, but now a radically new age has dawned, an age in which the sacramental sig-

[14] *Ibid.,* p. 231.

[15] Gabriel Vahanian, "Beyond the Death of God," *Dialog I* (Autumn, 1962), pp. 18–21.

nificance of the world has disappeared, and human existence has lost its transcendental dimension. Ironically, Christianity produced this Western culture which is now seen to be post-Christian, but the present cultural phenomenon of the death of God highlights the fact that modern man has adopted new thought patterns which make it impossible for him to accept the Christian message. Something has happened to the consciousness of Western man, says Vahanian, something overlooked by many theologians, but recorded in graphic terms by poets, novelists, artists, and playwrights. But, he continues, there is no univocal consent among these men regarding the import of such an event; in fact, one notices a decidedly bipolar reaction among these men. Some of them, like Camus and Beckett, assert that the self-invalidation of Christianity enables man to face his condition honestly and to assume the ambiguities of his self-understanding, while others, like Joyce, or Eliot, or Faulkner, or Ingmar Bergman, express a sense of being orphaned, and they contend that the death of God leads to a frustration of the creative imagination.

Western culture has been severed from its theological roots, its metaphysical foundations, and its sacramental significance. The one outstanding characteristic of the present era is the radical immanence which completely permeates the modern mentality, an immanence which compels one to conclude that Christianity has become irrelevant and meaningless. But the present situation is not analyzable simply in terms of a substitution of a scientific or technological world view for a mythological one; the transition is more radical and more profound than that. At the present time, Christian symbols have lost their claim upon men's consciousness because the inner core of the Gospel message and the classical Christian symbols are contemporaneous with a different historical situation. The complexity of today's crisis is compounded because modern man has become disenchanted with both religion and science—with religion because of the current phenomenon of the death of God, and with science because of the imminent threat of possible annihilation, due to man's scientific ingenuity and creativity. What is needed today, says Vahanian, is not a theological reformation, but a cultural revolution. Man has desacralized the world, forgetting that ultimately culture is a form of consecration of the world.

Therefore, a transfiguration of culture is needed today to restore things to proper perspective. Western culture is already slowly groping beyond its own devaluation of symbols for a new language, for a new dialect, for a new way to talk meaningfully about God. As a consequence of the present religious crisis, man has learned that God is not necessary, in the sense that he simply cannot be taken for granted. In a similar manner, man has also learned that God cannot be used as an hypothesis, whether it be epistemological, scientific, or existential, unless one wants to draw the degrading conclusion that "God is reasons." Such a conception of God denigrates the nature of God. Man cannot assume that God exists, says Vahanian, but he should realize that God must exist. In other words, God is inevitable, not necessary; he is wholly other and wholly present, and faith in him is still demanded on the part of man.

In *Wait without Idols,* Vahanian states that, according to the biblical understanding of God, the reality of God is independent of the cultural framework within which it is grasped.[16] He concurs with Karl Barth's judgment that there is no adequacy between our concepts and the reality of God; God always remains wholly other. Man, he argues, should come to recognize that the kerygmatic approach to Christianity is the only valid one, and that one should completely dispense with the apologetic approach. Man's concepts of God are culturally determined; they are valid only when they authentically reflect human experience and are formed within a given cultural framework. But organizations within such a cultural context can gradually overwhelm human experience and eventually distort or invalidate it, thereby invalidating the concepts related to that experience. God dies whenever man's concept of him becomes an idol or a cultural accretion, whenever man tries to objectify or domesticate God. The current cultural phenomenon of the death of God underlines the fact that God is now freed from cultural concepts and that modern man is now groping for a new and more meaningful concept of God.

To speak of the death of God means, then, that finally, at the end of the Christian phase of Western culture, the reality of

[16] Gabriel Vahanian, *Wait without Idols* (New York: George Braziller, 1964).

the living God is freed from the cultural concepts and other institutions that attempt to objectify and domesticate it. The death of God marks the end of Christian culture and, especially, of its attempt to assimilate *the other God,* the living God of whom our religion as well as our diffuse religiosity is a desperate caricature. This means that, man being a religious animal, we are groping for a new concept of God and a new attitude, a mode of being congruous with it; that a new religiosity is dawning. And a new era begins when a new religiosity appears, rises from the empty tomb of the dead God.[17]

Modern man has lost the awareness of the presence of God's transcendent immediacy. Secularity, man's involvement with the world, need not have become secularism. Religion has become pragmatic and utilitarian, degenerating into idolatrous religiosity. The present death-of-God syndrome indicates that transcendent values have been replaced by immanent ones.

Our present crisis stems from the fact that we have changed the biblical iconoclasm of the Christian tradition into the idolatrous post-Christian religiosity of our cultural institutions, be they social, political, economic, or ecclesiastical.[18]

In an article entitled "Swallowed up by Godlessness," Vahanian offers some of his reflections on the topic of Christian atheism.[19] His own designation for this movement is "Christosophy," and he argues that no real solution to the present crisis is to be found in capitulating to the immanent cultural framework of contemporary thought. This new Christosophy, he says, is no more relevant to modern man than the fossilized Christianity which it rejects. The best way to view the present situation is to consider the current state of godlessness as a valid alternative to faith in God. Christian atheism is a compromise position. Christosophy errs seriously in viewing secularism as the remedy instead of the sickness itself. Its own internal consistency is made possible only because it has capitulated to the atheistic exigencies of the contemporary world view. The death of God, in this context, simply becomes a new spring-

[17] *Ibid.,* p. 231. Italics in original.

[18] *Ibid.,* p. 234.

[19] Gabriel Vahanian, "Swallowed Up by Godlessness," *Christian Century* 82 (Dec. 8, 1965), pp. 1505-1507.

board for a new religiosity because it is transformed into an article of faith; it becomes an ersatz surrogate which is no less religious for being godless. In other words, the proponents of Christian atheism offer man the same old opium. Feuerbach was far more consistent when he reduced theology to anthropology.

One should realize, says Vahanian, that the reality of God was affirmed in spite of, not because of, the biblical world view. And no world view, immanent or otherwise, *ipso facto* invalidates faith or belief in God. But once man freely selects the atheistic alternative to Christian faith, he should recognize that the time has come to write a new Gospel and not simply to patch up the old. What is most needed today, Vahanian says, is clarity. Man must learn to realize that true secularity is the only truly religious mode of being. And true secularity is as different from secularism as it is from pantheism. The bible affirms the secular, while secularism is a condition that dissolves biblical faith and is a result of the separation of the secular from the religious, a separation of man's involvement with the world from his commitment to God. The demarcation line is not found between the sacred and the profane, the religious and the secular, the theistic and the atheistic, or one world view and another. Rather, it is to be found between God and the idol, the creator and the creature, iconoclasm and idolatry. And no world view, whether theistic or atheistic, can prevent either God's becoming an idol or man's self-deification.

In a book entitled *No Other God,* Vahanian has recently reiterated his objections to the radical proposal of Christian atheism.[20] An immanentist world view, he admits, might aid man's understanding of authentic faith, but radical immanentism should not be transformed into an article of faith. Godless Christianity is a weak substitute for authentic religious belief. When Feuerbach reduced theology to anthropology, he was far more consistent than the modern Christosophists.

Theology must indeed remain open to the world and its wisdom, but it must scrupulously avoid every temptation to fashion idolatrous substitutes for the transcendent and immanent reality of God. The world is the arena of God's creative and redemptive design. Vahanian suggests that, during the post-Christian era of the death

[20] Gabriel Vahanian, *No Other God* (New York: George Braziller, 1966).

of God, theological thinking should follow the direction of Calvin's thought as formulated in the *Institutes*. The salient features of Calvin's thought indicate the essential nature of the commitment to Christian faith and its tradition.

Thus, following Calvin's lead, Vahanian maintains that man's knowledge is essentially theonomous and that theology is Christological, pneumatic and ecclesial. From this perspective, man's natural, empirical understanding of himself invalidates itself whenever it cancels out the knowledge of faith. Man's knowledge of himself depends upon his knowledge of God. Unbelief is always mixed with faith. Furthermore, there is no other God than he who is accessible through Christ alone, the God who has revealed himself in the Christ-event. Although Christian theology must employ contemporary categories of understanding, it is not wedded to any single philosophical system or world view. Theology has an historical, cultural, political, and even a worldly dimension. Its development is oriented along these axes but it is not circumscribed or determined by these factors of human existence.

Modern secularism, Vahanian concludes, offers a serious challenge to authentic religious belief insofar as it denies both the transcendence and immanence of God. Only a cultural revolution, coupled with a reformulation of Christian theology following Calvin's insights, can bring about a satisfactory response to such a challenge.

11. An Evaluation

The results of Gabriel Vahanian's analysis of the current religious crisis revolving around the future of belief are very pessimistic. Only a cultural revolution, he concludes, can save modern man from his present idolatrous conceptualization of God. A new iconoclastic thrust is now needed if man is to rediscover the true nature of authentic religious belief. At this point, therefore, we must ask ourselves whether Vahanian's analysis of the modern crisis of unbelief is accurate. Is modern man actually living in a post-Christian era? Is the modern age completely impervious to Christianity? Is radical immanence the outstanding hallmark of contemporary Western culture? Has Christianity actually brought about its own self-invalidation through a process of self-destruction based upon the gradual transformation of authentic religious belief into a degenerate and idolatrous religiosity? Is a cultural revolution the only solution to the present situation?

Vahanian's central thesis is that the death of God is a religio-cultural phenomenon. God himself is not dead, but man's religio-cultural notion of God is dead because contemporary man has lost all awareness of the transcendent and all appreciation of the transcendent immediacy of God to the human situation. Although one might justly accuse Vahanian of exaggerating the extent of modern unbelief and religiosity, yet all available evidence seems to support his basic contention that modern Western man is very much ill at ease with the idea of the transcendent. Modern thought forms are, for the most part, secular and positivistic in character, reflecting a deeply ingrained immanence. Thus, the mental climate of the present era militates against a continued acceptance of the Christian world view. An intellectual rejection of belief in God is becoming more widespread today. More and more reflective people are discovering that, for them, the Judaeo-Christian God is either absent, hidden, withdrawn, irrelevant, non-existent, or dead. An increasing number of serious thinkers are concluding that God is completely irrelevant to their daily lives, and that for all practical purposes he might just as well be dead.

In the final analysis, whatever else one may say about the problem of God, one thing is certain: the existence of God is not a self-evident fact. Serious unbelief is not a phenomenon which is uniquely characteristic of the modern age. At the present time, however, reflective individuals are beginning to realize that an ultimate choice must be made between secular humanism and Christian theism if they are to live purposeful and meaningful lives. An analysis of the current death-of-God controversy underlines the sharp divergence of these two alternative views of reality. The two choices are mutually exclusive, and in the final analysis only one of them can be true. The hybrid proposal of Christian atheism offered by the contemporary death-of-God theologians is ultimately only an attempt at compromise: either man determines and establishes values according to his own immanent framework, or else they have a transcendent source which he should acknowledge. Vahanian is correct in his observation that the death-of-God theologians have capitulated to radical immanence and have mistaken the sickness itself for the remedy.

Vahanian concludes that the present phenomenon of the death of God is attributable to at least three basic causes: the emergence of radical immanence, the rise of scientific humanism, and the gradual self-invalidation of Christianity. Unquestionably, all of these factors have contributed greatly to a denial of the transcendent and to the progressive decline of religious belief in the Western world during the past three hundred years or so. But in portraying the present era as essentially post-Christian, an age whose outstanding feature is radical immanence, Vahanian seems to be overstating his case. For a significant number of serious thinkers today do not subscribe to the religiosity which Vahanian feels is so prevalent in today's world. They find they can successfully integrate their religious belief with their humanistic values, secular interests, and scientific knowledge, and still retain their basic convictions about the existence and nature of the transcendent God. They are unaware of any attempted compromise or intellectual dishonesty in their thinking. While it is certainly true that much of the thinking of contemporary man is fundamentally positivistic in tone and permeated with radical immanence, it is an exaggerated claim to assert that the thought patterns of Western man are primarily characterized by wholly immanent considerations. But Vahanian is correct in seeing a very serious challenge and threat to Christian thinking in the residual positivism and radical immanence of the present era. His fundamental insights into the inherent dangers of religiosity and radical immanence are completely valid.

Vahanian's contention that secularity, not secularism, is essential to Protestantism is important. It has relevance to the contemporary religious crisis. Modern man is currently searching for a viable understanding of the polar relationship which exists between the sacred and the profane. Vahanian is correct in insisting that man should not view his commitment to the world as something which puts his commitment to God in jeopardy. Rather than detracting from his commitment to God, man's commitment to the world should reflect his more basic and fundamental commitment to his Creator and Lord. This was certainly biblical man's view of the relationship which should exist between God and man, as is shown by a study of the theology of the covenant relationship between God and man which we find in the bible. As Vahanian says, authentic religious belief sets up no false dichotomy between these two commitments. Their polarized interaction should provide balance, purpose, and direction to human existence. Thus secularity —an awareness of, and a dedication to, the concrete and immediate sphere of man's activity in the world—is both valid and necessary for the Christian and constitutes the only possible religious mode of being for man in this world.

Another significant insight of Vahanian is his insistence that the reality of God is independent of the cultural framework in which it is grasped. A valid conception of God must reflect authentic human experience of God, both communal and individual, corporate and personal. The religious believer is aware that, in the final analysis, there can be no real adequacy between the transcendent reality of God and man's finite and limited comprehension or conceptualization of God. God always remains wholly other. The Hebraic concept of God in the Old Testament is not based upon the cosmological or cultural determinants of that era. In fact, it is set forth despite the predominant world view of that period. But, as Vahanian points out, those forces which are always operative within a given culture, those intellectual, social, moral, and religious forces which are normative or regulative within a given cultural framework, can distort a valid concept of God and transform it into an idolatrous concept, a pseudo-God, an ersatz substitute for God, a surrogate for God. It is against this background that Vahanian argues that the contemporary phenomenon of the death of God is a religio-cultural event rooted in the ersatz religiosity and radical immanence of the modern era.

For biblical man, as Vahanian indicates, there were only two basic realities: God and his creation. Despite the numerous anthropomorphic conceptions of God in the Old Testament narrative, the overall picture of Yahweh which eventually emerges is actually a delicately-balanced understanding of the transcendence and immanence of God. The sacred writers always postulate a distinct qualitative difference between God and man. According to the biblical view, man is defined by his relationship to God and to his fellow human beings. In this context, biblical faith is a dynamic response of the individual and the community to the revelation of the transcendent God. It is understood as a way of life, an orientation, a full commitment to live in a certain way. Accordingly, man does not inaugurate this movement toward God by searching out God on his own initiative. Rather, it is the Creator God who first reveals himself to man, thereby presenting man with the choice of accepting or rejecting his plan for man.

In concise terms, therefore, the biblical view of man is based upon a theocentric world view: God is the center and measure of all things. Modern secular man, on the other hand, subscribes to an anthropocentric world view in which man is the measure and standard of all things. When viewed from this perspective, Christian theism and secular humanism are seen to be diametrically opposed. Today's man of faith, clearly recognizing the real alternative to authentic religious belief, but firmly convinced that his faith is reasonable, despite real difficulties, freely chooses to live his life on a level other than that of sheer logical consistency. He puts his trust in the revealed Word of God. But in the eyes of the secular humanist religious belief is a form of voluntary delusion, a form of intellectual suicide, a desperate shot in the dark, or a means of avoiding the challenge to full responsibility in the pursuit of full human autonomy.

In the aftermath of the religio-cultural phenomenon of the death of God, Vahanian says, man now finds himself groping for a new and more meaningful concept of God. The previous culturally determined concepts of God have led only to the death of God. Thus, if religious belief is to survive, man must abandon all idolatrous concepts of God and come to realize that the transcendent reality of God cannot be circumscribed by human concepts. Vahanian argues that a return to biblical thought forms and classical Protestantism will not rectify the present situation. What is actually needed, he says, is not a theological reformation, but a cultural revolution. Modern man has lost an awareness of the sacramental dimension of human existence and culture. But unfortunately

Vahanian does not offer any concrete suggestions as to how such a cultural revolution can be brought about.

In the course of his analysis, Vahanian proposes the Barthian thesis of a purely kerygmatic approach to religious belief, rejecting any form of natural theology. He rejects the apologetic approach of Bultmann and Tillich. While acknowledging the many affinities which exist between existentialism and Christianity, he denies that any philosophical system can convey the truth of the Christian faith. The problem of man does not necessarily imply the problem of God, he says, and reason is completely indifferent since it can lead toward or away from God. Today's culture is anthropocentric and immanentist. The basis of culture has shifted from a sacral to a thoroughly secular foundation. Therefore, reasons Vahanian, only a cultural revolution can remedy the present religious crisis occasioned by the death of God.

In adopting the Barthian thesis of a strictly kerygmatic approach to the question of Christian faith, Vahanian severely limits the range of reason in dealing with the problem of the existence and nature of God. If one accepts the validity of analogous reasoning and analogous predication, then one is disposed to accept some form of natural theology and the possibility that certain philosophical systems can be used to convey religious and theological truth. But neither Barth nor Vahanian will accept the validity of analogous reasoning in dealing with the problem of God. The future of Christian belief may be dependent upon a combination of both the kerygmatic and the apologetic approach, rather than upon the strictly kergymatic approach urged by Vahanian.

II
WILLIAM HAMILTON

1. Introduction

Protagoras, in the 5th century B.C., is reputed to have said that man is the measure of all things. Such a statement could be a concise paraphrase of William Hamilton's anthropocentric vision of modern man living in the age of the death of God. Hamilton's writings are marked by a lively presentation of ideas and an attractive literary style. He views contemporary problems within the framework of radical Christianity. But his "religionless" approach is more *ethical* than psychological or theological. Fundamentally, he expresses complete agreement with Dietrich Bonhoeffer's inchoate theology of secular culture; he tries to interpret and extend some of Bonhoeffer's insights into what it means to be a Christian in the modern world. God is dead, says Hamilton. Modern man has come of age, and a new optimism is being offered to contemporary man. In schematic form, this is the new theological vision which Hamilton proposes to those who seek a solution to the ultimate meaning of human existence. Modern man must therefore acknowledge, affirm, and even will the death of God. He must learn to recognize that man is completely independent and autonomous in this world. He must learn to live with radical uncertainty, without the God-hypothesis, in a Godless world where love alone has the power to give meaning to human existence.

Hamilton's writings reflect his strong conviction that today's theologian must think in terms of power and rhetoric, and not in terms of logical structure and cohesive unity. Rejecting the traditional preoccupation of theologians with structural unity, he stresses the current need for a fragmented or segmented approach to theology. Theological insights, he maintains, must be interpreted in light of the predominant cultural and intellectual forces which shape the thinking of modern man. Theology is a time-conditioned enterprise, and if it is to have any current relevance, it must be constructed and presented within the framework of the social, cultural, and intellectual milieu of the modern world. Like Paul van Buren, he is interested in promoting personal righteousness and social justice. But unlike van Buren, he is not interested in presenting a carefully thought-out, systematized, logical framework within which to formulate his ideas, nor is he interested in offering a carefully worked-out scheme of secular belief. Theoretical speculation is of no interest to him; he is interested in movement and activity, and he constantly restructures his ideas as he goes along. He is mainly concerned with presenting a new theological vision rather than a systematized and structured pattern of secular Christianity. In fact, the only structural element which he attempts to introduce is the paradigmatic example of Jesus Christ. He is trying to describe a basic attitude or frame of mind which he finds to be part of the world outlook of modern man. His ultimate goal is the discovery of a viable Christian way of life in an age characterized by radical immanence and the death of God.

In the final analysis, most of his theological thinking centers around three basic themes or motifs which provide the basis for his radically new theological vision. These three fundamental themes are orchestrated in different ways in his various works with varying degrees of stress and emphasis. But together they hold the key to his theological vision. We find these themes clearly isolated and carefully delineated in an article he wrote entitled "The Shape of a Radical Theology," where he points out that the present radical movement in theology has three discernible focal points: (1) the death of God; (2) an interest in Christology; and (3) a new form of optimism.[1]

His main contention is that God is dead in the sense that modern man does not know, adore, possess, or believe in God. When he speaks of the death of God, he does not intend it in the sense of Hegel, Nietzsche, or Sartre. For him, it is a root metaphor

[1] William Hamilton, "The Shape of a Radical Theology," *Christian Century* 82 (Oct. 6, 1965), pp. 1219–1222.

which is meant to convey a sense of real loss; it indicates something irretrievable. The death of God is therefore to be distinguished from the "disappearance," the "eclipse," the "absence," the "withdrawal," or the "hiddenness" of God. Whatever the ultimate meaning of the phrase, Hamilton sees two immediate consequences to the death of God emerging at the present time. First of all, he says, it demands a redefinition of Protestantism. In the modern world, Protestantism must be understood as a movement away from God and toward the world, a movement away from the cloister and toward the world. Secondly, it signifies that today's Christian is invited to follow Christ more closely than ever before. During the time of the death of God, the only meaningful mode of existence available to the Christian is obedience to Jesus, that is, to the person of Jesus as presented in the New Testament documents. The individual Christian is invited to follow the suffering Christ in his selfless love of others. Since man cannot afford simply to sit around and contemplate his loss, he must look for ways of serving his fellowmen during this period. He must focus and channel his energies in a constructive way, and he must constantly put himself at the disposal of his neighbor. Further, since the traditional doctrine of Christian revelation is no longer acceptable, today's Christian cannot explain his following of Christ in "vocational" terms. When asked why he himself chooses to follow Jesus Christ instead of someone like Albert Camus, or Martin Luther King, or Francis of Assisi, Hamilton replies that there is something in Christ's words, his life, his way with others, and his death that he does not find elsewhere. Thus, the death of God is a summons for modern man to follow Jesus more closely than ever before as the exemplar and paradigm of human conduct. A profound awareness of the death of God should impel man to make a total commitment of himself to the love and service of his fellowman. This is what it means to be a Christian today: to be a man for others.

Another concept which is central to Hamilton's overall view of modern man deals with man's new movement from pessimism to optimism, a movement which he sees as a dynamic force operative in contemporary society. Socially, culturally, and even theologically, one finds that there are grounds for adopting an optimistic attitude toward the future. "Man come of age," to use Bonhoeffer's expression, is learning to live in a Godless age where love alone gives meaning to human existence. Christian faith and Christian hope in a personal, transcendent God are no longer possible for modern man; Christian love is the only virtue available to man at the present time. Modern man must learn to live with uncertainty, but at the same time he must acquire confidence in man's ability to solve his own problems, without recourse to the "God-hypothesis." Each individual is now faced with the existential choice of accepting or rejecting the change which is taking place. The radical Christian accepts the present situation, welcomes the new optimism, and looks forward to the day when the present darkness will be dispelled and a new meaning of faith will emerge. Currently, what is needed most is redefinition, reorientation, and restructuring, and in accordance with this new demand Hamilton redefines what it means to be a Protestant. Today's Protestant, he says, "has no God, has no faith in God, and affirms both the death of God and the death of all forms of theism."[2]

2. American Theology, Radicalism, and the Death of God

American theology is currently undergoing rapid change. Careful analysis indicates four clearly discernible camps of thought which act as focal points for theological reflection. These polarized groups, says Hamilton, can conveniently be categorized in the following manner. A large group of American theologians still feel at home in the ecumenical, Barthian, neo-Reformation tradition. Hamilton feels that this group may have its immediate future in the history of doctrine, Old Testament, and perhaps in ethics. A second group is the Bultmannians and the new hermeneutics people who are engaged in doing a great deal of solid New Testament work. Theologically this group is unstable, and one notices a drift, particularly at the left margin, toward the third and fourth groups. The third group consists of those theologians who

[2] William Hamilton, "The Death-of-God Theologies Today," *Radical Theology and the Death of God,* Thomas Altizer and William Hamilton (Indianapolis, Ind.: Bobbs-Merrill Company, 1966), p. 37.

are hopeful for a new kind of natural, metaphysical, or philosophical theology. In this camp, the ontological argument is being
restudied, along with the ideas of Wittgenstein, Whitehead, and
Heidegger. This growing, enthusiastic, intelligent group gives an
indication of the strength of liberal theology today. Finally, we
find a fourth group, a group of "radical" or "death-of-God" theologians. Hamilton points out that a number of names have been
applied to this group, none of which is entirely satisfactory. One
hears, for example, of the "new" theology, the "secular," the
"radical," or the "death-of-God" theology. In Hamilton's estimation, the term "radical" is perfectly adequate, provided that it is
carefully distinguished from other forms of radicalism.

> The death-of-God radical theologians, recently given far
> more visibility than they either desired or deserved, are men
> without God who do not anticipate his return. But it is not a
> simple not-having, for there is an experience of loss. Painful
> for some, not so for others, it is a loss nonetheless. The loss is
> not of the idols, or of the God of theism, but of the God of the
> Christian tradition. And this group persists, in the face of both
> bewilderment and fury, in calling itself Christian. It persists in
> making use of the phrase "death of God," in spite of its rhe-
> torical color, partly because it is a phrase that cannot be
> adapted to traditional use by the theologians today.
> The death-of-God tradition is beginning to see the work laid
> out before it: historical, exegetical, apologetic, ethical. It is
> not out to appeal to modern man or to "take him seriously,"
> nor is it enchanted with being new or relevant. Wisely, it
> knows that many secular modern men like their theological
> foes to be as orthodox as possible so they can be rejected as
> irrelevant.[3]

This new group of theologians is trying to discover a viable
mode of existence for the Christian in this age of the death of
God. In considering the relation of radical theology to traditional
Church structures and institutions, Hamilton observes that it must
be clear that this new theology has neither the power nor the
ability to serve the Protestant Church, at least in its traditional
forms. He writes:

[3] Hamilton, "American Theology, Radicalism and the Death of God,"
Radical Theology and the Death of God, p. 6.

I do not see how preaching, worship, prayer, ordination, the sacraments can be taken seriously by the radical theologian. If there is a need for new institutional forms and styles, however, this theology doubtless has a great deal to say. If theology is tested by its ability to shape new kinds of personal and corporate existence in the times in which it lives, then it would seem that radical theology may be able to pass such a test.[4]

For the most part, radical theology originated and now functions within a broad Christian framework. But on a different level, Hamilton says, there seems to be a psychological affinity between certain kinds of Protestants and certain kinds of Jews, and this may afford possible ground for dialogue between these two groups. For both the radical Protestants and the Jews are men caught between a having and a not-having, and neither group is satisfied with a verbal resolution of this plight. "The believing Jew is a man with God and without the Messiah; the death-of-God Protestant is a man without God but not without something like a Messiah."[5]

It is very difficult to discover the roots of the radical movement within the Christian framework or to point out any specific source of this movement. The appearance of Bishop J. A. T. Robinson's book, *Honest to God,* in 1963, brought into public focus the "radical" British movement in theology. This movement, however, has an American counterpart which actually antedates it in some areas, but not until very recently did the American movement begin to become somewhat organized and to assume the proportions of a movement. At the present time, this American form, popularly known as the death-of-God movement, seems to be more radical than that of the British "radicals." More radical, that is, on each of the three main points of *Honest to God*— God, ethics, and the Church. In the estimation of the American death-of-God theologians, Robinson's radicalism does not go far enough. Many feel that Robinson is far too confident concerning the possibility of God-language. Others object to his retention of a form of non-objectified theism, following van Buren's claim

[4] *Ibid.,* p. 7.
[5] *Ibid.*

that both objectified and non-objectified theism have been shown to be impossible according to the standards of modern philosophy.

But what exactly does contemporary man mean when he says that God is dead? How are we to interpret this statement? In his own analysis of the meaning of this phrase, Hamilton suggests that it is helpful to keep in mind Nietzsche's *Gay Science*. Nietzsche describes a scene in which a madman runs into the marketplace and, standing in the midst of the crowd, loudly proclaims the event of the death of God. "God is dead! God remains dead! And we have killed him!" After witnessing the silent, bewildered response on the part of the crowd, he gradually begins to realize that he has come too soon. Mankind has not yet learned of the event. For, just as it takes time for the light from the stars to reach the earth, so too the news of the event of the death of God takes time to reach men's ears. And yet, paradoxically, men have killed God! Hamilton quotes this entire section from Nietzsche's work so that the reader might have a good referent point from which to judge the meaning of the statement. Hamilton points out that today's radical theologian rejects all of those hypothetical meanings formulated within the limits of the neo-orthodox or biblical-theology tradition. In his own words:

Perhaps we can put it this way; the neo-orthodox reconstruction of the Christian doctrine of revelation seems to have broken down for some. It used to be possible to say: We cannot know God but he has made himself known to us, and at that point analogies from the world of personal relations would enter the scene and help us. But somehow the situation has deteriorated; as before, we cannot know, but now it seems that he does not make himself known, even as enemy. This is more than the old protest against natural theology or metaphysics; more than the usual assurance that before the holy God all our language gets broken and diffracted into paradox. It is really that we do not know, do not adore, do not possess, do not believe in God. It is not just that a capacity has dried up within us; we do not take all this as merely a statement about our frail psyches; we take it as a statement about the nature of the world and we try to convince others. God is dead. We are not talking about absence of the experience of God, but about the experience of the absence of God. Yet the death-of-God theologians claim to be theologians, to be Christians, to be

speaking out of a community to a community. They do not
grant that their view is really a complicated sort of atheism
dressed in a new spring bonnet.[6]

3. Death-of-God Theologies Today

To delineate the positions of the death-of-God theologians in
greater detail, Hamilton attempts to indicate the central ideas
of Thomas J. J. Altizer and Paul van Buren in a schematic manner. He then follows this brief exposition with a more detailed
presentation of his own views about the death of God. This synop-
tic projection of the predominant ideas of the death-of-God movement, from within the movement itself, affords a valuable insight
into the concerns and aims of the movement.

Turning first to the views of Thomas J. J. Altizer, Hamilton
says that Altizer's analysis of the contemporary religious crisis
begins with the cosmic event of the disappearance of the sacred.
His basic presupposition is that God has died in our history, and
he attempts to interpret this event in terms of a dialectical relation
between the sacred and the profane. In his analysis he prefers
mystical categories to either Christological or ethical ones. Part
of the background of his thought is found in Mircea Eliade's
studies of the meaning of the sacred in both archaic and modern
religion and in the Kierkegaardian idea of dialectic. The fundamental question which Altizer raises is: How can we recover that
connection with the sacred that modern man has lost?

Altizer rejects gnosticism, the negation of the profane in order
to reach the sacred, as a proposed solution to the present crisis,
but he admits that it is a powerful temptation, a temptation with
perennial appeal. He rejects Eliade's advice to return to some sort
of pre-cosmic primitivism and to recover the sacred in the way
that archaic religion did. His own solution to the present problem
is a dialectical one. Liberation, he maintains, is effected only by
strong affirmation: only by resolutely affirming the profane will
man find the sacred. This paradoxical resolution of the problem

---

[6] William Hamilton, "The Death-of-God Theologies Today," *loc. cit.*, pp.
27–28.

is based upon Altizer's understanding of the myth of the coincidence of opposites. For Altizer, a vehement affirmation of something—in this case the full reality of the secular, the profane, and the this-worldly character of modern life—will somehow provide the seeker with the opposite—in this case the sacred—as a gift he does not deserve. Man must therefore learn to say "yes," not "no," to the radical profanity of the modern age.

In Altizer's view, Hamilton says, man does not solve the problem of the death of God by following Jesus, but by being liberated from history by him. His radical new vision of man begins with man accepting, affirming, and even willing the death of God in a radical sense. It ends with man's willing participation in the present darkness occasioned by the death of God while he awaits a new manifestation of the sacred in this world. Altizer incorporates Nietzsche's vision of eternal recurrence into his own prophetic vision, asserting that liberation can only be occasioned by the collapse of the transcendence of Being, by the death of God. He adopts Nietzsche's portrait of Jesus, a Jesus who is the object of an eschatological faith which liberates the believer. "Altizer's vision," Hamilton concludes, "is an exciting one, logically imprecise, calculated to make empiricists weep, but imaginatively and religiously it is both sophisticated and powerful."[7]

Hamilton next turns briefly to the key ideas employed by Paul van Buren in his attempt to discover a secular meaning of the Gospel. He begins his treatment of van Buren's views by noting the sharp contrast in personalities which one encounters in comparing the approaches of these two men. "Altizer is all *élan,* wildness, excessive generalization, brimming with colorful, flamboyant, and emotive language. Van Buren is ordered, precise, cool." [8] Van Buren is primarily interested in finding a non-religious interpretation of the Gospel message, and he eventually discovers that the most adequate tool at his disposal is linguistic analysis. Employing the methodology and mechanics of linguistic analysis, therefore, he tries to understand the Gospel in a secular way. In the course of his search, he comes to reject the theological views of Karl Barth and his followers, on the grounds that, in their attempt

[7] *Ibid.,* p. 31.
[8] *Ibid.,* pp. 31–32.

to present a systematic theology, they have forfeited the world as we live in it today. He likewise comes to reject the views of the left-wing Bultmannians, men like Schubert Ogden, because, he says, they have given up the historical basis of Christian faith in favor of an idea of authentic existence.

Van Buren tends to assume that modern analytic philosophy has made all meaningful language about God impossible. Simple literal theism is to be rejected, he contends, and so is that kind of sophisticated and qualified non-objective theism encountered in the writings of men like Ogden and Tillich. Hamilton is not interested in discussing the question of van Buren's presuppositions regarding the valid extension of the methods of analytic philosophy. But he is interested in van Buren's conclusions, namely that man must learn to do without God and hold to Jesus of Nazareth during the time of the death of God. One immediately notices a certain affinity between the conclusions reached by Altizer and those reached by van Buren, despite the fact that they employ vastly different methods of analysis. Hamilton comments:

> Thus, the urban and methodologically scrupulous van Buren joins hands with Altizer, the ecstatic and complex proclaimer of the death of God. The tone of voice is quite different; indeed, the languages are not the same, but the meaning is unmistakable in both: God is dead. For Altizer the disappearance of the sacred is a sort of cosmic event; for van Buren it can be more precisely described: the rise of technology and modern science, the need in our thinking to stick pretty close to what we can experience in ordinary ways. Both are referring to something that has happened to them, not to someone else or to modern man in some generalized sense, and they are willing to admit it.[9]

In dealing with the death of God, Altizer relies mainly on mystical categories while van Buren finds a viable solution in the adoption of a Christological ethic. Although they agree concerning the fact of the death of God, their proposals represent two different ways of Christian living today.

The Christian without God is a waiting man for Altizer, daring to descend into the darkness, grappling with all that is pro-

[9] *Ibid.,* p. 33.

fane to wrest from it its potential sacral power. The Christian without God for van Buren is Jesus' man, perfectly free lord of all, subject to none.[10]

When it comes time to locate his own thought concerning the death of God within the ambiance of this general movement, Hamilton announces that his own starting point is bipolar; it has both a positive and a negative aspect. The negative aspect is associated with the perception of the gradual deterioration of the portrait of the God-man relation as found in biblical theology and the neo-orthodox tradition. Today, such a view has lost all power of persuasion. The positive aspect, on the other hand, consists in the attempt to redefine Protestantism within the profane context of the contemporary world.

For Hamilton, there are three distinct ways of viewing the Protestant Reformation: a psychological way, a theological way, and an ethical way. At the end of the last century, he says, the Reformation was viewed, on the psychological level, as a victory for the autonomous religious personality. Freed from the oppressive tyranny of hierarchy and institution, the individual found an unmediated relationship with God. At the beginning of this present century, the Reformation came to be understood, not in terms of autonomous religious personality, but as the theological discovery of the righteous God. Today, however, we need to find a new interpretation of the Reformation, one that is more appropriate to the needs of the modern world. This new interpretation must fit the experience of the Church and the world, and it would appear that it should be formulated in ethical terms, rather than in psychological or theological terms. Its primary focus should not be the free personality, or the concept of justification by faith, but the movement from the cloister to the world, because today's Protestantism consists essentially in a movement away from the sacred place.

Hamilton feels that his interpretation of the meaning of the Reformation, coupled with his preliminary negative comment, offers a kind of faith. But this form of faith is not a clinging by one's fingernails to the cliff of faith, not a terror-struck confession before the alien God. He writes:

[10] *Ibid.*, pp. 33–34.

It is not even a means of apprehending God at all. This faith is more like a place, a being with or standing beside the neighbor. Faith has almost collapsed into love, and the Protestant is no longer defined as the forgiven sinner, the *simul justus et peccator,* but as the one beside the neighbor, beside the enemy, at the disposal of the man in need. The connection between holding to the neighbor and holding to Jesus will be dealt with in a moment.

Here I reflect the thought of the later Bonhoeffer more than either van Buren or Altizer wants to or needs to. My Protestant has no God, has no faith in God, and affirms both the death of God and the death of all forms of theism. Even so, he is not primarily a man of negation, for if there is a movement away from God and religion, there is the more important movement into, for, toward the world, worldly life, and the neighbor as the bearer of the worldly Jesus.[11]

Something in the essence of Protestantism itself, Hamilton maintains, inclines one to move into the world. But that world to which one is driven is not the world of such modern writers as Henry James, Eliot, Yeats, Pound, Joyce, Lawrence, Kafka, Faulkner, or Beckett, all of whom are seeking freedom from a middle class society or even from society itself. For it is impossible, at least in some very important ways, says Hamilton, to affirm the values of the technological revolution, the legitimacy of the hopes and claims of the dispossessed, and the moral centrality of the Negro revolution in America, and still live comfortably in the world as they portray it. Thus, in many ways, today's Protestant is driven into the world they reject—the secular world of technology, power, money, sex, culture, race, poverty, and the city. "Thus the worldliness affirmed by Protestantism has a postmodern, pro-bourgeois, urban, and political character."[12]

But Protestantism is not only a movement toward the world; contemporary Protestantism demands a simultaneous movement away from God and religion as well. This factor underlines the unique and distinctive feature of this movement, namely the formation of a radically new form of Christianity: *religionless Christianity*. Today, Hamilton continues, there are at least two different schools of interpretation of Protestant religionlessness. The first

[11] *Ibid.,* pp. 36–37.
[12] *Ibid.,* p. 38.

school of thought is the moderate, or the *Honest to God* school, for which religion essentially means some sort of religious activity: the liturgy, counseling, going to church, saying prayers, and so forth. This group advocates radical experimentation in such areas as the form of the Church and the ministry. But there is a second school, popularly known as the death-of-God school, which is far more radical in its approach to religion. Religion, for this group, is not understood as man's arrogant grasping for God, in the Barthian sense, nor is it understood in terms of certain external forms of worship and ritual observance, as is the case with the moderate radicals. This group (or at least Hamilton) defines religion as any system of thought or action in which God (or the gods) serves as the fulfiller of needs or the solver of problems. Hamilton joins with Bonhoeffer in asserting the breakdown of the religious *a priori* and man's coming of age. Religionlessness, for him, is the combination of a certain kind of God-rejection and a certain kind of world-affirmation. In referring to the breakdown of the religious *a priori,* Hamilton means that there is no way, ontological, cultural, or psychological, to demonstrate that God is a necessary component in assessing the meaning of human existence. God is not a necessary Being; he is not needed to help man avoid despair or self-righteousness. God is merely one of the many possibles which present themselves in the radically pluralistic spiritual and intellectual milieu in which we find ourselves. For man come of age, God is not necessary.

This is just what man's coming of age is taken to mean. It is not true to say, with Luther, *entweder Gott oder Abgott.* It is not true to say, with Ingmar Bergman, "Without God, life is an outrageous terror." It is not true to say that there are certain areas, problems, dimensions to life today that can only be faced, solved, illumined, dealt with, by a religious perspective. Religion is to be defined as the assumption in theology, preaching, apologetics, evangelism, counseling, that man needs God, and that there are certain things that God alone can do for him. I am denying that religion is necessary and saying that the movement from the church to the world that we have taken as definitive of Protestantism not only permits but requires this denial. To assert that we are men moving from cloister to world, church to world, to say that we are secular men, is to say that we do not ask God to do for us what the world is qualified to do. Really to travel along this road means that we trust the world, not God, to be our need-ful-filler and problem-solver, and God, if he is to be for us at all, must come in some other role.[13]

Hamilton feels that his position is to be distinguished from ordinary Feuerbachian atheism. In proposing his own version of Christian atheism, he is firmly convinced that his synthesis reflects the best elements found in Altizer's mysticism and van Buren's Christological ethic. He is searching for the best way of handling the historical experience of the death of God. First, he is in complete sympathy with the idea of "waiting" which he finds in Altizer; this introduction of an element of hope or expectation distinguishes this form of atheism from the classical forms, and it removes a large amount of the anguish and gloom which one might expect in the wake of the death of God. Man may someday come to discover what it really means to delight in God. Secondly, he notes that the theme of the Christological ethic worked out by van Buren fits in quite easily with his own emphasis on contemporary Protestant worldliness.

By way of a provisional summary: The death of God must be affirmed; the confidence with which we thought we could speak of God is gone, and our faith, belief, experience of him are very poor things indeed. Along with this goes a sharp attack on religion which we have defined as any system using God to meet a need or to solve a problem, even the problem of not having a God. Our waiting for God, our godlessness, is partly a search for language and a style by which we might be enabled to stand before him once again, delighting in his presence.

In the time of waiting we have a place to be. It is not before an altar; it is in the world, in the city, with both the needy neighbor and the enemy. This place really defines our faith, for faith and love have come together in the interim of waiting. This place, as we shall see, is not only the place for the waiting for God; it is also a way to Jesus Christ.[14]

In an effort to describe graphically the present state of affairs in American theology, Hamilton employs literary types taken from classical Greek drama and Shakespeare as symbolic theo-

---

[13] *Ibid.,* p. 40.
[14] *Ibid.,* pp. 41–42.

logical guides for modern man. The two literary analogues which he singles out as particularly descriptive of the present situation in American theology are the characters of Orestes and Prospero. The character of Orestes represents an advancement in maturity when compared with that of Oedipus, and the character of Prospero represents an advancement in maturity when compared with that of Hamlet. Hamilton suggests that a comparable evolution in maturity is discernible in the development of American theology in recent years.

He begins his comparison by saying that one might describe the state of American theological thought during the past thirty years as being in the Oedipal stage of development. But the time has now come for theology to move into a more mature post-Oedipal situation, where the representative hero of this new situation becomes Orestes. On the psychological level, Oedipus stands for the individual as he moves into his central crisis of growth and self-identity, as he solves the problems of his adolescence or his coming of age. He demonstrates the individual's psychological bondage, his lack of freedom, and his lack of clear direction. In the theological mode, Oedipus represents the confused and questioning man who is trying to find the inner meaning of love, authority, rebellion, fatherhood, and so forth. "The Oedipal believer," says Hamilton, "is a man standing still and alone in a desolate place. He is looking up to the heavens; he has no eyes of flesh, only eyes of faith, and he is crying out his questions to the heavens."[15]

However, on the psychological level, Orestes represents the individual as having gone beyond this identity crisis in the maturation process. His character manifests the freedom of the individual and his struggle for consistency and harmony. Unlike Oedipus, Orestes does not act under the influence of inexorable fate; his actions are performed in the light of a destiny based on a free and deliberate choice. It will be remembered that Oedipus inadvertently kills his father, while Orestes, through loyalty to his father, freely chooses to kill his corrupt mother. Orestes underlines man's need to master and accept anxiety and to find a meaningful and constructive role in society. Thus, Orestean theology means an

[15] *Ibid.*, p. 43.

end to preoccupation with inner conflict, to the agony of faith, and to the careful confession of sin. Modern man must learn to be completely open to the world and to be available to his fellow-man. In theological thought, therefore, Orestes can be proposed as a paradigmatic hero for contemporary man. Orestean theology indicates that, in order to overcome the death of the father (the death of God) in our lives, the mother (the mother who represents religion, security, warmth and authority, but who has become corrupt) must be abolished, and we must give our attention and devotion to the *polis,* to the city, to politics, and to our neighbor. Modern man must kill the mother to discover the as-yet-unformed meaning of his loyalty to the father. Hamilton writes:

> Thus, Protestant men, Protestant churches, and, most important here, Protestant theology, belongs in the street if it is to be truly Orestean. The academy and the temple can, for now, no longer be trusted as theological guides. Not only our action but our thought belongs with the world of the city, which in our time means power, culture, art, sex, money, the Jew, the Negro, beauty, ugliness, poverty and indifference. Thought and action both must make the move from Oedipus to Orestes, from self and anxiety and crying out to the enemy-God, to the neighbor, the city, the world.[16]

An Elizabethan counterpart to the movement from Oedipus to Orestes is found in the movement from Hamlet to Prospero. Today, Hamlet theology is at an end, Hamilton says, and Prospero has become the paradigmatic hero in theological thought. Hamlet was faced with deciding whether to acquiesce to the demands of his father's ghost or whether to rebel. In a similar way, Hamlet theology is concerned with authority and with the father. "The Hamlet theology, thus, is one in which man is largely alone, in which he is obsessed by his own and his people's rottenness, and in which he, in his solitariness, wonders about God and what God wills." [17] The new theological hero for man come of age is Prospero, the man who gives up his charismatic power and magic, the man who releases Ariel, the man who leaves the place of magic and mystery and returns to his dukedom in Milan. Pros-

[16] *Ibid.,* pp. 44–45.
[17] *Ibid.,* p. 45.

pero represents the man who moves from the sacred, from the realm of magic and religion, to the world of the city.

Hamilton insists on the importance of realizing that the death of God must not be taken as symbolic rhetoric for something else. The death of God, he says, consists in a real sense of loss, of not believing, of not having. Man has lost not only the idols or gods of religion, but God himself. Also, the death of God is a public event in man's history, since it is not an experience peculiar to a neurotic few, nor is it entirely inward and private. Despite all this, however, man waits and hopes that something may emerge on the other side of the profound darkness of unfaith that presently envelops the modern world. In the meantime, man cannot remain content to simply sit and wait for the darkness to be dispelled; he must learn to concentrate all his energies and passions on the specific, the concrete, and the personal. He must learn to turn from the problems of faith to the reality of love. Man come of age is aware that there is no need for God or religion in the modern world. The question of God is an irrelevant problem. But the world of experience is real, and it is both necessary and right to be engaged actively in helping to change its patterns and structures. Thus, modern man refuses to consent to the traditional interpretation of the world as a shadow-screen of unreality which masks or conceals the eternal, considered to be the only true reality. Hamilton notes:

> The death-of-God Protestant, it can be seen, has somewhat inverted the usual relation between faith and love, theology and ethics, God and the neighbor. We are not proceeding from God and faith to neighbor and love, loving in such and such a way because we are loved in such and such a way. We move to our neighbor, to the city and to the world out of a sense of the loss of God. We set aside this sense of loss or death, we note it and allow it to be, neither glad for it, nor insistent that it must be so for all, nor sorry for ourselves. And, for the time of our waiting we place ourselves with our neighbor and enemy in the world.[18]

To differentiate his position of Christian atheism from that of sheer atheistic humanism, Hamilton asserts that our way to our neighbor is not only mapped out by the secular or profane social,

[18] *Ibid.,* p. 48.

psychological, and literary disciplines, but it is also mapped out as well by Jesus Christ and the example of his way to his neighbor. Further, Jesus is found in the concrete work carried on in the world today. He finds that basically there are two forms of the presence of Jesus Christ in the contemporary world. At times the work of the Christian is to discover Jesus under the masks of the world, for he may be concealed in the world, in the neighbor, in the struggle for beauty, clarity, and order. Moreover, in this process of continually searching for Christ, the Christian also discovers himself. But there is also another form of the presence of Jesus Christ in the contemporary world. Under this form, the individual Christian strives to become Jesus in and to the world. In pursuing this goal, the Christian life, ethics, and love become first of all a decision about the self. This is then followed by a movement beyond the self into the world of men. Hamilton says that man should not waste time looking for Jesus "out there," in such places as scripture, tradition, sacraments, Ingmar Bergman movies, or in the world behind a mask; let him become a Jesus to other men.

Hamilton admits he may be proposing a too simple marriage between Christology and ethics, but he suggests that the Christian of today will find a viable form of Christianity in the adoption of one or both of the paths to Jesus that he proposes. In formulating his radically new concept of Christianity, a Christianity without a supreme being, he is convinced that today man must learn to follow Jesus more closely than ever before, without letting the silence, the loneliness, and the deprivation occasioned by the death of God hinder his commitment to Christ and his fellowman.

4. The Religious Vision of Dostoevsky

Hamilton tells us that his immersion into the thought of Dostoevsky was a decisive influence in his transition from the neo-orthodox to the radical school of theological thinking. In the final analysis, the two forces which ultimately effected this change of mind were an analysis of the character of Ivan Karamazov and the inchoate theological vision of Dietrich Bonhoeffer. Hamilton believes that an insight into Dostoevsky's own religious vision can be revealed through a careful study of the characters in the novel *The Brothers Karamazov*. Dostoevsky can certainly teach us what our despair is like, he says, but can he teach us how to believe or how to live? Hamilton writes:

> The theme or problem of the novel is the existence of God, though the problem so defined is not identical with the plot. The plot turns on the rivalry between Dmitry and his father for the favors of Grushenka, with the murder of old Karamazov forming the climax. Dmitry is falsely accused, but he accepts his suffering and is changed by it. Smerdyakov, the true murderer and a follower of what he takes to be Ivan's ideas, hangs himself. Ivan partly comes to see that he is the true murderer, collapses under the strain, and may or may not be healed at the end.
>
> The plot begins to fit into the problem as soon as we note that both the literary and theological center of the book lies in the character of the three (legitimate) Karamazov sons, Ivan, Dmitry, Alyosha, and their relationship to the death of their father. The three brothers, taken together, are a portrait both of Russian man and of Dostoevsky himself: what he knew he was and what he hoped to become. He *is,* indeed, *The Brothers Karamazov.*[19]

The Karamazov family as a whole, Hamilton says, is marked by unique character traits: shame and self-pity, sensuality and unbelief. All of the brothers, in one way or another, desire the death of the father, and each of them (if we exclude the "brother" who is the actual murderer) participates to some degree in the death of the father, which Hamilton sees as probably standing for the death of God. Dostoevsky seems to identify the plot (the story of the murder) with the theme (the problem of God) by having both speak of the father's death. Thus, all of the brothers participate in some way in the death of God. But how can one return to the Father when he is dead? This, Hamilton suggests, is Dostoevsky's real religious problem in the novel. Dostoevsky is disturbed by the actual emptiness of man's life in this world, but it is the possible emptiness of the heavens that really terrifies him. The thoughts and actions of the three sons are actually reflections of his own religious vision.

[19] William Hamilton, "Banished from the Land of Unity," *Radical Theology and the Death of God,* pp. 54–55. Italics in original.

Dmitry Karamazov, noble but uncontrolled, rake and trouble-maker, is perhaps the truest *external* portrait of Dostoevsky, but the real *inner* tension in Dostoevsky is that symbolized by the struggle between Ivan and Alyosha: Dostoevsky's own struggle with the problem of God. But this struggle is not simply a bipolar tension between Alyosha as believer and Ivan as unbeliever. The struggle is complex and multi-dimensional, for there is a strange mixture of belief and unbelief which characterizes the psychological state and mental attitudes of each of the three brothers. In varying degrees, each of the three brothers represents the sensuality of the Karamazovs looking for the new man to be born. The similarities and differences among the three brothers come into sharper focus if we analyze the character of each one in detail.

Dmitry is presented to us as coarse and crude, but also as full of compassion and longing. In the end, he undergoes a type of conversion and is willing to suffer for a crime he did not commit in order to wipe away the sufferings of Russia. He rejects both suicide and cynicism because he sees that God will be present even in the mines to which he will be sent. "If they banish God from the earth," he cries, "we shall need him under the earth! . . . And then shall we, the men beneath the ground, sing from the bowels of the earth our tragic hymn to God, in whom there is gladness!" [20] On earth there is neither God nor human brotherhood, but both will be affirmed from the underground. Dmitry's future, Hamilton observes, is apparently one of salvation and hope, but his ultimate religious vision is a pagan one. He has undergone some sort of conversion, but it is a conversion to the earth, and perhaps even to a mystical vision of a united nation, but not to the Christian God. His eschatological vision is not Christian, because the foundation of the new unity between God and man in suffering is rooted in an identification of man with Mother Earth.

Turning to a consideration of the character Ivan Karamazov, we find that there is a theological, as well as an existential or personal, dimension to his struggle with the problem of the meaning of human existence. Literary critics, Hamilton says, usually emphasize the second aspect. The Karamazov vitality and lust for

[20] Cf. *ibid.,* p. 57.

life is certainly very much in evidence in the life of Ivan, but he is also the reflective man of reason bent on understanding the life he is living. Despite his search, he finds no simple solution to the problem of God and the problem of man.

> The warmth of his love and the coldness of his mind give Ivan two different answers to the problem of the freedom of the will. His mind affirms that man is free. His "poem" about the Grand Inquisitor tells us this; and this freedom is what finally leads him to rebel against God. But Ivan's actions convince him that there is no freedom, that all men are fated to be parricides, that no one can escape the curse. So man's denial of God is not a free choice; it is a mysterious and fateful necessity.[21]

In the course of the novel, Ivan gradually comes to realize that he is responsible for his father's death, and he decides to acknowledge his responsibility. But at the trial his testimony is confused and disordered because he is already seriously ill with brain-fever, and this development leaves Dmitry worse off than before. But Ivan's future, like that of Dmitry, seems to be one of salvation and hope. Alyosha remarks that the decision to confess and to try to assist his unjustly accused brother was a decision for virtue on the part of a man who did not believe in virtue.

But what factors influenced Ivan's decision? What was the problem which caused him so much anguish? Hamilton suggests that the problem of God was the focal point of Ivan's struggle to determine the meaning of human existence. He writes:

> So Ivan's struggle is more than a conventional one between logic and life, between emancipated intellectualism and the unshakable Karamazov lust. It is mainly a struggle about God. Is God dead? This is the real question that drives Ivan mad, for he cannot give a simple "yes" to it. The same question drove Nietzsche mad, and it may have very nearly driven Dostoevsky mad as well.[22]

Thus, Ivan's struggle with the meaning of life is complex. He is completely bewildered and confused by the existence of evil and

[21] *Ibid.,* p. 59.
[22] *Ibid.,* pp. 60–61.

suffering in the world, and he candidly confesses his inability to see life in more than three dimensions. In his tavern confession to Alyosha, he says that perhaps God is not dead, but is simply "accepted" by man. In the final analysis, it seems that it is not God that Ivan rejects, but the world that he has created. The reason for this rejection is that human suffering makes both God and the world incomprehensible. Thus God exists, but Ivan rejects his absurd world and returns to him the ticket of admission. This confession of the existence of God reveals a totally different aspect of Ivan's character. From time to time in the course of the novel, the hypothetical statement: "If God does not exist, then everything is permitted," is attributed to Ivan. But only on one occasion, Hamilton says, does Ivan directly declare his disbelief in God, and that instance is found in a somewhat playful discussion over brandy with his father. This hypothetical assertion seems to be a mask that Ivan hides behind, a statement he enjoys making at parties. Actually, his serious problem is not at all with the non-existence of God; in fact, the existence of God causes him more anguish than the non-existence of God ever could. Ivan's unbelief is not ordinary atheism. Ivan tests God against the standard of justice, and God fails the test. Even if God exists, Ivan still freely chooses to reject his world, for he considers it unjust that so much pain and human suffering should be necessary.

Therefore, Ivan (and perhaps even Dostoevsky himself) accepts God and yet refuses to believe in him or his world. He is a man in whom belief and rebellion are fatefully conjoined. This strange mixture of perversion and insight, rebellion and belief, is clearly in evidence in Ivan's poem about the Grand Inquisitor. Most commentators, Hamilton says, find it extremely difficult to discern what meaning, if any, this legend possesses. His own opinion is that the legend is deeply unclear. It is impossible to discover the root message contained in it because neither Ivan nor Dostoevsky knew himself well enough to express himself clearly and without ambiguity. Thus, after careful consideration of three different interpretations of the legend offered by D. H. Lawrence, Romano Guardini, and Nicholas Berdyaev, he concludes that the Godless Christ of the legend is not the Christian figure of Christ. The image of Christ in the legend is unclear because Ivan

had not made up his mind whether to praise or disparage Christ.
In both Ivan and Dostoevsky one finds an ambivalent mixture of
love and hatred for Jesus. In a summary evaluation of the import
of the legend, Hamilton writes:

> In his discussion of the relation of the ultimate to the penulti-
> mate, Dietrich Bonhoeffer points to two false ethical solutions
> which he calls compromise and radicalism. Compromise sees
> what needs to be done, and in order to do it, accepts the
> world in all its brutality. The Grand Inquisitor stands here.
> Radicalism sees only the goal, and every other consideration
> is rejected. Dostoevsky's Christ is here. Neither way is possi-
> ble, though Dostoevsky showed us only the two: the anarchy
> of love, or the ruling elect giving man what he wishes. Today
> we know too much to be satisfied with this simple set of alter-
> natives, but too little to coherently state a third way. The love
> of Christ, freely accepted by man, does make us truly free.
> But we also know something else. Men may do without spir-
> itual bread; they may even do without love; but they cannot
> do without earthly bread.[23]

Thus, Hamilton concludes that the religious vision of Dostoevsky, as projected in the thought and action of both Ivan and
Dmitry, is internally unclear. Which way does he want to go?
Does he want to go the way of Dmitry's sensual humility, singing
the praises of the earth-god from the subterranean depths? Or
does he want to go the way of Ivan, holding to God for fear of
annihilation, but hating him and his world? All of this remains
completely ambiguous. The God of Ivan's confession in the tavern
scene is unclear, the Godless Christ of the legend is unclear, and
the earth-god of Dmitry is unclear. It is impossible to relate any
of these ideas to distinctive Christian affirmations.

Many commentators argue that Dostoevsky was tempted to
go Ivan's way, but that in the course of the novel he surrendered
to the way chosen by Alyosha. The youngest brother, they say,
is Dostoevsky's sole claim to be taken seriously as a religious
guide. Hamilton concurs with their judgment that Alyosha is
certainly presented by Dostoevsky as a religious guide, but he
questions whether Alyosha's vision is any clearer than that of

[23] *Ibid.,* p. 72.

Ivan or Dmitry. Like the rest of the Karamazov family, Alyosha's character exhibits a mixture of belief and unbelief. He is a serious monk who at times has grave doubts concerning God. His religious faith is strong, but it is also unsophisticated and inadequately trained.

Instructing Alyosha just before his death, the saintly Father Zossima recommends that he fall upon the earth, embrace it, kiss it, and attempt to enter into spiritual communion with it. He also urges him to love all men and all things. Besides, he cites the resurrection theme of John 12: 24, and he urges Alyosha to remember this. After the death of Father Zossima, Alyosha expected that his body, like the bodies of holy men in the past, would be exempt from corruption. But when he returns to the elder's cell after his death, he finds that the body has already begun to decompose. Then he hears Father Paissy reading the story of the miracle at Cana, the first Johannine sign, and not the resurrection theme of John 12: 24. Seeing the corruption, Alyosha finds that his innocence is shattered by the ultimate finality of the event, and he leaves the cell and goes to Grushenka in an attempt to fathom the mystery of death. After seeing her, he returns to the cell and prays.

Hamilton says that all of this indicates that Dostoevsky is preparing us for a miracle of grace, for a transformation. Father Zossima is about to rise from the earth, but not in the literal sense. He is to rise in the form of Alyosha, the monk in the world. There is a resurrection theme present, but the biblical image associated with Cana is thought more appropriate than the Johannine resurrection motif to indicate the precise nature of Alyosha's conversion. Alyosha goes out into the starry night and falls upon the earth. Suddenly, feeling a great love for it, he embraces it, kisses it, and finds his whole being suddenly transformed. He is grasped by a powerful new force and filled with ecstasy and love, a love of the earth and all men. When he finally rises, he is armed with a new resoluteness and determination.

Hamilton says that this is not a description of a Christian experience. It is a conversion to something, but it is not clear precisely to what. There is a resurrection theme, but it is full of pantheistic and humanistic overtones. We are presented with a vision that points toward the highest possible development of man on earth, through the affirmation of such values as life, goodness, and beauty. But this basic insight is not new; it reflects the "religion of humanity" motif of the 19th century. Hamilton admits that Dostoevsky possessed prophetic vision, but he insists that his answers are fatally confused. In the final analysis, he proposes a vague populism and a quietism that tries to love all things, without facing the fact that we can only love particulars. Although he cannot tell us how we should live, he is still important.

> Dostoevsky is important because he can and does teach us how in fact we do believe, for he has understood, as only a great artist can, the struggle between belief and unbelief.
> Dostoevsky began as an atheist and a revolutionary in his twenties, and before his exile into Siberia he had been a profound explorer of the underground depths of man's nature. While in Siberia he was converted to a sort of mystical populist faith which ultimately came to be directed toward the Russian people as bearers of God, a nation-church. The twin strands of belief and unbelief were always together in him, and it seems as if he never really rid himself of either.[24]

Finally, Hamilton argues that Dostoevsky was simultaneously both a convinced atheist and a convinced believer. He even rejects Dostoevsky's own claim, made at the close of his life, that he had broken through his doubt and had moved into a kind of faith. The novel, also written toward the close of his life, does not support this claim. Dostoevsky continually oscillates between the polar extremes of belief and unbelief, and he seems never to have resolved the tension in his own life. In the end, Hamilton suggests, it is perhaps best not to claim to have discovered the final secret of Dostoevsky's religious vision. But whether it is Dostoevsky's fundamental lack of clarity or our own blindness that prevents our acceptance of the view of Alyosha, nevertheless, we do find a self-portrait of ourselves in Ivan's picture of himself. Hamilton says: "The God that is dead for him is dead for us; and his Karamazov-God of tension and terror is often the only one we are able to find." [25] Thus, Ivan does not tell us how to live or how to

[24] *Ibid.,* p. 81.
[25] *Ibid.,* p. 84.

believe, but his vision does tell us how in fact we do believe. It seems that clarity and certain faith are part of an eschatological vision, the reality of which can never be enjoyed now.

5. The New Theologian

In an essay entitled "Thursday's Child," Hamilton presents his ideas regarding the emergence of a new type of theologian.[26] The essay, he says, is not entirely autobiographical. The device of using an ambivalent narrator is employed to keep the reader off guard by having him argue with a series of moods and happenings rather than with the author himself. In this essay, he has attempted to portray in graphic terms the new American theologian searching for a viable mode of existence in a confused and rapidly changing world. He argues that the theologian of today and tomorrow has far to go, as the title of the essay indicates, for he is a man without hope, without faith, with only the present, with only love to guide him and to provide a meaning for his life. Hamilton attempts to demonstrate the validity of this assertion by comparing the historical triad past-present-future with the operational triad faith-love-hope, and then applying this model to the actual experience of today's theologian.

Non-theological observers, Hamilton remarks, have described the American as someone fated to be a man without a sense of the past and without a sense of being able to count on a stable future. Profane and secular America has traveled farthest along the road from the cloister to the world that Luther and the Reformation mapped out. But in the course of this development, it lost something; for Western Europe and the Communist world have a kind of spiritual substance and vitality which is lacking in America. The foundations of faith have been lost.

Hope, says Hamilton, is the way of declaring one's future open and assured, and love is the way of standing before your neighbor in the present moment. Thus, if we consider faith, hope, and love together, it seems that the American can really live in only one of them at a time, perhaps only one in a lifetime. If this is true,

[26] William Hamilton, "Thursday's Child," *Radical Theology and the Death of God,* pp. 87–93.

reasons Hamilton, and if it is true that the American is fated to be a man without a sense of the past or the future, then the contemporary theologian is found to be a man without faith, without hope, with only the present, with only love to guide him.

In trying to present a composite picture of the attitudes, interests, and activities of the new theologian, Hamilton begins by noting that the theologian in America today is a man without faith, and he proposes that this state of affairs should not only be acknowledged but even willed. Such a theologian, of course, has a doctrine, or doctrines, concerning God, but "he really doesn't believe in God, or that there is a God, or that God exists," because he has suddenly discovered a void, a disappearance, an absence, at the center of his thoughts and meditations. In other words, he has found himself to be without faith.

Other discernible characteristics are also evident in the new American theologian. One notable feature of the new theologian is that he does not go to church. Why? Because he finds himself alienated from God, from Christendom, from Christianity, and from the Church. Although, in the past, he tended to immerse himself in Church works, in preaching, speaking and so forth, slaking his thirst for worship and Word in more protected communities, today's theologian is now admitting to himself and others that he can no longer believe in God or the Church and that he should not go to church. He is saying "no" openly. As a result of this decision to say "no" to the Church, he is neither despairing nor hopeful about the Church; he is simply not interested in the Church. He is not troubled because of this decision; he feels neither pride nor guilt. He has candidly admitted his unbelief to himself and decided to confess this unbelief publicly.

Today's theologian neither reads nor writes much serious theology. If he does happen to write, the motivation usually springs from sheer professionalism and not from any real and sincere interest in the topic. His reading in the area of theology has gradually narrowed down to paperbacks, articles, and reviews. He is familiar with the bible from a professional standpoint, but it has become a strange book for him, and he can no longer view it as the revealed Word of God to men. Yet on occasion he finds that certain isolated pieces or fragments suddenly come alive for him, but he is unsure why this happens or how it takes place. He must learn to cope with this alienation.

> The theologian is alienated from the Bible, just as he is alienated from God and the church. This alienation may not last. If it doesn't last, fine; if it does last, the theologian will have some piercing questions to ask of himself. But there are wrong ways (Karl Barth) and right ways to overcome this alienation, and for now he has to be honest with himself, with the God before whom he stands in unbelief, and he must wait.[27]

If this, then, is the actual state of affairs, how does such a theologian conduct himself? On the public and professional side of his life, Hamilton observes, he is likely to employ two different masks. "One is modestly devout, earnest and serious, one which he uses for his teaching and Church work. The other is a modestly worldly mask for his non-religious friends and for the forms of their common life."[28] But in his private life, in the inner core of his being, he realizes that these are masks and nothing more, and honesty and integrity impel him openly to admit his unbelief and faithlessness.

> He knows that his rebellion and unbelief is both deeper and uglier than his bland worldly mask suggests, and he knows also (a bit less assuredly?) that his devout mask is too vapid. To be a man of two masks is, he knows, to be less than honest. Thus, he has had to come out into the open about his faithlessness, even though he may suspect and hope that beneath it is a passion and a genuine waiting for something that may, one day, get transformed into a kind of faith even better than the one he has willed to lose.[29]

Part of the new theologian's trouble today centers around the doctrine of the nature of the Church. Professionally, he finds himself confronted with three quite different understandings of the Church. Only the third makes genuine sense to him, but he finds that it is far too imprecise to be very helpful to him. The first unsatisfactory view of the Church is the one operative in ecumenical

[27] *Ibid.*, p. 90.
[28] *Ibid.*
[29] *Ibid.*, pp. 90–91.

work or in Roman Catholic-Protestant dialogue, where the Church is defined by the classical marks: that is, in terms of unity, holiness, catholicity, and apostolicity. A second unsatisfactory way of viewing the Church is the one which asserts that the Church is found where the Word of God is preached and the sacraments rightly administered. Today's new theologian, however, finds that he has come to define the Church in a third way, a way which sees the Church as being present whenever Christ is being formed among men in the world. This view is based upon a sense of community, even though this community has no outlines, no preaching, no sacraments and no liturgy.

Thus, the new theologian whom we see emerging in today's world is a man who realizes that he has lost faith, God, and the Church. Although he is acutely aware of his loss and regrets it, he is not driven to despair. He remains a patient and passive man, a man silently waiting for a clarification of his unbelief, and perhaps even for a new form of belief. His waiting reflects none of the existential moodiness found in many quarters today. Although, in a sense, he is also deprived of hope, and although he cannot accept any single Christian doctrine, he refuses to despair, choosing to follow the example of Christ suffering in the garden of Gethsemane.

The theologian today is thus both a waiting man and a praying man. His faith and hope may be badly flawed, but his love is not. It is not necessary to probe the cultural, psychological, or even marital reasons for this, but simply to note it as a fact. In Christology, the theologian is sometimes inclined to suspect that Jesus Christ is best understood as neither the object nor the ground of faith, neither as person, event or community, but simply as a place to be, a standpoint. That place is, of course, alongside the neighbor, being for him. This may be the meaning of Jesus' true humanity and it may even be the meaning of his divinity, and thus of divinity itself. In any case, now—even when he knows so little about what to believe—he does know where to be. Today, for example, he is with the Negro community in its struggle (he will work out his own understanding of what "being with" must mean for him), working and watching, not yet evangelizing. He is also with all sorts of other groups: poets and critics, psychiatrists and physicists and philosophers. He is not in these places primarily to make things happen—a new solu-

tion to the science-religion problem or a new theological literary criticism—but just to be himself and to be attentive, as
a man and therefore as a theologian. This is what the form
of love looks like. It is a love that takes place in the middle
of the real world, the ugly, banal, godless, religious world of
America today.[30]

As viewed by Hamilton, therefore, the contemporary American
theologian is a man without faith and without hope; he is a man
without God and without the Church. The only dynamic force
which gives his present existence any real meaning is human love.
And to make love an operative force in his life, today's theologian
finds that he should perhaps reinterpret Jesus Christ. Rather than
viewing him as the personal object or ground of faith, today it is
perhaps better to define him as a place to be, a standpoint. In treating of the nature of this love, Hamilton writes:

> His love is not a secure and confident one, and thus it is not
> condescending. It is not, therefore, what some men call *agape*.
> It is a broken love, one that is needy and weak. It is thus a
> little like what men call *eros*. To be sure, his whole project may
> be swept away in a moment, if it can be shown that the theo-
> logian is just fleeing from one kind of religion-as-need-fulfill-
> ment to another. Perhaps someone will be able to show him
> that his weak and needy love has some points of connection
> with the love of the Cross.[31]

Hamilton believes that some help in this situation might be offered by Dietrich Bonhoeffer, whose theological writings open up
new possibilities for the American theologian in his search for the
meaning of Christian love in a world come of age.

6. Dietrich Bonhoeffer

Hamilton feels that the writings of Dietrich Bonhoeffer—the
young German theologian executed by the Nazis on April 9, 1945,
at age 39—are exerting a decisive theological influence on the
younger generation of Protestant thinkers in the United States.
After reading Dostoevsky and Bonhoeffer, Hamilton himself de-

[30] *Ibid.,* pp. 92–93.
[31] *Ibid.,* p. 93.

cided to cross the line separating the liberal and the radical schools of theological thought. In Hamilton's estimation, Bonhoeffer provides the only recent theological writings which enable American theologians to understand adequately the new era into which we are moving. Vahanian calls it post-Christian, and Kenneth Boulding calls it post-civilized. Hamilton notes that Bonhoeffer is not an important or influential figure in West Germany or Switzerland, the traditional intellectual centers of Protestant theology. But in the United States his writings are teaching a few Protestants what it means to say "yes" to the 20th century and still stay recognizably Protestant. A radically accelerating pace of secularization characterizes the present era, and modern man is searching for a viable form of Christianity, a form flexible enough to assimilate recent changes. Religion has become more and more unimportant, powerless, and irrelevant in the modern world. Man now lives in an age of rapidly expanding technology, of mass media, of great danger and experimentation.

Hamilton contends that one of Bonhoeffer's most important contributions to this new climate of theological thought is his book *Letters and Papers from Prison,* which was edited and published posthumously. He focuses his attention on three key concepts which he feels provide the basic framework for a new style of Protestantism.

The first concept he singles out for interpretation is Bonhoeffer's affirmation that the world has "come of age." This statement, says Hamilton, reflects Bonhoeffer's conviction that the world has finally moved out of its adolescence and reached an adult phase. In accordance with this newly acquired maturity, Bonhoeffer suggests that modern man adopt a full, ungrudging, affirmative attitude toward the secularizing process which has been gradually developing in the West since the 13th century. Christians have always been offended by the self-assurance of Western secular man, but the traditional Christian uneasiness in the presence of such anthropocentric confidence, assurance, and independence is wrong. God is not a working hypothesis, and man must learn to live without him, *as if* he were not there. This movement toward secularism, autonomy, and away from God is to be approved for theological reasons; dependence and need are not proper descriptions of man's relationship with God. Thus the modern Christian is asked to accept the world without God as something given and unalterable. In a world come of age, man can no longer be religious, if religion be defined as the system that treats God, or the gods, as need-fulfillers and problem-solvers. Reflecting on this view, Hamilton comments:

> There are thus no places in the self or the world, Protestants who listen to Bonhoeffer go on to say, where problems emerge that only God can solve. There are problems and needs, to be sure, but the world itself is the source of the solutions, not God. God must not be asked to do what the world is fully capable of doing: offer forgiveness, overcome loneliness, provide a way out of despair, break pride, assuage the fear of death. These are worldly problems for those who live in this world, and the world itself can provide the structures to meet them.[32]

Therefore, no longer should man view the world without God as something incomplete or broken. The modern world can do without God, and thus the idea of the innate religiousness of man, or the religious *a priori,* must be rejected. Not all men's hearts are restless until they rest in God.

Turning his attention to a second important idea that Bonhoeffer proposes—a religionless form of Christianity—Hamilton writes:

> The second idea which marks Bonhoeffer's influence and importance is his plea for a non-religious or religionless Christianity. Because the world is grown up and has moved out of its dependency situation, the God of religion, solving otherwise insoluble problems, meeting otherwise unmeetable needs, is impossible and unnecessary. Thus man cannot be said to need God at all; God is not necessary to man. With this affirmation, the substance of whole libraries of Protestant preaching, evangelism, apologetics and Christian education seems a little thin. If man does not need God, if he is not necessary to our lives, how can there be a God for us? Doesn't this lead to a fatal blurring of the line between belief and unbelief? Is it really possible to pull off, without sophistry or deceit, a definition of the Christian as the godless man?

[32] William Hamilton, "Dietrich Bonheoffer," *Radical Theology and the Death of God,* p. 116.

There are some Protestants who are definitely moving in this direction, seriously considering our time as the time of the death of God whose full advent Nietzsche's madman predicted. Others stop short and claim that we may be able to distinguish between using God and enjoying him, between *uti* and *frui*. Thus, we need to seek out the ways in which the unneeded and the unnecessary God may be enjoyed.[33]

The Christian viewpoint, Hamilton continues, is not a necessary one; it is merely one of the different possibilities available to man in the prevailing competitive and pluralistic spiritual situation. What Bonhoeffer is actually doing is undermining the traditional Christian assurance and confidence that it can persuade an indifferent world that it really needs God. Today, man is discovering that he can make it without God, without guilt and despair. Through his writings Bonhoeffer is forcing the contemporary Christian to shift his attention from the area of theology, apologetics, communications, hermeneutics, and so forth, and to begin to focus his interests and energies on the shape and quality of human life. Modern man is entering a time of confusion between theology and ethics, with the result that the communication of the Christian with our world is likely to be essentially ethical and non-verbal for some time to come. Today, therefore, the truth or falsity of the Christian message is determined by the degree of dynamic commitment of Christians to the modern world.

Hamilton devotes only a half paragraph to Bonhoeffer's enigmatic new vision of modern man as being offered an invitation to participate in the sufferings of God. He writes:

The time when the real vitality of Protestantism was intellectual and centered in the Academy is at an end. The Protestant continues to engage his unbelieving brother, but he is likely to be engaging him by working alongside him. What distinguishes the Christian from his non-Christian comrade? If there is any answer to that, it may well be found by meditating on the third, and most elusively powerful, of Bonhoeffer's ideas, written nine months before he was hanged: "Man is challenged to participate in the sufferings of God at the hands of a godless world." [34]

[33] *Ibid.,* p. 117.
[34] *Ibid.,* p. 118.

7. The New Optimism

The apparent movement from pessimism to optimism in contemporary American culture today provides a theme of interest to the radical Christian theologian. Analyzing this modern trend, Hamilton attempts to indicate how some theological responses to this recent movement may be developed. He admits that there are no methodological tools available for connecting the general spirit of optimism with the new optimism currently informing theology. As Hamilton uses the term, optimism refers to a willingness to count on the future and to hold a firm belief in the possibility of its real improvement.

Most people, he says, are gradually realizing that the neo-orthodox-ecumenical-biblical-kerygmatic theology has begun to weaken. This deterioration of established theology can be attributed both to theological and non-theological factors. In analyzing the theological reasons for this disintegration, Hamilton concludes that the death of God has played a predominant role.

> The theological reasons for the deterioration of neo-orthodoxy are beginning to become clear. Neo-orthodoxy was a striking protest against the liberal confidence that God could be possessed, and its return to the dialectic of the presence and absence of God testified to the way believers felt during the years before and after World War II. The reason neo-orthodoxy is not working today surely has something to do with the collapse of this dialectic, a collapse which is the overcoming of the presence of God by the absence that men are calling the death of God.[35]

Among the non-theological reasons for this recent deterioration of neo-orthodoxy, Hamilton finds that its doctrine of man played an important role in bringing about the present situation. From the Depression era up until the 1950's, neo-orthodoxy provided an interpretation of the despair and tragedy of daily events, an interpretation with strong pessimistic overtones. In the 1950's it assimilated psychotherapy, existentialism, and the I-Thou philosophy, and more and more it focused man's attention on his inner world and

---

[35] William Hamilton, "The New Optimism—from Prufrock to Ringo," *Radical Theology and the Death of God*, p. 157.

this turned his attention away from the world of politics which contributed so much to its formation in the 1930's and 1940's. Ironically, although neo-orthodoxy was born as a radical protest against liberal conformism, it now began to justify inner submission, prudent realism, and mature acceptance of the tragic structures which society was imposing on men. Men ceased being angered by injustice, and they gradually learned to delight in life's complexities and richness, despite the tragic dimension of human existence. A tragic sense of life, it was discovered, is congruent with nice manners, fine clothes, sensitivity to interpersonal relations, and a good conscience about the ratrace of daily living. Men simply sought the courage to accept the unchangeable and the inevitable. Thus, neo-orthodoxy contributed greatly to the creation of men skilled in avoiding unprofitable commitments, careful about risks, and very wise in knowing how not to make fools of themselves in their daily lives. Gradually, man learned to become quite at home in the world. Neo-orthodoxy helped to mold shrewd, realistic believers whose wry view of self and others could be as well confirmed by the poet, the existentialist novel, or one's analyst, as by theology.

But today all of this has changed. A radical transformation of attitudes is now in evidence in almost every sphere of human involvement. The earlier pessimism seems to have lost its persuasiveness and gradually given way to an increased sense of the possibilities of human action, human happiness, and human decency. If one were forced to select a date for this change of fundamental attitudes, Hamilton suggests that January 4, 1965, might be appropriate: the day on which T. S. Eliot died in London and Lyndon Johnson delivered his State of the Union message. Existentialism, he says, never enjoyed the extensive popularity in America or Britain that it enjoyed on the Continent, because the early writings of T. S. Eliot provided an adequate description of man's not being at home in the world. Johnson's speech, on the other hand, called attention to man's broadened horizon of possibilities and reflected a renewed confidence in man's ability to change the world around him. In symbolic terms, Prufrock has been superseded by Meersault.

Recently, sensitive authors like Saul Bellow have begun to write about the end of pessimism, the end of the wasteland era, the end of the hollow men. Moses Herzog, in Bellow's novel *Herzog,* vi-

olently rebels against the fashionable pessimism of modern intellectual life and lashes out against those who continuously speak of
dread, alienation, inauthenticity, and forlornness. This current
change of attitudes, especially in America, is described by Hamilton in the following terms:

> Is it possible to note, some forty years after the publication of
> Eliot's *The Hollow Men,* that the world has ended neither
> with a bang nor a whimper? There was a period in the recent
> past when the fear of the bang was acute, but in spite of Viet-
> nam today, America is not afraid, and it once more is
> beginning to take seriously the fact that it has a real future.
> Prufrock, the typist, the hollow men, never really connected
> with the real world; they were afraid of it. "In short, I was
> afraid." But on the night of Eliot's death, President Johnson
> invited his fellow countrymen not only to enter the world of
> the twentieth century but to accept the possibility of revolu-
> tionary changes in that world. Johnson's speech was just po-
> litical rhetoric, one can say, and he would be correct. But it
> was somehow unlike political rhetoric of other eras—it was
> believable. And the legislative record of the first session—on
> domestic issues—has partly confirmed the rhetoric. This shift
> we are charting from pessimism to optimism can also be de-
> scribed as a move from alienation to politics, from blues to
> the freedom song.[36]

This change of sensibility, he maintains, is clearly discernible in
at least three areas of modern life: in the social sciences, in art, and
in the civil rights movement. First, he finds that a vote of confidence
for a new optimism is being cast by representative men within the
field of the social sciences. Two men in particular, Kenneth Boulding and Marshall McLuhan, are especially confident about the future. In his recent book, *The Meaning of the Twentieth Century,*
Boulding expounds the thesis that modern man is moving into a
post-civilized society. Man should rejoice over this transition because he is learning to say "yes" to change, to technological ad-
vances, to automation, to widespread experimentation, and to mass
media communication. Today there is no apparent limit to man's
creativity, ingenuity, and ability to cope with the difficulties of human existence. This same basic sentiment is expressed by Marshall

[36] *Ibid.,* pp. 159–160.

McLuhan in his recent book, *Understanding Media,* where he urges contemporary man to participate in the exciting changes currently taking place in our post-civilized society. He criticizes literate Western man for rejecting new media of communication such as television and insists that such media should be viewed as extensions of consciousness, extensions which put us in contact with human projects everywhere. Developments in this area affect all levels of society; they reach the educated and the uneducated alike. Western man can no longer afford to remain aloof and disinterested in the affairs of men. Each individual is now totally involved in everything that happens, and he must therefore begin to acquire a certain degree of empathy and depth of awareness.

Hamilton feels that these two men are isolated but, at the same time, eloquent and prophetic voices crying in the wilderness. These two men, and a few others, see the actual situation as it really is, and they invite modern man to responsible and enthusiastic participation in molding the future of man.

The vote for optimism which was cast in the field of the social sciences is seconded by certain representatives in the field of art. Lionel Trilling, for example, in a recent essay entitled "The Two Environments," attacks the proposal that literature should serve an almost religious function and the suggestion that alienation and despair are the artist's only gift to the moral life of man. Some of his views parallel Bellow's recent concerns. Another example of this newly emergent spirit of optimism in the arts is found in the music of John Cage, a leading opponent of the modern tradition of art as a form of self-expression. Cage rejects the idea of art as the imposition of the artist's selfhood and creativity on the chaotic components of human existence and experience, the idea that art is work, something serious, and intended to bear serious value. The end of art, according to Cage, is not order or value, but purposeless play. Art is not the uncovering or portrayal of the human condition; it is selfless celebration or play, reflecting an interest in the ordinary experiences of human existence. According to this view every man has the capacity to be an artist, and the only materials he needs to practice his art are the ordinary moments of his daily life. A similar concept of art, Hamilton says, is encountered in certain forms of contemporary art as exemplified, for instance, in the

work of Robert Rauschenberg where the ordinary things a technological society rejects, Coke bottles, used cans, old newspapers,
tires, and so forth, can be reassembled by the artist into something
attractive and beautiful. This protest against artistic self-expression is also encountered in the theater of the absurd, some recent
film-making techniques, the anti-novelists of France, and even in
the currently popular music of the Beatles. Hamilton feels that a
basic undercurrent of new optimism is found in the Beatles' music
and in their first movie, *A Hard Day's Night,* particularly in the
surrealistic scene of their jumping, dancing, and abandon in an
open field. The movie reflects a festive mood of celebration and re-
joicing characteristic of this generation.

But the most decisive piece of evidence indicating this move
from pessimism to optimism, in Hamilton's estimation, is provided
by the civil rights movement where we find gaiety, an absence of
alienation, and a vigorous and contagious hope. The dynamic principle underlying this movement is a clearly discernible optimism,
an optimism beyond tragedy, beyond alienation, and beyond existentialism. This optimism is clearly mirrored in its songs, such as
"We Shall Overcome." Thus a new enthusiasm is now becoming
manifest, and we seem to be out of the 1950's, says Hamilton, the
era when the young were tame, safe, and cool, the era when the
mysterious recesses of consciousness and inner identity were explored under the leadership of J. D. Salinger and William Golding.
The 1960's, he adds, may prove to be the time for celebration,
play, and hope.

It seems that ultimately all forms of pessimism—political, theological and cultural—are coming to an end. But what does theology
make of this new optimism? There are some, Hamilton says, who
contend that this new anti-pessimism compels modern man to look
up some optimistic parts of the Christian tradition, and who suggest that the life of Jesus with his disciples should be the theological
center of the new theology, just as Paul's struggle with the law was
the foundation of the post-liberal development. In other words,
man should move from the "pessimism" of Paul to the eschatological optimism of the synoptics to provide a biblical base for the new
optimism. But Hamilton is not interested in searching out biblical
or theological foundations for something that has already taken

place. Yet he is convinced that there are some theological reasons, in addition to some of the cultural factors cited, which help to explain the emergence of this new optimism. In general terms, the current phenomenon of the death of God has made this new optimism possible. One begins to see the connection between the death of God and the new optimism after analyzing the real meaning of tragedy.

Some intellectuals, Hamilton says, are saying that there are no tragedies around today and that there cannot possibly be any, for the presence of tragedy requires the presence of God or the gods, and that presence is precisely what we do not have today. According to these men, then, the death of God has brought about the death of tragedy. Hamilton calls attention to George Steiner's thesis, as formulated in *The Death of Tragedy,* which states that we have not had tragedy since the 17th century, and that the disappearance of the tragic man is the consequence of the disappearance of the presence of God who makes tragedy possible. But Hamilton does not agree with this analysis. He thinks Steiner correct in insisting on the end of tragedy and the tragic man, but wrong in simply identifying the death of tragedy in the 17th century with the death of God. He is also wrong, Hamilton continues, in his simple affirmation that the presence of tragedy and the tragic man requires the presence of God. In his own evaluation of the real nature of tragedy, Hamilton concurs with the judgment of Lucien Goldmann, as expressed in *The Hidden God,* that tragedy thrives not on the mere presence of God but on the dialectic between his presence and absence. Tragedy is at an end today because that dialectic has broken down. Hamilton writes:

> The death of God, only hinted at in the seventeenth century, is the breakdown of the dialectic between the presence and absence. Absence has won a decisive victory over the presence. The madman predicted it, the plays of Ibsen work out the transformation of God into the conscience of man, and with Karl Marx the divine reality becomes the historical process. The greatest holdout in the nineteenth century was perhaps Dostoevsky, in whose very soul the struggle between the presence and the absence of God took a classical form. He was both Ivan and Alyosha.[37]

[37] *Ibid.,* p. 168.

Hamilton concludes that the new mood of optimism which now pervades modern attitudes seems to indicate that tragedy is culturally impossible or unlikely at the present time. Man is confident that he can solve any problem which might arise, no matter how difficult it might be. Besides, it seems that tragedy is also theologically impossible today, due to the death of God, to the definitive breakdown of the dialectic between presence and absence, and to the rupture of that polar equilibrium which is an essential component of tragedy. With the death of tragedy, a new spirit of optimism is emerging.

> This is not an optimism of grace, but a worldly optimism I am defending. It faces despair not with the conviction that out of it God can bring hope, but with the conviction that the human condition that created it can be overcome, whether these conditions be poverty, discrimination, or mental illness. It faces death not with the hope for immortality, but with the human confidence that man may befriend death and live with it as a possibility always alongside.
>
> I think that the new optimism is both a cause and a consequence of the basic theological experience which we today call the death of God.[38]

8. The Significance of the Death of God

For Hamilton, the death of God is not an abstract idea, but a real and concrete event, an event which occasions terror for some and a joyous sense of liberation for others. Hamilton and other radical Christian theologians are definitely members of the second group. In an article entitled "The Death of God," which appeared in the August 1966 issue of *Playboy* magazine, Hamilton tries to clarify some of the various meanings that the term "death of God" might have for modern man.[39] He begins his presentation by describing the idea as difficult, complex and mysterious. First of all, he says, one must realize that the death-of-God theologians are not talking about the absence, the eclipse, the withdrawal, the disap-

[38] *Ibid.,* p. 169.
[39] William Hamilton, "The Death of God," *Playboy* 13 (August, 1966).

pearance, or the silence of God—all of which are legitimate ideas
within the context of the orthodox Christian tradition. The death-
of-God theologian does not expect the return of the Christian God
under any form. He has experienced the death of God, and he
suspects that others have shared this same experience. In accordance with the intellectual and spiritual relativity of the present
age, he readily admits the relative character of his viewpoint. He
is primarily interested in trying to communicate his own experience
of this event, and he is not interested in trying to reduce Christianity to a non-controversial minimum which will be acceptable to
scientists, rationalists, and freethinkers.

Hamilton indicates that there are many *possible* meanings for the
term "the death of God," but he is content to enumerate only ten of
these possible meanings in some detail. The proposed meanings
cover a whole spectrum of different interpretations. Only the
second one is singled out for special comment.

> It might mean that there once was a God to whom adoration,
> praise and trust were appropriate, possible and even neces-
> sary, but that there is now no such God. This is the position of
> the death-of-God or radical theology. It is an atheist position,
> but with a difference. If there was a God, and if there now
> isn't, it should be possible to indicate why this change took
> place, when it took place and who was responsible for it.[40]

The death-of-God motif is found to be present, both directly and
indirectly, in the works of Goethe and the romantics, William
Blake, Hegel, Strauss, Feuerbach, Marx, Ibsen, Strindberg,
George Eliot, Matthew Arnold, Hawthorne, and Melville. Hamilton argues that the coming and death of Jesus makes God's death
possible, that the 19th century makes it real, and that contemporary
man must come to understand it and accept it. In a sense, God
died with Jesus on the cross. In another sense, he died in the last
century in Europe and America. And in a third and final sense, he
has died today in the experience of man.

The death-of-God theologian is not trying to convince others of
this event; he simply calls attention to his own experience of the
event. His affirmation that God is dead is not based on any single

[40] *Ibid.,* p. 84.

or startling discovery; rather, it is the result of the convergence or confluence of many factors, a congeries of many elements, insignificant in themselves, but overpowering when seen in conjunction. Hamilton cites two reasons why he personally believes that God is dead. First, God is no longer necessary for man as a problem solver or as a meeter of needs. Some men may still need God, but there are some who do not. There is no longer any dimension to human existence which man must call God. Secondly, man is faced with the problem of unmerited suffering, and it seems impossible to reconcile the reality of suffering with the alleged goodness and power of God. The problem of Job, Ivan Karamazov, and Albert Camus now confronts us. After Auschwitz, the Christian God became impossible. Hamilton continues:

> Let me put this in another way. The death of God means two closely related things: that some of the human experiences to which men have traditionally given the name of God must be redescribed and renamed, and also that some of those experiences are no longer ours. For example, religious men have often pointed to experiences of dependence, awe, reverence, wonder, mystery, tragedy as signs of the incalculable and mysterious character of life, saying of these experiences taken together, "Something like this is what we mean by God." There are, of course, such things about us, and the only point I wish to make here is that one needn't give any of them the name of God. They are real facts of our life; we have human sciences and arts to clarify them, and they point to mystery and wonder, but not to God.
>
> But a second thing is just as true. There are experiences that men have had in the past and which they have traditionally understood as pointing to God that are simply not available to us in the same way today. Take the experience of dependence, especially in the presence of nature. Listen to a research biologist or a doctor or a physicist or a space scientist talk about his work. He is talking about mastery, control and power, not about a sense of his smallness before the universe. . . . Are there other traditional religious experiences that we're losing touch with? The death of God lives in this kind of world.[41]

The death-of-God theology, he adds, does not attempt to reduce life to the dimensions of the scientifically knowable or the imme-

---

[41] *Ibid.*, p. 138.

diately relevant. It accepts the mysterious, the sacred, the holy, and the transcendent, but it does not call these things God. It attempts to discover Godless forms of the sacred, new forms whereby such realities as sex or death can assume sacred dimensions.

How, then, should man react to the death of God? The death-of-God theology replaces God with the human community—not as it is now, but with a view of what it might become—and with Jesus, the man. Man has learned that the traditional attributes of God—forgiveness, consolation, judgment, and so forth—can be exercised by the human community. In the second place, Jesus, the man for others, is an appropriate surrogate for God when viewed as the focal point of obedience or the object of trust and loyalty.

Hamilton concludes his presentation in the following terms:

At the start of this article, the question was posed whether the death of God might be a non-event, fashioned by nothing more substantial than the eager and empty publicity mills of our day. We radical theologians have found, I think, that it is something more. It is a real event; it is a joyous event; it is a liberating event, removing everything that might stand between man and the relief of suffering, man and the love of his neighbor. It is a real event making possible a Christian form of faith for many today. It is even making possible church and ministry in our world.[42]

9. An Evaluation

William Hamilton's main reason for postulating the death of God is that he himself has personally experienced it in his own life, and he suspects that others have had basically the same experience. The modern world, he argues, has witnessed the gradual deterioration of the traditional image of the God-man relationship found in biblical theology and neo-orthodoxy. The death of God, he insists, is a public event, and not a private affair limited to the experience of a few neurotic individuals. It is a spiritual and intellectual reality. Because of the death of God in modern society, contemporary man has discovered that faith or belief in a tran-

[42] *Ibid.,* p. 139.

scendent, personal, spiritual Being and hope in such a Being are simply impossible today. His only reliable guides for the future are love and the example of Jesus Christ. Since modern man has now *come of age,* to use Bonhoeffer's expression, he must now assume full responsibility for his own future destiny, without any reference to, or dependence upon, the "God-hypothesis."

Is Hamilton's evaluation of the present religious situation accurate? Has modern man lost all ground for Christian faith and hope? Is God really dead? If he is dead, when did he die? In response to questions of this nature, we might begin by saying that one cannot quarrel with Hamilton's contention that the death of God is a personal experience in his own life. Furthermore, his suspicion that others have had fundamentally the same experience seems to be well founded, for it appears that a rather large segment of humanity today has lost all faith and hope in the Judaeo-Christian God. Many now find that they must strive to attain full maturity and autonomy within the immediate context of the world around them. They seek a new destiny rooted in purely anthropocentric and immanent values, since the Judaeo-Christian God has ceased to be an operative force in their daily lives. Thus, Hamilton is certainly not alone in his profession of disbelief.

Most serious religious believers find that it is difficult to point to a single reason which provides complete justification for the validity of their religious belief, attributing such a judgment to a convergence of a number of different factors. Thus it is not surprising to discover that Hamilton claims to be able to find no single reason for postulating the death of God, but argues that his unbelief is a judgment resulting from a confluence of many different factors. The rise of science, the emergence of radical immanence, the existence of evil and suffering in the world, and other aspects of the human condition all militate against a continued belief in a transcendent and personal God. Although these different components are not logically compelling when viewed in isolation, says Hamilton, they assume persuasive proportions when seen in close conjunction.

One serious objection to Hamilton's thesis regarding the death of God is that his statements concerning the precise nature of this event are extremely unclear and ambiguous. The phrase "the death of God," he insists, conveys a real sense of loss, indicating something irretrievable, something more than the mere absence, withdrawal, silence, or eclipse of God. But what precisely is this "something more"? In discussing some of the possible meanings the phrase might have, Hamilton focuses upon the following: "It might mean that there once was a God to whom adoration, praise and trust were appropriate, possible and even necessary, but that there is now no such God. This is the position of the death-of-God or radical theology." [43] But when and how did God die? Why did God die? According to Hamilton, God is always dying, as is shown by man's continual rejection of God as a problem solver, a meeter of needs, a necessary or useful hypothesis, and so forth. In a more decisive sense, God died in Jesus Christ, for the coming of Christ showed men that they no longer needed gods in the old religious sense. God died in a more definitive sense in the 19th century in Europe and America. In a final sense, God has died just now. Thus, Hamilton gives a three-part answer to the question of when this event took place. God is dead because man has discovered that he is unnecessary.

Hamilton insists that it is foolish to believe that the death-of-God advocate wants to reduce life to the scientifically knowable, the empirically verifiable, or the immediately relevant. Man should appreciate the mysterious, the awesome, the sacred dimension of human existence, he says, but he should not call that dimension God. Understood in this way, ultimate human realities such as love, sexuality, and death can assume the aura of the sacred.

But in the final analysis, Hamilton's treatment of the topic of the death of God is extremely vague and ambiguous. All that he says concretely about the phenomenon of the death of God at the present time is that modern man experiences the death of God in his daily life, and he finds this experience reflected in literature. At times Hamilton seems to imply that a real, personal, transcendent, spiritual Being whom men called God has actually died, while at other times he seems to indicate that God was only a psychological projection on the part of man, a projection that man has gradually learned to do without. Is Hamilton's dead God a person, a process, or an idea? Altizer, at least, makes an effort to delineate carefully

[43] *Ibid.*, p. 84.

what he means by the phrase "God is dead," and van Buren chooses not to speak of the death of God at all. Hamilton's treatment of this theme, however, is far too vague and nebulous to be either convincing or satisfying. At times, moreover, one gets the impression from reading Hamilton that the death of God is not as definitive and irrevocable as one has been led to believe.

In the aftermath of the death of God, Hamilton suggests that the only meaningful mode of existence available to the Christian is obedience to Jesus. Man come of age must learn to replace the dead God with Jesus and the human community. The human community alone cannot be expected to provide all of the functions previously associated with God. Although deprived of Christian faith and hope, contemporary man can still look to Jesus for inspiration, while relying upon the resources of love. While patiently waiting for a new form of faith and hope to appear, today's radical Christian should adopt a form of "religionless" Christianity, a way of life modeled on the life of Christ, a mode of belief that balances God-rejection with a form of world-affirmation.

In his theological thinking, Hamilton is more of a reductionist than either Altizer or van Buren. He does not insist, for example, upon retaining traditional Christian terms in verbalizing or formulating the new beliefs of radical Christianity. He frankly admits that the new radical theologian must be honest with himself and with others, openly saying "no" to the Church since he no longer believes in either God or the Church. He openly confesses that his Protestant has no God, no faith in God, no Church, and no sacraments. The only truly Christian dimension to Hamilton's fragmentary theology is the example provided by the life of Jesus Christ which serves as the sole integrating factor in his version of radical theology. Using Christocentric principles, Hamilton recommends the pursuit of personal righteousness, social justice, and a strong commitment to man and the world as being among the most important pursuits of man at the present time. Modern man should look to Jesus Christ for inspiration during this period of the death of God if he wants to discover what constitutes meaningful human existence in an atheistic framework. Rejecting all forms of traditional systematic theology, Hamilton advocates the adoption of a fragmentary approach to theological thinking, since this is what the present situation seems to demand. Theology, he argues, is a time-conditioned enterprise, and contemporary theology should be fragmentary if it is to reflect the intellectual, social, and cultural movements of the present era. The new theologian must learn to abandon structural unity and systematic consistency if he is to discover theological meaning. Thus, today's Christian is not compelled to accept a system of truths or a body of belief; he is free to retain certain elements of belief while abandoning others as he moves forward in his search for theological meaning.

It might legitimately be objected that Hamilton's fragmentary approach to theology is too unstructured. Perhaps the weakest point in his proposed version of Christian atheism is his emphasis upon Christocentric considerations. Why should modern man, now that he has come of age, model his life on the example provided by a Galilean peasant who lived almost 2,000 years ago? There have been many individuals in the history of mankind who have manifested a strong independent spirit and whose lives were characterized by a selfless love and a devotion to humanity. What is so outstanding in the life of Christ that would recommend him so strongly to Hamilton as the supreme paradigm for meaningful human existence in an atheistic framework? Why not choose a more contemporary figure? In response to questions of this nature, Hamilton is content to remark that he finds something in the New Testament writings about the life of Jesus which he does not find elsewhere.[44] But he never indicates precisely what this vague and nebulous "something" is. If Jesus is so important to his theological vision, then one has the right to expect far more clarity on this point.

Hamilton openly confesses that he cannot accept the personal, transcendent God of the Judaeo-Christian tradition, the scriptures, the Church, the sacraments, and so forth. He does not argue, as does Altizer, that the real meaning of the Christian message has been basically misunderstood by orthodox Christianity; he does not engage in mental gymnastics, as does van Buren, in a vain attempt to find a certain congruence between the fundamental intention of traditional Christian doctrines and the secular thought patterns of modern man. His Protestant is a man without God and

---

[44] William Hamilton, "The Shape of a Radical Theology," *loc. cit.*, p. 1221.

without a Church, but a man who uses Christ as a paradigm for daily living. In this sense, therefore, Hamilton's vision can be called a form of Christian atheism, despite the unusual juxtaposition of terms, and despite the fact that Hamilton never actually demonstrates any real intimate connection between his atheism and his Christology. During the time of the death of God, the radical Christian is invited to participate in the death of God by imitating the suffering Christ, the Christ of Gethsemane and the cross, the Christ who was truly the man for others.

The Jesus who forms the center of Hamilton's Christological reflection is a very elusive figure. Jesus, he concludes, is not so much a person as a place to be, and the place to be today is in the world of men, immersed entirely in the interests and concerns of men. This blurring of the Christological focus of Hamilton's version of Christian atheism causes one to ask: Just how Christian is this version of Christian atheism? In the final analysis, Hamilton's version of Christian atheism appears to be a conjunction of secular humanism and an idealized image of Jesus of Nazareth.

Why not select a more contemporary example? Why not select a man like Gandhi or Martin Luther King or John F. Kennedy or any other extraordinary individual who might possess highly valued characteristics—unusual freedom· and selfless dedication to the concerns and interests of mankind? Why should man come of age look back to this Galilean peasant for inspiration? This last question is particularly appropriate, in light of the fact that Hamilton's new radical vision is future-oriented. His new vision of Promethean man would seem to demand a more contemporary model than Jesus of Nazareth.

In his insistence upon the adoption of a fragmentary theological method, Hamilton overlooks the major Christian thinkers of the past 2,000 years, preferring to read the New Testament through the eyes of Fyodor Dostoevsky and Dietrich Bonhoeffer. He feels that his theology reflects the overtones of optimism which one detects in the present culture. His theology reflects modern man's sense of confidence and self-assurance that he has finally learned to live without God and that he is now fully capable of molding and shaping his own future along purely humanistic lines.

Ultimately, however, because of his failure to show any real connection between his atheism and his Christology, Hamilton's presentation of Christian atheism remains unconvincing both to the orthodox Christian and the secular humanist. But a careful analysis of Hamilton's ideas does serve a useful function for the serious Christian thinker within the orthodox tradition, for it forces him to attempt to clarify his own ideas in such areas as the nature of religious belief, secularity, the nature of God, the nature and function of Christ, and the relationship between God and man.

III
PAUL VAN BUREN

1. Introduction

The recorded history of both the Eastern and the Western world provides abundant and eloquent evidence that men of all ages and cultures have attempted to make meaningful statements about the existence and nature of God, and to express significantly the content of their religious belief. Such statements have been articulated within particular cultures, some more advanced than others. Available evidence also indicates that every age has possessed its share of skeptics and non-believers, men who question the accepted religious beliefs of their predecessors or their contemporaries. Belief and unbelief are two formative and polarized components. The tension between them has contributed greatly to the religious and intellectual history of man. It seems that man has always attempted to justify his religious belief both to himself and to others; conversely, the skeptic or the non-believer has always tried to justify his own position.

But in recent years the very possibility of making meaningful theological statements about God or the content of religious belief has been questioned by an ever increasing number of serious thinkers. Such opposition to significant theological predication finds its most articulate expression in the writings of logicians, philosophers of science, linguistic analysts, and logical positivists. Fundamentally, they all question the ability of the human mind to reach a trans-empirical object through a rational process of inference. By what right, they ask, can one take the terms of ordinary human experience, such as father, son, person, love, good, and so forth, and apply them with a significant shift and extension of meaning to something which we cannot directly experience? Must not the new elements introduced into the concepts, when applied beyond our own experience, be necessarily devoid of positive meaning? In other words, how does one justify analogous predication of divine attributes?

Some linguistic analysts, for instance, contend that metaphysical or theological questions are, of their very nature, unanswerable. These men assert that all meaningful discourse is empirical, and since metaphysical and theological statements are neither propositions of empirical science nor tautologies of logic or mathematics, they are therefore nonsensical and meaningless. Such statements are not factual; they are actually pseudo-statements which resemble factual statements in external form only. In actual fact, however, they are totally devoid of meaning, and this becomes evident under close logical scrutiny. The function of philosophy, they maintain, is to clarify statements in order to determine what meaning, if any, they possess.

But there are other linguistic analysts who argue that theological and philosophical statements can and do possess some real meaning. This meaning is discernible by the application of strict semantic analysis and depends upon linguistic usage within a given logical context. Thus, by analyzing statements of a philosophical or theological nature against the framework and background of their formulation, one can discover their meaning and import.

One modern thinker concerned with the contemporary problem of meaningful theological predication is Paul van Buren of Temple University. The starting point of his analysis is the predominantly secular orientation of modern man, and the principal methodological technique employed is linguistic analysis. Before investigating how van Buren arrives at a determinate secular meaning of the Gospel, it will be profitable to pause to consider in some detail the precise nature of linguistic analysis.

There are many different forms of analysis: mathematical, scientific, clinical, historical, literary, structural, and so forth. Linguistic analysis shares the same basic characteristics. It is fundamentally and essentially a tool, a method, a technique, and not a doctrinal philosophy or a school of philosophical thought. And because it is a tool, it does not offer a *weltanshauung*. As a tool or a method, it finds its justification and validation in pragmatic application. Insofar as it represents a trend or a movement rather than a monolithic school of thought, it resembles existentialism. But unlike existentialism, it does not attempt to make value judgments. Its sole function is to clarify and refine the contextual meaning of statements.

More precisely, we might say that, as a methodological technique, it analyzes concepts rather than words; it seeks to refine and clarify the ideas conveyed by words. Hence it is the study of language and its myriad complexities, but not in the manner of linguists, philologists, grammarians, or lexicographers. Its ultimate aim is to free everyday language from confusion and ambiguity by systematically applying the acuity of semantic analysis to proposed statements to determine their real meaning, if any. It demands clarification prior to speculation, and it insists on strict adherence to logical structure. Thus, linguistic analysis basically consists of a functional analysis of language, of a detailed and systematic examination of the way that language is used. It is a critical and rigorous study of contextual meaning.

Further, it is imperative that linguistic analysis should not be confused with logical positivism, despite their many similarities. Linguistic analysis traces its roots to British empiricism, while "logical positivism" was the term first coined in the 1920's to characterize the viewpoint of a group of philosophers, scientists, and mathematicians referred to as the Vienna Circle. Actually there are many characteristics which distinguish linguistic analysis from logical positivism, but for the purposes of this study it is necessary to differentiate between them on two levels only: the level of language and the level of verification. On the level of language, we find that logical positivism deals with an artificially constructed language, a scientifically structured propositional calculus. Linguistic analysis, on the other hand, is the study of ordinary language. On the level of verifiability, we find that logical positivism essentially denies the objective truth of statements which cannot be verified empirically. The exponents of this view see the methodology of the physical sciences as the only self-justifying and self-validating method of acquiring truth. Any other approach to the acquisition of truth is considered to be uncritical and unjustified. Viewed from this perspective, therefore, all philosophical and theological statements which purport to express something significant become meaningless because they are unverifiable according to the principle of empirical verification. There are many linguistic analysts who would concur with the logical positivists in their judgment regarding the meaninglessness of philosophical and theological statements, but most linguistic analysts adopt a more flexible, more refined, more sophisticated standard of verification than that employed by logical positivists.

Most linguistic analysts, following the insights of the later Wittgenstein, adopt a deceptively simple methodological principle: the meaning is in the use. According to this view, the meaning of a term is identical with its use; the meaning of a statement is discovered by a functional analysis of it within its proper contextual framework. Meaning is not something lying beneath the surface of a statement, something uncovered by patient analysis. Use determines the meaning.

In his later thought, Ludwig Wittgenstein came to reject a number of his earlier ideas regarding the nature and function of language. Language, he concluded, is actually multi-functional and multi-dimensional. In other words, ordinary human language manifests a great diversity of functions. Words are like the tools in a toolbox, to use Wittgenstein's own image; they can be used in an endless variety of ways. Another useful analogue to clarify the diversity of language is to consider words as chess pieces whose meaning is defined in terms of their various functions. In the case of linguistic usage, meaning is not found in the actual naming of a thing, but rather in the technique involved, since there are different ways of naming things. Thus, it is wrong to suppose that there is only one common function of all language: namely, a descriptive use. Furthermore, there can be no single structural element underlying all forms of language, although it never occurs to us to stop thinking of language as a mathematical model. The only basic component common to all forms of language is that of logical structure.

Another way of demonstrating this diversity of function in all human language is to consider language as a type of intellectual game. According to this view, each language game has its own language, its own logic, and its own rules of inference. Each game is a discrete and completely autonomous unit. To play the game correctly, one must become acquainted with all three components: the language, the logic, and the rules of inference which pertain to the particular game. Meaning is determined by analysis within the system, within the conceptual framework of the particular game, and all significant reference points must lie within the contextual dimensions of the game being played.

Linguistic analysis operates in a systematic manner, and therefore it is not interested in the unique use of a term or the unique meaning of a term. The meaning of a term or a phrase can be determined only after detailed and systematic analysis of its functional use. This interpretation of meaning differs from that proposed by existentialist thinkers who agree that meaning is to be found within the context of the particular situation, but who argue that there is no systematic way of determining meaning because every case is unique.

This brief perusal of the nature of linguistic analysis provides a sufficient basis for considering the views of Paul van Buren about contemporary secular man and his use of linguistic analysis as a tool for discovering the secular meaning of the Christian message.

2. Van Buren's Use of Linguistic Analysis

At the very beginning of his book, *The Secular Meaning of the Gospel,* van Buren indicates the central question around which all of his considerations revolve. "How," he asks, "can the Christian who is himself a secular man understand his faith in a secular way?" [1] Van Buren's main concern in this book is to find an ethical, active, and socially relevant form of Christianity, one dedicated to the life, interests, and commitments of the secular world. It is axiomatic, from his point of view, that modern man is irretrievably secular in orientation, thought, and dedication. The empirical or secular standards of contemporary thought thereby become normative and regulative for man today. Man must learn to make his value judgments in accordance with the empirical criteria em-

---

[1] Paul van Buren, *The Secular Meaning of the Gospel* (New York: Macmillan, 1963), p. xiv.

ployed by the modern world. Science, technology, valuation, and all forms of human endeavor take place within a culturally determined conceptual framework rooted in empirical attitudes. If Christianity, therefore, is to offer a viable mode of existence for contemporary man, it must operate within this secular context. It must not attempt to impose an outmoded metaphysical or supernaturalistic mentality on contemporary man. It must utilize the empirical categories so prevalent in our scientific and technological age. Since the orientation, the interests, the works, the pleasures, and the goals of modern man are all grounded in empirical attitudes, the only meaningful statements which can be made are either scientific assertions about the nature of physical reality or historical and ethical assertions about the nature of man. The historical dimension of life and the human problems of valuation, decision, and commitment are the crucial areas which today demand man's full attention and consideration. One cannot accept the traditional Christian view of God and the nature of religious belief and still live comfortably in the modern world. Contemporary secular man finds that he has no need of the God-hypothesis. Thus the Christian must learn to accept this without regrets and immediately set about restructuring his value system along the lines of current thought patterns.

In searching for a secular meaning of the Gospel, says van Buren, all references to a personal, transcendent God must be omitted. The spiritual, the supernatural, the metaphysical, and the trans-empirical are all meaningless concepts within the context of modern attitudes and thought. They are to be rejected, not so much because they are not scientifically verifiable or demonstrable, but because a functional analysis of these terms indicates that they are devoid of positive meaning in contemporary discourse. Such concepts are foreign and alien to the mentality of modern man.

The central methodological principle which van Buren employs throughout his entire study of the meaning of the Christian message is a modified version of the principle of empirical verification. This provides him with a consistent, empirically-grounded, systematic way of determining the meaning of any given statement. As seen above, this principle states that the meaning of any term is identical with its use. The employment of this technique enables

him to analyze not only empirical facts of history, but also such intangible realities as love, honor, duty, commitment, and so forth.
Meaning, then, is not something invisible hidden behind the word
itself. No new insights are required; all one has to do is analyze the
functional use of language to discover the meaning of a statement.

Van Buren points out the obvious fact that he is certainly not the
first modern thinker to address himself to the problem of finding a
suitable reformulation of Christian belief. He notes, for example,
that the Protestant theologian Rudolph Bultmann has attempted to
demythologize the New Testament message and to interpret it in
terms of the existentialist philosophy of Martin Heidegger. Bultmann argues that the mythological form of the kerygma, the original apostolic proclamation, is incomprehensible to contemporary
man as it is expressed in the New Testament. But if man strips the
kerygma of its mythological form and begins to interpret it existentially, then the event of Christ becomes the center of both faith and
theology. Only when existential categories are employed, says
Bultmann, does the event of Jesus Christ, his appearance in history, his words, and his death, become a dynamic force. Viewed in
this light, the Christian kerygma offers man the possibility of
realizing a new and authentic mode of existence.

Van Buren is in basic agreement with Bultmann's presentation
of the problem, but he does not agree with Bultmann's proposed
solution to that problem. Van Buren suggests that there are other
ways to pose the contemporary question of faith which may prove
more fruitful. Starting with the conviction that the Christian kerygma expresses the heart of the Gospel, he argues that the whole
tenor of modern thought makes the biblical and classical formulations of the Gospel unintelligible. He suggests that the recent developments in linguistic analysis might provide the most useful tool
for operating upon the contemporary problems of theology. He
explicitly rejects, however, the approach of logical positivism to
such questions. Theological or philosophical questions, he says,
cannot be summarily dismissed as being meaningless simply because they are neither assertions of logic or mathematics nor statements which can be verified or falsified empirically. Linguistic
analysis, he notes, utilizes a much more sophisticated and refined
version of the verification principle. This approach takes into con-

sideration the different levels and uses of language and employs a much more flexible conception of language than logical positivism. The modified verification principle helps the linguistic analyst to determine the precise functional use of a term within a given contextual framework.

He accepts the fundamental insights of existentialist writers in the problematic area of theological predication, but he feels that such an approach to the problem does not do justice to the secular or empirical character of modern man. His own task, therefore, as he sees it, is to describe and arrange three pieces of the theological puzzle: the current concern for Christology, the "liberal" concern with a contemporary way of thinking, and a logical analysis of theological statements. "A careful, functional analysis of the language of the New Testament, the Fathers, and contemporary believers will reveal the secular meaning of the Gospel." [2] His intention is not to make Christianity understandable or palatable to the unconvinced non-believer. His book is designed to be a conversation "from faith to faith" and therefore addressed to the convinced Christian believer who is also a secular man. Furthermore, he insists that the term "secular" must remain flexible since the secular world has not yet developed any univocal empirical viewpoint or decided precisely how its empirical attitudes are grounded.

In addition to his initial assumptions regarding the secular character of modern thought and his use of the modified version of the principle of empirical verification, van Buren has to incorporate two more working principles into his analytic study of the Christian message. First, he finds it useful to adopt R. M. Hare's theory of non-cognitive *bliks*. A *blik* is defined as a viewpoint, a fundamental attitude, an orientation, a commitment to see the world in a certain way. It is not achieved by empirical inquiry. According to this view, religious or theological statements are not statements about how things are, but how we see them. Second, he finds it helpful to adopt R. G. Collingwood's theory of history. For Collingwood, meaning in history refers to the attitude or the interpretation of the viewer and not something discovered underlying the empirical facts. In other words, the meaning reflects the *blik* of the viewer. Thus, a conjunction of these principles enables van Buren to ex-

[2] *Ibid.*, p. 19.

plain the relativity of Christianity while at the same time providing him with an historical anchor.

Despite a lack of references to the death of God, so commonplace in the writings of Hamilton and Altizer, and despite the fact that he has publicly dissociated himself from the death-of-God movement, the conclusions reached by van Buren indicate a close connection between his thinking and the death-of-God camp. He insists that, since modern man cannot accept the traditional Christian idea of God as a personal, transcendent Being operative in the world of men, a reformulation of the meaning of the Gospel message demands that all such references be carefully excised. Any literal, philosophical, biblical, or mystical understanding of the Gospel that uses such concepts must be jettisoned if the Gospel is to have any meaning for contemporary man. The empirical criteria of the present era compel one to reject both literal theism as wrong and all forms of qualified theism as meaningless. To use circumlocutions such as experienced non-objective reality, or to attempt to use indirect, oblique, or analogous language about God is a waste of time, because such modes of predication only appear to function as proper modes of discourse. The "God" of qualified theism dies the death of a thousand qualifications.

Although all references to a personal, transcendent God must be removed from a modern reformulation of belief, Christ still remains the historical and logical center for any reconstructed theology. What men were looking for in God, says van Buren, they find in Jesus Christ. Christ was a man for others and his uniqueness lies in his extraordinary freedom and his availability. Furthermore, after his death, his freedom began to manifest a certain contagious quality, enabling other men to share in that freedom to some degree.

In the final analysis, therefore, van Buren's theology is thoroughly Christocentric, and he feels that, although his reformulation of Christianity pares down Christianity to its historical, ethical, and intentional dimensions, it nevertheless retains all of the essentials. Thus, all of the doctrines which are central to the Christian message can still be professed by modern secular man.

3. Evaluations of Chalcedon

Orthodox Christology finds its classical expression in the Chalcedonian decree of 451. Van Buren is interested in tracing in broad outline the theological developments which led up to this formulation and then evaluating this doctrine in light of contemporary standards. According to his analysis, a significant choice was made at the beginning of Christological thought: namely, the choice to understand Jesus as the incarnate Logos. The Logos doctrine, as formulated by Justin Martyr, became the predominant Christological view by the middle of the 2nd century, eventually prevailing over a type of Spirit Christology, according to which Jesus was viewed as a man possessed by the Spirit of God. For Justin, Jesus was a man like ourselves, yet distinct from all other men because he was the man in whom the God-Logos was incarnate. His origin set him quite apart from the rest of men. Following the familiar Stoic conception of the Logos as the all-pervasive rational principle of the universe, Justin taught that this rational principle had taken on a human body, soul, and spirit: that is, all the parts which make up a human being. Yet one is also justified in worshiping him as Lord, he argued, for this man was the Logos of God.

The evolution of Christological thought during the patristic era was guided by two distinct forces which exerted a decisive influence on the final formulation of the Christological problem as enunciated in the Chalcedonian decree. During this era, Christological thinking tended to polarize around two distinct schools of thought, one located at Alexandria in Egypt, the other at Antioch in Syria. The Alexandrian thinkers, especially Origen, began to conceive of the Logos as almost equal to God. But another form of Christology, a Christology which preferred to view Jesus as being in the closest possible relationship to the Logos which dwelt in him essentially, comes to light in the teaching of Paul of Samosata. The roots of Paul's thought lay in the early Spirit Christology, and he seems to have understood Jesus as a man, born in a special way by God's decree, who, because of a unique indwelling of the Spirit of God in his person, gradually became the perfect man and was consequently adopted as God's Son. This doctrine, van Buren points out, reflects a strong interest in the historical person of Christ, and it is this particular emphasis which recommends his thinking to some theologians today. Paul's teaching, however, was condemned at the Synod of Antioch in 268 which decreed that the difference between Jesus and all other men was one of kind and not simply of degree.

At this point, van Buren notes, a real problem arose. No one questioned the common idea of the impassibility of God since the divine was by definition incapable of suffering any change. But the Gospels said that Jesus died on the cross. The simple Christology of Justin Martyr was unable to assimilate both the Alexandrian emphasis that the Logos was in the closest possible relationship to God, approaching identity, and the Antiochene emphasis that Jesus was in the closest possible relationship to the Logos, which dwelt in him essentially.

At this point, three alternatives seemed possible. One could say that an exchange was made and that Jesus did not actually die, or a distinction could be made between the Logos which is divine and the man Jesus who suffered and died, or a distinction could be made between the Logos incarnate in the suffering Jesus and God. The logical consequence of the third alternative would be that the Logos would not quite be God, and Arius, of course, made that precise conclusion. Van Buren writes:

> Arius' solution was logical, but his decision to draw the line between God and the Logos undermined the earlier defense against the charge of worshiping a man rather than God. Fundamentally, this solution implied that what was seen in Jesus was something less than God; God himself might be other than that which was revealed in Jesus, perhaps a God of wrath rather than love. So serious a threat to the New Testament witness could not go unchallenged, and regardless of the Arian logic the Council of Nicea in 325 A.D. insisted that the Logos or the Son of God was of one essence with the Father.[3]

Thus the Nicene definition eliminated the third alternative. Meanwhile, the Alexandrian school tended to adopt the first alternative, minimizing the suffering and the concrete historicity of Jesus, while the Antiochene school, on the other hand, tended to

[3] *Ibid.,* p. 28.

adopt the second alternative, stressing the real sufferings of Jesus and his real death, an emphasis which forced them to draw a line between the suffering man and the impassible Logos. The traditional way of categorizing or classifying these two different types of Christology, van Buren notes, is to refer to the Alexandrian version as the Logos-flesh type and the Antiochene version as the Logos-man type.

The final stage on the road to Chalcedon began with a reaction to the teaching of Apollinaris, Bishop of Laodicea. Having carried the Alexandrian or the Logos-flesh type of Christology to its logical conclusion, Apollinaris taught that in the incarnation the Logos took on a human body vitalized by a human soul. According to him, a man is composed not only of a body and its animating principle, the soul, but also of *nous,* the rational principle of man. In Jesus, the human *nous* was replaced by the divine Logos. The teaching of Apollinaris was condemned in 362, and the tension between the two schools of thought increased until a compromise formula was decided upon in 451. Van Buren comments:

> The last stage on the way to Chalcedon was marked by the struggle between the advocates of the two basic types. Cyril of Alexandria, the final leader of the old Egyptian tendency, stressed the unity of Christ at some cost to the reality of his manhood, and the theologians of the Antiochene tendency stressed the reality of Christ's manhood at some cost to the unity of his being. The compromise which was agreed upon at the Council of Chalcedon, and which prevailed after long hesitation and many reconsiderations in the following centuries, combined the affirmations of both tendencies. This compromise was prepared for by a development of the terms "nature" and "person" or (to use the original word and to avoid confusion caused by our very different use of the word "person") *hypostasis.*[4]

A gradual clarification of the technical terms "nature" and *"hypostasis,"* therefore, made a compromise formula possible. Although the two terms were used interchangeably in the beginning, they gradually came to be clearly distinguished. By the 5th century, they were sufficiently distinct to allow a new Christological

[4] *Ibid.,* p. 30.

formulation, the Chalcedonian statement. But it was not until the 6th century that the complete difference between them was definitively clarified. At the time of the Chalcedonian decree, the "nature" of a being was considered to be that which marked it for what it was, while its actual existence, that which allowed it to be at all, was termed its *"hypostasis."*

> The final patristic answer to the Christological problem was that the hypostasis of the Logos, having already a divine "nature," took on a human "nature" also. This human "nature" did not exist prior to or apart from this assumption (it was anhypostatic); it began to be in the moment of being assumed by the hypostasis of the Logos (it was enhypostatic). The manhood of Jesus Christ, therefore, was considered to be constituted of a human "nature" and the hypostasis of the Logos. Freely translated, the late patristic Christological answer asserted that Jesus was indeed a man as we are men, but the fact that he existed as a man was totally dependent on the fact that God the Word, the eternal Logos, had called him into being to be the historical bearer of this divine Word.[5]

The conclusion of Chalcedon was refined by Leontius of Byzantium, and it was given its classical expression in the writings of John of Damascus. In its final form, it tried to integrate both Christological tendencies as expressed in the doctrine of the hypostatic union: a union of the divine and human "natures" in one "hypostasis," that of the Logos. According to this doctrine, both natures are considered to be inseparable and indivisible, thereby satisfying the Alexandrian tendency. Yet they do not lose their identity or become mixed, thereby satisfying the Antiochene tendency. This is not a temporary or an accidental union, but a permanent one grounded in the one hypostasis of the Logos. Considered separately—that is, theoretically—the human nature of Christ had no hypostasis of its own. Considered actually and concretely, the humanity of Jesus had its existence in that of the Logos.

Van Buren admits that, for the Eastern mind, the formula may be important, not so much as a definition of how things actually are, but rather as an indication of where the Fathers understood the mystery to lie. But it is modern man, he adds, who is trying to

[5] *Ibid.*, p. 31.

understand what was meant by this ancient Christology. It is difficult to grasp the significance of the Christological formulas because modern man is far removed from the world of thought in which this formulation took place. Despite this difficulty, van Buren expresses his intention to try to comprehend the Chalcedonian decree and the statements of the Fathers in a sympathetic manner.

Much of the present depreciation of patristic theology, he observes, is due to the influence of Albrecht Ritschl and Adolph von Harnack who proposed the thesis that, as the early Church moved into the Hellenistic world, the original, dynamic, and historical faith of the Church, as expressed in the New Testament writings, became Hellenized. As a result of this process, the Gospel was transformed into a static, speculative, and metaphysical theory about the person of Christ and the Godhead. Modern theology, they contended, should abandon the hopelessly metaphysical thought of the Church Fathers who were responsible for the Christological dogmas, and return to the original, dynamic, Hebraic mode of thought.

A positive approach to patristic Christology, however, is found in the writings of Karl Barth, who, in attempting to formulate his own interpretation of the Christ event, has tried to remain faithful to Chalcedonian and classical Christology. Although he would not place the teachings of the Fathers on a level with the New Testament, his intention has been to learn something from them about how to read the New Testament, with the result that he approaches patristic Christology with deep sympathy. In the final analysis, the doctrine of the incarnation is, for him, a sound exposition of the news that the Word of God, who is God himself, has participated fully in human existence. The Word actually became flesh, participating in the sinful condition of humanity, and it came to terms with sin precisely in the sinful situation of man. In the teaching of Barth, as in that of the Fathers, primary stress is put on the divine hypostasis, but he insists more radically than the Fathers did that the divine Word accepted the whole burden of human sin. For him, the glory of God the Word consists in the fact that he humbled himself even to death on the cross. Faith and theology, he contends, must stand before the mystery of the incarnation, trying with the aid of past theological reflection to grasp the seriousness of the mystery, and trying to reach, at the present time, the answer of the apostles to the question of who is Jesus Christ.

In offering his own evaluation of patristic Christology, van Buren says that a sympathetic understanding of the patristic mentality only goes so far. He argues that, considered from a modern perspective, orthodox patristic Christology did not do justice to the manhood of Jesus of Nazareth. Patristic anthropology differed from that which is currently in vogue today, and this difference led to a different reading of the New Testament witness to Jesus of Nazareth. In Justin Martyr's Christology, Jesus is like us, but he is not really one of us. Justin's idea of perfect manhood is compatible with a view of man based on the model of a machine or with a view of man as simply a biological organism composed of certain component parts. But this view of man is deficient. In general, patristic writers neglected one very important aspect of Jesus—namely, his compassion, his interest in the affairs of men, his relationship with other men. Modern theologians, on the other hand, tend to look upon this feature of Christ's life as being the hallmark of his true humanity.

Van Buren insists that, despite strong protestations to the contrary, orthodox patristic Christology considered Christ to be qualitatively different from other men. Thus, it is questionable whether the true manhood of Jesus is actually retained in the patristic doctrine. He writes:

> Our condition as men is that of beings who have our own hypostasis, whose existence in history is, apart from what may be said by the doctrine of creation and providence, grounded in history. According to orthodox classical Christology, Jesus did not share this condition. He entered into the place where we are, but he was not grounded in this place as we are. He was a visitor, not a member of the family. In this respect, orthodox classical Christology is inadequate to meet its own goals.[6]

The Greek Fathers, he claims, tended to neglect history. They were inclined to view the incarnation more as a condition than an event. When modern theologians begin by defining the hu-

[6] *Ibid.*, p. 40.

manity of Jesus in terms of his being-for-others, his involvement, and his deep compassion for his fellowmen, they are speaking as men who are interested in history and who find such a paradigm of far more value than the patristic concept of "nature." Van Buren argues that, although the proposal of Paul of Samosata was admittedly inadequate and without historical foundation or textual support, and although it represented a naive conception of the interrelation of freedom and destiny in human life, his approach still offered promise and possibilities and therefore it should not have been completely rejected. Its promise lay in its basic orientation, in its suggestion of a more dynamic, personal, and historical conception of Jesus, and in its stress on the whole relationship of God and man in Jesus' history.

The entire development of classical Christology, van Buren maintains, was colored by the patristic idea of God. It was presupposed by the Fathers that God and his Word must be impassible because change was the mark of the imperfect, a sign of corruption and decay. But such an approach raised the problem of trying to explain the meaning of Christ's suffering and death. If the Fathers had not made this presupposition, Christian theology would have evolved along completely different lines.

> If they had been more consistent in saying that God is unknown apart from his self-revelation and that we must begin with Jesus Christ in order to know anything about God at all, they might have been able to begin with the cross as the event of self-revelation of a God who is quite able to take suffering to himself and whose glory is so great that he can also humble himself. Had this been done, the course of the development of classical Christology would have been quite different.[7]

The Fathers, however, strove to maintain their commitment to the bible. They believed that there was one God and one history of revelation, and their Christology reflected this conviction. This one God was known through his self-revelation, in the Law and the prophets, and finally in a definitive way in the person of Jesus Christ. The life, death, and resurrection of Jesus was viewed as an act of God himself. Each aspect of classical Christology

[7] *Ibid.*, p. 42.

expresses the patristic concern to interpret and preserve the apostolic witness without dilution or distortion.

The thought patterns of the Fathers, however, were quite different from those of modern man. Recent developments in the area of biblical studies have provided the contemporary theologian with new and more meaningful categories for the construction of a new Christology. The centrality of the covenant, the dynamic and historical character of the event of God's self-revelation, and the importance of obedience as the proper response of man in God's covenant played only a minor role in patristic Christology, but they offer a new and promising framework for the formulation of a modern Christology. Van Buren suggests that it is helpful to reread passages in the New Testament, not in terms of the traditional Logos interpretation, but according to the covenant paradigm. The term "Son of God," for example, takes on a new significance when viewed in this light. In the Old Testament, the title "Son" implied serving obedience, and it was first used as a designation for Israel. Then it was a designation for those who represented the people of the covenant in a special way, such as the king or the high priest. Using the paradigm of the covenant, Jesus becomes a man called by Yahweh to play a particular role in history for the sake of the world. He is the obedient bearer of a specific election or commission. Following its usage in the Old Testament, therefore, this title "Son of God" provides a basis for the development of a Christology of "call" and "response." Jesus of Nazareth is seen as Yahweh's faithful new Israel, the Son of God. Van Buren writes:

Yahweh's decision expresses his very heart. The prologue of the Gospel of John summarizes this idea by saying that God's Word is God himself, from the "beginning." It was possible to identify Yahweh with his decision because the New Testament authors conceived of God always in relation to the decision enacted in Jesus of Nazareth. In the beginning there was a decision that there should be one for the many, and that the many should come to know themselves to be involved with the one. And "in the fullness of time," this purpose was enacted concretely in the history of Jesus of Nazareth. It became flesh, a plan enacted, and Yahweh's purpose dwelt among us in that Jesus dwelt among men. What Yahweh had to say to man, what he had in mind for men, was to be seen and heard in the form of this man, who was, therefore, the very Word of Yahweh.

So long as a word is not thought of as an ideal entity, but as an action leading to a relationship, the assertion that the Word actually became Jesus does not involve us in the pagan idea of a transmutation of the divine into the physical. An intention became an action; a plan was enacted. To ask whether the plan exists apart from its enactment, or whether it has been transformed into its enactment, indicates that one is thinking of a plan or a word as a quasi-physical substance. It is simply a plan, and its enactment is simply what results when the plan is realized. To summarize this idea in naive terms, Yahweh determined in his heart of hearts upon having his faithful Son, Jesus, and through him a faithful creation. He created this world and called his people Israel for this purpose. He realized this purpose concretely in history when he called this man into a role in history upon which he had decided "before the foundation of the world." [8]

Further, when it comes time for a consideration of the human nature of Christ, this new biblically-grounded Christology is able to overcome many of the deficiencies which are found in the patristic approach. The reason for the uniqueness of Jesus is that he bore a particular calling from Yahweh, a call to which he responded wholeheartedly in his own particular history. He was singularly obedient to this calling, and the Easter event is Yahweh's proclamation of this obedience. Part of his special calling demanded that he be a man-for-others, and from what we know of his historical existence and his social relationships, he was thoroughly and willingly involved with the concerns and interests of men. He was a human being and in no sense "more than a man."

This man, moreover, though fully man and in no sense "more than a man," is not to be confused with other men. He stood apart from them for the very reason of his solidarity with them: he was the one man who truly existed for others. His calling was to be the one for the many, whereas the calling of all other men is to let him be that for them: the way, the truth, and the life. He stands apart from all the others also in that he was obedient to his calling, whereas they are not obedient to theirs, or they only learn obedience by relying solely

[8] *Ibid.*, pp. 52–53.

on the obedience of him whom they know and confess as Lord
and Savior.

This interpretation of Jesus and the Gospel is an example of
the kind of Christology which is being developed in many
quarters by men influenced by biblical theology, and it is
intended to be faithful to the concerns evident in the Christology of the Fathers. We have presented that tradition and suggested this contemporary interpretation of it in order to make
clear what conservative theology has held to be the constitu-
ent elements of the Gospel. At the center stands the person
of Jesus of Nazareth. But although such an interpretation may
be called "orthodox," it is still, from the point of view of the
theological "left," sadly mythological in form, if not in content.[9]

4. Existentialist Interpretations

The theological "left," van Buren observes, has been particularly interested in finding a contemporary interpretation of the
Gospel message. One segment of his study is therefore devoted to
an analysis of the views proposed by men like Rudolph Bultmann
and Schubert Ogden. Ogden passes beyond Bultmann, because
he feels that Bultmann does not go far enough in making the Gospel
understandable to modern man. Therefore van Buren considers
Ogden to be the more helpful of the two. Accordingly, van Buren
begins this section of his study with Ogden's analysis of Bultmann's
thought. Bultmann and Ogden both agree that the fundamental
problem facing modern man in his attempt to understand the New
Testament is that he can no longer accept the mythological
world-picture in which the New Testament message is enclosed.
A mythological world-picture, writes Ogden,

> . . . is one in which (1) the non-objective reality that man
> experiences as the ground and limit of himself and his world
> is "objectified" and thus presented as but another part of the
> objective world; (2) the origin and goal of the world as a
> whole, as well as certain happenings within it, are referred to
> non-natural, yet "objective" causes; (3) the resulting com-
> plex of ideas comprising the picture takes the form of a double
> history.[10]

[9] *Ibid.,* pp. 54–55.
[10] Cf. *ibid.,* p. 58.

Commenting on this, van Buren writes:

The New Testament pictures the world as having three stories. Heaven, which signifies the transcendent, is conceived spatially as being "above" the earth. The New Testament "objectifies" heaven by representing it as a sphere "within the inclusive world of objective reality." The world is thought to have originated in a supernatural act, and supposed interventions of the divine in this world are almost commonplace in the biblical documents. Finally, a superhuman, divine history runs parallel to human history. Ogden points out that Bultmann has defined myth carefully. A concept of a three-storied universe is only a bit of primitive science. What makes the primitive science mythological in the New Testament is the belief that the upper and lower realms are transcendent. The heart of Bultmann's definition lies in the idea of *objectification* of "the non-objective reality that man experiences as the ground and limit of himself and his world." [11]

Behind the mythological structure of the New Testament, Bultmann believes, there lies a basic understanding of the nature of man, an interpretative expression of how man understands himself and his relation to the world around him. The New Testament mythology conveys the believer's basic understanding that he is not lord over himself, and that his freedom from such forces as selfishness and despair is ultimately grounded and rooted in his dependence on transcendent powers. Thus, myth is not simply to be eliminated; rather, it must be interpreted in its proper context as the expression of man's existential self-understanding.

Fundamentally, Bultmann operates on the principle that there are basically only two kinds of statements: those which give information and those which demand a decision on the part of the listener or hearer. The kerygmatic statements of the New Testament, he maintains, are of the second type, demanding a decision on the part of the reader as to how he shall understand himself. According to Bultmann, the very nature of the New Testament witness and the nature of faith itself demand an existential interpretation. Thus, it is erroneous to view the New Testament as a source of information, and faith as an assent to what is said. Van Buren comments:

[11] *Ibid*. Italics in original.

According to Ogden, "Bultmann reduced the entire contents of the traditional Christian confession to one fundamental assertion: *I henceforth understand myself no longer in terms of my past, but solely in terms of the future that is here and now disclosed to me as grace in my encounter with the Church's proclamation.*" [12]

Much of Bultmann's thinking is heavily impregnated with Martin Heidegger's ideas concerning the philosophy of existence. Man not only exists; he knows that he exists and he is able to search and to probe for the meaning of that existence. Man is responsible for himself and he is obliged to make his own decision about who he is. One of the outstanding hallmarks of human existence is this: each individual undergoes a ceaseless questioning process in his search for self-identity, whereby he tries to discover who he is both in himself and with respect to the rest of mankind. But in a theological context, the question immediately arises whether the historical occurrence of Jesus is necessary for the realization of authentic existence. Is Jesus necessary for faith—faith as a new form of self-understanding?

For Bultmann, the realization of authentic existence does depend upon the historical occurrence of Jesus of Nazareth. According to the New Testament, man lost the factual possibility of authentic existence. Even his knowledge and understanding of that authenticity have been perverted, with the result that he thinks it is his to command. But if man is to realize authentic selfhood, then he must learn that he cannot free himself. He must be set free, and this liberation is actually realizable only because God has already given himself for man in Jesus Christ. This saving and redemptive act of God takes place as a present reality when a man responds to the New Testament message and decides to understand himself as crucified and dead to his own past and now open solely to the future offered to him in Jesus' name. The "objective fact" connected with the Easter event was the disciples' response of faith to God's gracious offer: this new possibility of realizing authentic human existence. This event signifies the institution of the ministry of reconciliation. Thus, Bultmann insists upon the historical grounding of the kerygma even though

[12] *Ibid.*, p. 59. Italics in original.

the saving event is something realized here and now by the individual believer. Ogden has summarized Bultmann's fundamental theses in the following terms:

> (1) Christian faith is to be interpreted exhaustively and without remainder as man's original possibility of authentic historical (*geschichtlich*) existence as this is more or less adequately clarified and conceptualized by an appropriate philosophical analysis. (2) Christian faith is actually realizable, or is a "possibility in fact," only because of the particular historical (*historisch*) event of Jesus of Nazareth, which is the originative event of the Church and its distinctive Word and sacraments.[13]

Evaluating Ogden's statements, van Buren agrees that Bultmann is trying to maintain two incompatible theses. He writes:

> The incompatibility is evident in the double use of the word "possibility." Either faith has always been possible in fact, regardless of the appearance of Jesus of Nazareth, and every man is responsible for believing in God, or faith is not an unconditional possibility for man, and he may not be held responsible for not believing in God or charged with being without excuse (Rom. 2, 1). The critics to the right and to the left disagree as to how to settle this dilemma, of course: those to the right hold for the second thesis and deny the first; those to the left make the opposite choice. Both sides agree that Bultmann's position will not do as it stands because of this inconsistency.[14]

In the presentation of his own ideas, Ogden offers a revised version of the two Bultmannian theses, a revision intended to overcome the weaknesses of Bultmann's position. Except for the words "historical" and "to be more or less," his rewording of the first thesis is identical with that ascribed to Bultmann. Van Buren argues that Ogden understands Christian faith to be simply the real possibility of authentic existence, something which Heidegger has already adequately defined. His second thesis is more radically altered and reads:

> Christian faith is always a "possibility in fact" because of the unconditioned gift and demand of God's love, which is the

[13] *Ibid.*, pp. 61–62.
[14] *Ibid.*, p. 62.

ever-present ground and end of all created things; the decisive manifestation of this divine love, however, is the event of
Jesus of Nazareth, which fulfills and corrects all other manifestations and is the originative event of the Church and its distinctive Word and sacraments.[15]

Van Buren argues that this variation of Bultmann's second
thesis is not much of an improvement. It changes "only" to "always" and it replaces the event of Jesus of Nazareth by a universal
and omnipresent prerequisite. Finally, it makes room for faith
without Christ, at least without the historical Jesus—"an inter-
esting, but not original, conclusion."

In considering the proposed formulations of the theological
"left" within the framework of the problem of God, language,
and history, van Buren concludes that their proposed reconstruc-
tions of the Christian message are objectionable on two levels.
Theological reconstruction should not only be logically consistent,
but it should also do justice to the thinking of contemporary man
and to the major elements of the Gospel. Both Bultmann and
Ogden violate this standard on both levels. First, neither one does
justice to the secular or empirical tenor of modern thought. Secondly, both neglect the historical character of the Gospel.

In support of the first assertion, Van Buren offers three arguments. First, the expression "experienced non-objective reality," as
it is used by Ogden, is meaningless within the context of modern
thought, for if one applies the principle of verification to the
expression: "an experience of the ground and end of all things" or
"experienced non-objective reality," he finds that there is no way
of knowing what counts for or against something that is the ground
and end of all things.

In the second place, it is also meaningless to speak analogically
and existentially about God. Oblique language about God, van
Buren contends, is no more useful than "objectifying" language
about God. The problem lies in the word "God" itself and in any
other word which supposedly refers to the "transcendent." Neither
Bultmann nor Ogden demonstrates how human predication can be
made applicable to God, whether the term "God" refers to a
personal being or the end and ground of all things.

[15] *Ibid.*, p. 63.

Thirdly, van Buren denies Bultmann's assertion that statements of faith and of the kerygma are existential statements only. He maintains that the New Testament kerygma contains statements that are clearly empirical, as well as some that are clearly existential. Its typical statements are actually a mixture of these two types, and their empirical aspect cannot logically be ignored.

Having raised these objections to the position of the theological "left" on the level of empirical considerations, van Buren then proceeds to present two further objections on the level of historical considerations. He begins by pointing out that the existentialist "left," as represented by Ogden, replaces the historical event of Jesus of Nazareth by the existential response of the believer. One cannot legitimately speak of the cross as an "eschatological event" since the New Testament does not speak of the cross in this way—in any ordinary use of the verb "to speak." Existentialist theologians substitute a figurative use of language for the literal use, and thus fail to do justice to the historical dimension of the event of Jesus of Nazareth, a necessary prerequisite for any serious analysis of the Christian message.

Secondly, by circumventing the Easter event in defining the relationship of faith to Jesus of Nazareth, both Ogden and Bultmann overlook the historical character of the Gospel. Easter faith for the primitive Church, according to them, was the Church's way of responding to the ministry of the historical Jesus. The issue had come into sharper focus with the death of Jesus, but the basic nature and ground of faith in Jesus remained unaltered. The resurrection, therefore, plays no central role in Ogden's proposal. For him, it is sufficient to say that what was always and everywhere man's possibility eventually became concrete in the life of Jesus. The disciples actualized this possibility in their own lives by their response of faith in Jesus. But other men, Ogden admits, have realized authentic existence quite apart from Jesus or the resurrection, and therefore Jesus is not an indispensable condition for realized self-authenticity. This conclusion, van Buren indicates, does not meet Ogden's own demands.

In his overall evaluation of the radical alternative of the left wing, van Buren concludes that both versions of the first thesis set up a particular philosophical analysis of human existence as the final norm for faith. In concrete terms, the existential-theological left wing is committed to the freedom of man as defined by Heidegger. Furthermore, Bultmann's second thesis is an empirical statement in appearance only, and the only way to preserve any logical consistency is to conclude that Bultmann is actually proposing two norms: Jesus and the New Testament, on the one hand, and Heidegger's philosophical analysis of man, on the other. Ogden objects to the exclusiveness of Bultmann's second thesis because it seems to deny human responsibility, and therefore he restates the thesis in his own terms. But neither Bultmann nor Ogden, in van Buren's opinion, considers the logical necessity of any confession of faith containing an element of exclusiveness, insofar as it reflects the commitment of the believer to the object of his faith. In the final analysis, Ogden's conclusion is no less restrictive than Bultmann's because he fails to consider the logic of confessional statements.

Van Buren feels that Ogden does not fully appreciate the dilemma of modern man. The juxtaposition of faith, as expressed in traditional terms, and man's ordinary way of thinking, van Buren says, culminate in a type of spiritual schizophrenia. The secular empiricist must work out the meaning of the Gospel for himself. This necessity to understand its meaning arises from his own situation and his own desire to be a responsible and self-integrated Christian. This necessity is prior to the apologetic and evangelical concerns of the left wing.

In concluding his analysis, van Buren says:

> The conclusion of the theological "left" leaves us with the difficulty of speaking about "transcendence," "ground and end of all things," or some other oblique phrase substituted for the word "God," which simply begs the empiricist's question. It leaves us with the center of the New Testament kerygma, Jesus the Messiah, displaced by an analysis of existence by a modern philosopher. Ogden protests against the Christological interest of the conservative position and is convinced that the heart of the Gospel is represented by Theology rather than by Christology. But if the choice is between "God," however subtly hidden in oblique language, and the man Jesus of Nazareth, the empirically-minded secular "believer" can only choose the latter, for he does not know what to do with The-

ology. Analogical as well as literal language about God makes
no sense to him. He may or may not find existentialism's
analysis of the Gospel enlightening, but if he wishes to understand the Gospel, he cannot responsibly circumvent Jesus
and the peculiar way in which his history is presented by the
documents of the New Testament. Because the situation of
"modern man" is in us and not outside of us, our analysis of
the theological "left" as well as of the "right" leads us to reconsider the language of the New Testament concerning Jesus
of Nazareth.[16]

5. The Problem of Theological Predication

The central theological problem today, van Buren suggests, is the
apparently meaningless language used by contemporary theologians.
Modern secular man, with his grounding in empirical attitudes,
finds such language unintelligible. The existentialist theologians
attempt to resolve this problem by rejecting any "objectification"
of God and introducing indirect, oblique, and analogous language
about God. But any "non-objective" use of language, van Buren
argues, allows no verification and is therefore meaningless. Once
one begins to use the term "God" in a qualified sense, he begins
to kill his assertion by the "death of a thousand qualifications,"
to use Anthony Flew's expression, and he ends up making no
assertion at all. Modern man has discovered that he does not need
the literally nonsensical entity called God. Contemporary man
questions the very possibility of speaking about God in a meaningful way. Van Buren notes:

> The empiricist in us finds the heart of the difficulty not in
> what is said about God, but in the very talking about God at
> all. We do not know "what" God is, and we cannot under-
> stand how the word "God" is being used. It seems to function
> as a name, yet theologians tell us that we cannot use it as we
> do other names, to refer to something quite specific. If it is
> meant to refer to an "existential encounter," a point of view,
> or the speaker's self-understanding, surely a more appropri-
> ate expression could be found.[17]

[16] *Ibid.*, p. 79.
[17] *Ibid.*, p. 84.

Attempts have been made in recent years to resolve the problem by trying to vindicate the meaningfulness of religious assertions. One such defender, van Buren says, is R. M. Hare, who begins by conceding to Flew that if religious assertions are taken as statements about "how things are," then they must be judged meaningless. But if religious statements such as "God loves all men" or "Jesus Christ is Lord" are viewed as confessional statements and not as empirical statements, then they can be shown to have a real meaning. In his attempt to show that man's faith and theology can still possess a meaning, Hare proposes his theory of "*blik*." A *blik,* in Hare's terminology, signifies a fundamental attitude, an attitude which is not the result of empirical inquiry. It reflects basic presuppositions we have concerning the world, which are not verifiable and yet determine everything we do. But these presuppositions, Hare cautions, should not be viewed as explanations. This is the error that Flew makes.

Van Buren points out that Flew disagrees with Hare's theory of *blik.* Both agree, however, that a simple literal theism is untenable, and that a qualified "non-objective" theism is meaningless since it dies the death of a thousand qualifications. For if God is wholly other, then we cannot speak of him at all. Their disagreement centers around the nature of Christianity. In Flew's estimation, the statements of the Christian faith form a collection of cosmological assertions concerning the nature and activities of a personal, transcendent being. On the other hand, Hare sees them as expressions of a *blik,* as expressing a basic attitude, a commitment to view the world in a certain way, and as reflecting a way of life following inevitably upon this orientation. Hare's theory of *blik,* therefore, enables him to defend a non-theistic meaning of religious language.

Van Buren says that another defender of the meaningfulness of religious language is Ian T. Ramsey, who offers support for Hare's concept of *blik* and tries to add a further dimension to it. In introducing Ramsey's contribution, van Buren writes:

He argues that the language of faith combines the language of discernment, of an admittedly special sort, with the language of commitment, of a sort which covers the totality of life and the world. Statements of faith direct our attention to certain kinds of situations: situations of disclosure, when "the light dawns" and the situation becomes alive and new. The emphasis is not only on the disclosure or discernment, but also on the resulting commitment, whereby what we now "see" becomes important and determines our subsequent seeing. In such situations, the believer makes use of odd words like "God." [18]

To indicate how such religious words function, Ramsey employs the idea of models and qualifiers. The model of "father," for example, points in a certain direction, and when the model "father" is qualified as "eternal" or "omnipotent" we indicate that the word "father" is only a model and that we should push on and on in an effort to discern the situation in depth. A disclosure or discernment situation, he says, is found in the revelation of God's name in the tautological statement of Chapter 3 of Exodus: "I am who I am." This tautology marks the ultimate limit of religious language. One encounters a parallel limit-statement in cases of human loyalty where the final and indisputable explanation for any action is the statement, "because I'm I."

Within the conceptual framework of Ramsey's approach, words like "resurrection," "duty," "love," and "God" direct us to a type of situation in which a discernment fundamental to our whole conception of life and an appropriate response of commitment may take place. Situations of this type transcend empirical description, even though such description may be necessary in a given discernment situation. In effect, Ramsey is offering a further development of Hare's concept of *blik*. Van Buren summarizes Ramsey's application of the idea of discernment and commitment to the area of Christology in the following terms:

A "blik" involves a perspective entailing a commitment, and Ramsey has clarified this with his analysis of the language of discernment and commitment. When this analysis is applied to the language of Christology, it discloses two sorts of languages: one is the language of a "blik"; the other is that of a straightforward empirical observation. Both sorts of language are used about the same person, Jesus of Nazareth. But the language of Christology is appropriate only to one who himself has discerned what Christians discern, for whom Jesus

[18] *Ibid.*, p. 87.

has become the occasion for a new discernment involving his whole perspective. We can summarize by saying that the language of Christology is language about Jesus of Nazareth on the part of those for whom he has been the occasion and remains the definition of their "blik." [19]

A further development from Hare and Ramsey is found in the proposal of T. R. Miles who recommends what he calls "the way of silence qualified by parables." As a substitute for the language of simple literal theism or that of qualified theism, Miles urges the course of silence in which no claims or assertions are made. The believer may, however, qualify his silence to some degree by employing what Miles calls a "theistic parable." For example, he may decide to picture the world as having been created by a loving Father. But one must recognize, Miles insists, that this is a matter of personal conviction rather than the conclusion of a rational argument. A theistic parable simply invites one to view the world in a certain way with the result that one's whole perspective or *blik* is affected.

In van Buren's estimation, a radical and important contribution to the analysis of the language of faith has been made by R. B. Braithwaite. He begins by proposing that the primary question today is not whether a religious statement is true or false, but rather the problem of trying to determine how such a statement can be known to be true or false. Until this has been ascertained, a religious statement cannot be said to have a discoverable meaning. Braithwaite finds that such a criterion is provided by the verification principle of linguistic analysis: the meaning is found in the use. The meaning of the term is identical with its use. Against this background, Braithwaite defends the thesis that religious assertions are in fact used as moral assertions. Moral assertions share with religious assertions the characteristic of being neither logically necessary nor empirical; yet they have a determinate function, that of guiding conduct. And religious statements, he insists, also reflect the intention to follow a certain way of life. For Braithwaite, a moral belief is the intention to act in a certain way. A religious belief is also the intention to act in a certain way, with the added dimension of using certain stories or

[19] *Ibid.*, p. 91.

myths associated with that intention in the mind of the believer. A psychological and causal relationship exists between the story and the intention.

Not all linguistic analysts, van Buren observes, would go along with the proposals offered by Hare, Miles, and Braithwaite. Some, for example, would insist that there is a transcendent dimension to religious belief. Arguing from contingency and design, these men claim to reach the non-contingent and the transcendent, and they adopt a form of natural or undifferentiated theism. Many, appealing to Jesus as an authority, contend that, although religious statements cannot be verified here and now, in the *eschaton,* on the final day, such statements will be verified. Thus, statements of faith are in principle verifiable, and therefore meaningful, as cognitive assertions.

But van Buren prefers to follow the non-cognitive or *blik* conception of faith rather than a cognitive conception—and this for both logical and theological reasons. On the logical level, he argues that the cognitive approach involves speaking of God by analogy, yet the believer is unable to indicate to what extent such analogies are proper and appropriate. Further, no one knows what empirical attitudes would be possible or proper from an eschatological viewpoint. On the theological level, the cognitive approach to theological language is based on a natural sense of the divine, on natural religion, and on natural revelation, but the work of Karl Barth has shown that such an approach terminates in a dead end. Secondly, the cognitive approach leads to inner contradictions where it becomes difficult to reconcile the Christian God of grace and self-revelation with the neutral "it" of natural theology. Finally, the cognitive approach to religious language contradicts the empiricist's point of departure because it implies that there is a separate "religious" way of knowing, in contrast to other ways of knowing.

Thus, van Buren rejects the cognitive and adopts a non-cognitive approach because he feels compelled to follow what he considers most consonant with the tenor of modern thought. After studying various proposals concerning the nature of theological predication, he eventually concludes that simple literal theism is wrong and qualified theism is meaningless, that the language of faith does have a meaning, a meaning which can be explored and clarified by the use of linguistic analysis, and that one can take Christianity seriously, as a way of life, even though a straight-forward use of the word "God" must be abandoned. The key to the understanding of the language of faith lies in the actual func-tion of religious language. Some clarification of the problems of the language of faith has been achieved by a frankly empirical method of analysis which reflects the thinking of an industralized, technological, and scientific age. Certain empirical attitudes char-acteristic of modern thought have been seriously adopted and accepted without qualification, and these empirical criteria lead some linguistic analysts to choose Jesus rather than God, and Christology rather than theology. The word "God" is dead today. People do not know how to use the word any longer. The verifica-tion principle of linguistic analysis, however, provides modern man with the means to determine a secular meaning of the Gospel, and it offers the background for the construction of a new theology. The language of faith is now seen to be only one of a number of complex and diversified language games. Although confessional statements are not empirical statements about the way things actually are, nevertheless, their meaning is empirically verifiable. Religious language reflects a non-cognitive *blik,* and modern Christians should take care not to give the impression that their religious statements are empirical statements of fact.

6. History and the Easter Event

Since Christianity is an "historical" religion, in the sense that it is centered on the historical person of Jesus of Nazareth, the first task of the contemporary theologian is to find a suitable working definition of history. Van Buren finds a useful definition in the concept of history proposed by R. G. Collingwood. He says that history is to be understood as the answering of questions about *human* action in the past. Such an approach, van Buren says, does not attempt to speak of a "God" who is an actor in history, and it has no room for language about trans-empirical realities such as angels. History is therefore to be understood as secular and profane history. Thus Bultmann's distinction between profane history and the history of salvation and his disjunction between universal history and personal history are unacceptable in light of modern man's empirical standards.

Van Buren adopts Collingwood's thesis that meaning in history refers to the attitude of the viewer or speaker and not to some hidden reality underlying the empirical historical data. In other words, meaning cannot lie in history itself. Historical meaning points out the way in which an observer sees history. It indicates the discernment and commitment resulting from the study of a piece of history which influences the observer's manner of viewing the rest of history and his own life. In simple terms, therefore, to find a meaning in history is to have a certain perspective or *blik*. Van Buren comments:

> The expression "meaning in history" belongs to the language-game of reading or hearing history and discerning it in a way which leads to a new commitment. To speak of meaning in history is to speak of the insight and commitment which has arisen out of or is reinforced by one's reflection upon history. To say that there is no meaning in history is to say that in reading or hearing history, no *new* perspective has arisen which might lead to a commitment. Previously held commitments which might have led a man to say that history is bunk, or that it consists only of bare facts, might have been reinforced. A "bare-facts" historian would also be a man with a "blik," though his "blik" would differ from Collingwood's.[20]

According to the canons of historical analysis, the historian should attempt to enter sympathetically into his subject and seek to share its experiences. But the Christian historian, van Buren says, is faced with two difficulties from the outset. First, it is difficult to enter sympathetically into the history and the perspective of Jesus because there is a radical difference between modern attitudes and the outlook and attitudes of Jesus. Secondly, the Christian historian must deal with the problem of Easter, because the New Testament is now seen as confessional documents owing their inspiration to the experience of the Easter event, the turning point in the disciples' view of Jesus.

Van Buren's main interest does not lie in a search for the

[20] *Ibid.*, p. 114.

historical Jesus, but in an analysis of the language function of the New Testament kerygma. He makes a passing reference, however, to Albert Schweitzer's *The Quest of the Historical Jesus,* and he briefly indicates the views of Bultmann and Barth regarding the historicity of the New Testament narrative about Jesus.

> The choice left at the end by Schweitzer was that either of accepting the evidence that Jesus was so radically oriented toward Jewish apocalyptic thinking as to be beyond our understanding today, or of knowing almost nothing about him at all. Bultmann led the dominant trend of the second quarter of this century in making the second, more skeptical choice. In this he was joined by Barth. Both agreed at least in the conviction that the documents at our disposal do not provide the careful historian with the material for a biography of Jesus, or even for a reasonably probable interpretation of him as a man. A few of the major themes of his preaching, the general location of his activity, and the place and date of his execution at the hands of the Roman authorities are about all that the historian can discover. All the rest—from legends of his birth, through stories concerning his relationship with his disciples, to details of his arrest and execution—has come to us through the preaching of the early Christian congregations. This material was not intended to be documentary evidence of historical or biographical "facts." It was a story in the service of the Easter kerygma.[21]

Van Buren observes that neither Bultmann nor Barth is unhappy about this state of affairs. Bultmann's central concern is essentially rooted in the kerygma of the cross, and he is unconcerned about the historical and biographical details in Jesus' life and what he may have thought about himself. In Barth's view, the most important consideration for faith is the fact that God has acted in raising Jesus from the dead and in commissioning the apostles as witnesses to this.

In recent years, van Buren says, a number of New Testament scholars have inaugurated what has been called a *new* quest for the historical Jesus. Employing a revised technique, these men begin by admitting that the New Testament documents are confessional documents. At the same time, however, they claim that these

[21] *Ibid.,* pp. 117–118.

documents provide us with an indirect source of knowledge about Jesus of Nazareth, since the faith which produced the New Testament was a response to his person and mission. These documents present us with history in the form of incidents rather than a biographical study. By analyzing these fragmentary episodes, all of which center around the figure of Jesus, one can gradually piece together a representative mosaic of his originality and distinctiveness and the way in which the early Church responded to him.

New Testament scholars like E. Fuchs, G. Ebeling, and G. Bornkamm, working within the framework of the new quest for the historical Jesus, have focused on different aspects of the personality of Christ which emerge from a study of the New Testament evidence. One of the predominant features of his personality seems to have been his remarkable freedom. This exceptional freedom, in van Buren's estimation, is the outstanding hallmark of the composite picture of Christ as presented by the New Testament witness to him. All his other characteristics can be grouped around this central concept. Jesus was an exceptionally liberated person whose freedom is glimpsed in his authoritative statements, his openness, and his assured self-identity. He manifested a freedom from familial claims, religious obligations, the need of status, and even the forces of nature. In addition to these negative aspects of freedom, he was a man free from anxiety and the need to establish his own identity, and above all he was free for his neighbor. He was truly a man for others. He preached the freedom of service, and his own life manifested a deep compassion for others, a true openness to all, and a selfless humble service to others. His extraordinary freedom attracted some and repelled others.

But historical knowledge of Jesus, van Buren continues, is not faith. Prior to the Easter event, the historical Jesus did not elicit faith, in the sense of the faith response of the early Christian to the Easter event. To determine the precise relationship of Christian faith to the historical Jesus one must analyze the Easter event which stands between Jesus and the believer and between Jesus and the New Testament witness to him. Van Buren says that one is faced with two sides of an apparent paradox in this study: faith is not based simply on a picture of the historical Jesus, yet the historical Jesus is indispensable for faith. Clarity in this matter can be achieved only through a detailed study of the Easter event as proclaimed in the New Testament.

As an historian and a linguistic analyst, van Buren prefers not to speak of the Easter event as a "fact," at least not in the ordinary sense of the word. One can say something about the situation before Easter and something about the consequences of the Easter event, but the resurrection does not lend itself to being spoken of as a "fact" since it defies empirical description. We know that the disciples were changed men after the event, but we are not in a position to say what happened. In the final analysis, all that one can say is that something happened.

Following the norms of linguistic analysis, statements such as "The Lord appeared to me" or "I saw him" are to be put in the category of "sense-content" statements. Regarding the nature of such statements, van Buren writes:

> Statements of sense-content cannot be verified by common-sense or empirical means. That is to say, they cannot be verified by a shared sense-experience, since they do not say what "all of us" can see but only what "I saw." Nor can they be checked against empirical data open to any and every competent investigator who cares to examine them, for again, a sense-content statement is about what "I saw," not about what is "there for everyone to see." Only "I" can record what was "on the mirror of my mind." But this is only to say that sense-content statements are not common-sense or empirical assertions, and more cannot be said against them. The way to verify a statement of sense-content is to see if the words and actions of the person who makes the statement conform to it. The test is one of consistency. If Hamlet claims to have seen his father's ghost *and* to have learned from the ghost that his father was murdered, his claim is verified by his setting out to avenge his father's death. His actions tend to support his claim of what he had seen and heard. In like manner, Peter's statement of sense-content, which identified the one he saw with a man who had lived a certain kind of life, is verified by Peter's subsequent life.[22]

Linguistically, the statement "Jesus is risen" functions as an odd juxtaposition of words from two dissimilar language games, van Buren observes. The word "Jesus" functions as a proper

[22] *Ibid.,* pp. 129–130. Italics in original.

name, while the word "risen" functions like the term "kingdom of God." This latter group of words function as "end-words"; that is, they point to the end and goal of all existence. They are employed in order to commend a certain attitude to the hearer or reader as being worthy of serious consideration. End-words, like sense-content statements, are ultimately verified by the conduct of the man who uses them. Thus, in accordance with this standard, the Petrine version of the Easter event appears to have been validated.

The Easter event, which provided the basis for the New Testament kerygma, emerges from the New Testament narrative as a discernment situation for the disciples. Suddenly the disciples had the experience of seeing Jesus in a wholly new way and of sharing in the freedom which had been his, a freedom to be for others. Unexpectedly, the freedom of Jesus began to be *"contagious,"* and his disciples began to share in this extraordinary freedom. This was not a purely subjective experience; something actually happened to them. Jesus became the focal point of a perspective covering the totality of life, the world, and history, as well as their understanding of themselves and others. This is what they meant in confessing that Jesus was Lord over the whole world. And in saying that *God* raised up Jesus, they indicated that what had happened to them was fundamental to their life and thought.

Van Buren's study of the Easter event is concluded in the following terms:

We shall summarize our interpretation of the language of the Easter event. Jesus of Nazareth was a free man in his own life, who attracted followers and created enemies according to the dynamics of personality and in a manner comparable to the effect of other liberated persons in history upon people about them. He died as the result of the threat that such a free man poses for insecure and bound men. His disciples were left no less insecure and frightened. Two days later, Peter, and then other disciples, had an experience of which Jesus was the sense-content. They experienced a discernment situation in which Jesus, the free man whom they had known themselves, and indeed the whole world, were seen in a quite new way. From that moment, the disciples began to possess something of the freedom of Jesus. His freedom began to be "contagious." For the disciples, therefore, the story of Jesus could not be told simply as the story of a free man who had died. Because of the new way in which the disciples saw him and because of what had happened to them, the story had to include the event of Easter. In telling the story of Jesus of Nazareth, therefore, they told it as the story of the free man who had set them free. This was the story which they proclaimed as the Gospel for all men.[23]

7. The Language of Faith

As a result of the apostolic proclamation of the Gospel, other men came to understand themselves as sharers with the apostles in a freedom defined by Jesus' freedom and in a totally new view of life and the world. Van Buren points out that, although traditional theology has accounted for this experience of conversion by referring to the work of the Holy Spirit, such an explanation is obviously not an empirical assertion. A statement of this nature is empirically grounded only in those instances where the listener shares the same viewpoint as the speaker, at least in basic detail. In this case, van Buren interprets the reference to the Holy Spirit to be an indication that the new freedom and perspective are received as gifts by the believer and that they are of fundamental importance to him.

Hearing the New Testament kerygma preached and reflecting upon its meaning can become a situation of discernment for an individual. The language of faith employed by the Christian believer contains an exclusive element: it claims the universal significance of a particular historical individual, Jesus of Nazareth. For the Christian, Jesus defines what it means to be a man and becomes the focal point of one's entire perspective. The Christian is forced to admit, however, that there are no empirical grounds for denying that something similar could happen to a disciple of a free man like Socrates. But the language of the Gospel contains not only exclusive claims; it reflects a universal aspect as well, for it maintains that in the history of Jesus of Nazareth something universal, eternal and absolute—something it calls "God"—was mani-

[23] *Ibid.,* p. 134.

fested. Contemporary empirical standards, of course, prohibit any transcendent interpretation of the word "God," as though the term actually referred to a personal, transcendent reality.

The earliest and most basic Christian confession, "Jesus is Lord," signified the acceptance of a particular perspective upon life and history. It ascribed universality to a particular man, indicating that Christian faith is a response to the life and teaching of Jesus, a response which culminates in a new understanding of self, man, history, and the whole world. The Christian perspective, van Buren continues, is not simply one point of view among many. It is not a point of view selected by the believer, for it is not the conclusion to a logical chain of reasoning. Essentially, it is a *blik* which grasps the believer. Christian faith is a gift, and it can even be called transcendent, in the sense that it grasps the individual from without.

Paradoxically, the man who has been seized by the Christian *blik* finds himself suddenly set free, for the Christian *blik* has a liberating effect. The freedom of Jesus becomes the criterion for the public and private life of the individual. The Christian perspective, van Buren says, is both historical and personal. It is historical insofar as it is radically rooted and grounded in the historical person of Jesus Christ. It is personal insofar as it becomes the personal possession of the believer. The Christian confesses that Jesus is Lord over the whole world, thus signifying that the freedom of all men, and not only of believing Christians, is rooted in the contagious freedom of Jesus.

In van Buren's estimation, then, Christian faith is best understood in terms of Hare's concept of *blik*. Although the assertions of the Gospel are meaningless if they are taken as straightforward empirical statements, nevertheless, they do have a use and a meaning when taken as the formulation of a *blik*. The Gospel is an adequate expression of the Christian *blik*. For the individual a *blik* arises, as Ramsey has suggested, out of a situation of discernment or disclosure, suddenly seen in a new way demanding a commitment on the viewer's part. The decisive discernment situation for Christianity is Easter and the Easter proclamation concerning Jesus of Nazareth. But seeing things in a new way implies that there was an old way. Thus, just as the Easter faith of the disciples depended on their memory of Jesus, so the Christian faith of later ages requires a minimal acquaintance with the Gospel narratives.

Van Buren feels that Braithwaite's understanding of religious statements as assertions of an intention to act in a certain way, together with the entertainment of certain stories, is helpful but inadequate. Braithwaite does not do justice to the historical aspect of the Gospel and completely neglects the peculiar "story" of Easter. Van Buren ascribes to Miles the presentation of faith as the somewhat qualified way of silence, but he feels that the Christian can qualify his silence with something more than a parable. He writes:

> Certainly the Christian possesses no special sources for the scientific description of the universe. Before such questions as whether there is some absolute being, even "Being itself," which is "behind" or "beyond" all we know and are, some final "ground and end of all created things," he will be wise to remain silent. He may qualify his silence, however, by telling something besides a parable. What he has to tell is the history of Jesus and the strange story of how his freedom became contagious on Easter.[24]

One can legitimately ask whether this interpretation of Jesus, Easter, and the Gospel, with its careful avoidance of any objective use of the term "God" and of such circumlocutions as "transcendence," "being," or "absolute," is really a Christian interpretation. The answer to this question can be found, van Buren suggests, by measuring this interpretation against the Christological assertions of the New Testament. He begins this comparison by calling attention to the pericope found in Chapter 14 of the fourth Gospel, where Jesus says that those who have seen him have seen the Father. According to his own exegesis of the text, van Buren concludes that "Father" is the word which Jesus apparently used frequently in cases where his contemporaries might have used the word "God." Thus, many inherent difficulties begin to disappear, he continues, if we understand the author to mean that we should

[24] *Ibid.*, p. 144.

stop looking for the "Father," for we shall not find him, and the quest is beside the point in any case. In other words, the New Testament gives its answer to the problem of God by pointing to the man Jesus and saying that whatever men were looking for in "God" is to be found in Jesus of Nazareth. However one understands the word "God"—whether as the goal of human existence, or as the truth about man and the world, or as the key to the meaning of life—"he" is to be found in Jesus Christ, "the way, the truth, and the life" for all men.

The author of the fourth Gospel makes many assertions regarding the functional equivalence of "Jesus" and "God," but there is also strong emphasis on the submission of Jesus to the "Father." Van Buren argues that such references should not be understood as empirical propositions. They are intended to call attention to Jesus' humility, his service, his being for others.

> Undoubtedly Jesus believed he was obeying some "one," whom he called "Father," but the Gospel of John, as well as the logic of language, forces us to silence before all questions concerning that "one." We can only follow the recommendation of the evangelist to look at Jesus himself; questions about "God" will receive their only useful answer in the form of the history of that man.[25]

Some aspects of the New Testament message are more difficult than others to interpret in a meaningful way. For instance, Paul's words, "In Christ God was reconciling the world to himself," are difficult to understand because the statement is so largely a "God" statement.[26] Since the verification principle rules out any transcendent meaning for the word "God," van Buren recommends that one focus attention on the particular sort of reconciliation revealed in the history of Jesus. The Christian understanding of reconciliation has unlimited application because it indicates the freedom of Christ which has set all men free. The Christian's reconciliation with his neighbor has been possible because he has been set free for the service of his neighbor.

[25] *Ibid.*, p. 148.
[26] 2 Cor. 5, 19.

Turning to a consideration of the meaning of the phrase, "Christ died for our sins," van Buren finds that once again the key concept which unlocks much of the meaning in the New Testament message is the idea of Jesus' freedom. Being free from self-concern, he was thereby open to the concerns of others. His whole life was characterized by compassion and mercy, by an openness to others, by a solidarity with all men. And since his death was actually the consequence of his life, one may justly regard his death as the measure of the freedom by which he set other men free.

This freedom of Christ became contagious in the Easter event. But when does the actual liberation of the believing Christian take place? Analysis of the language of a discernment situation indicates that what is suddenly "seen" was somehow objectively present prior to the discernment situation. Thus it is true that, psychologically, the actual liberation of the believing Christian takes place when this new perspective is achieved. However, the language of a discernment situation reveals this freedom to have been objectively present beforehand.

The Christian also possesses the "eschatological" hope that the contagious freedom he has seen in Jesus and the reconciliation with which it is closely associated will ultimately prevail among all men. This is not a prediction, van Buren observes, but a conviction on the part of the believer, since "eschatological" hope means that "one would die rather than abandon it. It indicates the unqualified, undebatable aspect of the Christian's historical perspective." [27]

In the final analysis, there can be arguing about *bliks,* for one cannot demonstrate the superiority of one *blik* over another. For the Christian, Jesus of Nazareth is the sole referent point for historical perspective, while other individuals may find the key to understanding life or history in Buddha or Karl Marx. The modern Christian should rest assured that he can remain a Christian and still maintain his empirical attitudes. He should not attempt to demonstrate the superiority of his perspective over others. This confidence of the modern Christian, according to van Buren, is founded upon two basic principles. The first, intended to satisfy

---

[27] Paul van Buren, *op. cit.,* pp. 154–155.

the valid concerns of the theological "left," is expressed in the following terms:

> Statements of faith are to be interpreted, by means of the modified verification principle, as statements which express, describe, or commend a particular way of seeing the world, other men, and oneself, and the way of life appropriate to such a perspective.[28]

The second, intended to satisfy the valid concerns of the theological "right," is expressed in the following terms:

> The norm of the Christian perspective is the series of events to which the New Testament documents testify, centering in the life, death, and resurrection of Jesus of Nazareth.[29]

8. The Language of Christology

The apostolic message proclaimed the contagious freedom of Jesus. Previous analysis has shown its statements to be not cosmological assertions but formulations of a particular historical perspective. Its statements are cosmological assertions only in form, not in intention. Analysis of the language of the Gospel indicates that its main intention was to express, define, and commend a certain historical perspective. The search for a secular meaning of the Gospel entails analysis of the Gospel message and not of its form.

Theology has an obligation to remain faithful to the intention of both the apostolic message and the Chalcedonian Christology. Van Buren feels that his interpretation satisfies both requirements. Chalcedonian Christology was faithful in its own way to the intention of biblical Christology, and in turn the new Christology is faithful in its own way to the intention of Chalcedonian Christology. The cardinal principle which van Buren invokes to demonstrate this is that fidelity to intention demands transformation of language. To grasp the significance of the secular transformation

[28] *Ibid.*, p. 156.
[29] *Ibid.*

of the apostolic preaching, van Buren suggests that we reexamine
how the apostolic preaching was transformed by classical Christology. This principle of transformation may help us to understand
van Buren's paradoxical statement: "To clarify the function of
the language of Chalcedonian Christology, precisely by being dis-
loyal to its assertions, is to show that our intention is faithful to
the Chalcedonian intent." [30]

The traditional doctrine of the incarnation says that God entered
the realm of human history in the person of Jesus Christ. Such a
proposition is a statement of faith and cannot function as an
empirical proposition, as is shown by an application of the verification principle. For van Buren, the incarnation indicates the source
of the Christian perspective, whereby a piece of human history
becomes a situation of disclosure for Christians. The final character of this Christian perspective is seen in the Church's rejection
of Arianism. According to the early Church Fathers, the divine
Logos incarnated in Jesus of Nazareth was nothing less than God
himself. For van Buren, this belief signifies that there is no God
"above" or "beyond" that which is "revealed" in Jesus Christ. In
other words, the Christian perspective is not dependent upon any
other. The Nicene Creed, which formulates the belief of the
Church regarding the relationship of Jesus to God, was an attempt
to define the basis of the historical Christian perspective. Van
Buren comments:

> When the confession is understood in this sense, its trinitarian
> structure is significant. First, Christian faith consists of a single,
> complete orientation to the whole world. Second, this orienta-
> tion is that of a life lived in freedom and love for men, which
> has its norm in the history of Jesus of Nazareth. Third (and
> here we include the later development of the third article,
> concerning the Holy Spirit), the Christian acquires this orien-
> tation by being "grasped" by its norm. When this happens to
> him, he becomes free to acknowledge this norm and live
> accordingly.[31]

[30] *Ibid.*, p. 159
[31] *Ibid.*, p. 161.

A functional analysis of religious language indicates that, when the Christian asserts that the Logos or the divine Son is "eternal," the word does not function empirically, in a cosmological, astronomical, geological, or biological sense. Rather, it reflects the Christian conviction that this criterion of human existence, seen as concretized in Jesus of Nazareth, was always the norm of human existence.

Furthermore, it is the contagious freedom of Jesus which enables the Christian believer to explain himself in terms of "I'm I," as a root explanation. Therefore, van Buren concludes, it is not surprising to find the Christian using "final" words in speaking of Jesus, words of wonder, awe, and worship. In this context, such expressions as God of God, Light of Light and very God of very God become appropriate and understandable.

"Very God of very God," but according to his humanity, he was consubstantial with men. Since Jesus defines for the Christian believer what it means to be a man, the Christian perspective presents its concept of man in terms of freedom: to be human is to be free for one's neighbor. The freedom of Jesus provided the basis for the assertion of classical Christology that Jesus was without sin. The extraordinary character of that freedom is seen in the Easter event which provides the foundation for the Christian commitment to understand all other men in the light of Jesus. As true man, Jesus was like all other men in all things except sin. The likeness of Jesus to all other men is not jeopardized by the scriptural stories of the virgin birth of Jesus, except by an insistence that they must be understood to be factually true, since this would threaten Chalcedon's doctrine of the full manhood. Once one sees that they are simply literary devices or techniques designed to convey a sense of thanksgiving, awe, and joy over the coming of this man, they become meaningful.

Turning to classical Christology, van Buren notes that the Fathers taught that the human "nature" of Jesus had no independent existence apart from the existence of the Logos—i.e., the human "nature" has its existence only in that of the Logos. The meaning or function of this assertion in the Christian perspective is to say something about the relationship between the free man Jesus and the contagiousness of that freedom. In its negative form, "this doctrine means that the free man Jesus had no compelling interest for the believer apart from the consequences of Easter." [32] In its positive form, the form which orthodox theologians decided to use, "its meaning is that the Christian can only conceive of Jesus of Nazareth as a man whose freedom has become contagious." [33]

According to the Chalcedonian formulation, the two "natures" of Christ, the divine and the human, form a perfect union in the hypostasis of the Logos, united inseparably and indivisibly. A functional analysis of language, van Buren maintains, indicates that this formulation of unity deals with the relationship of the perspective of faith to the history of Jesus. There are two components in this union: the historical Jesus who manifested an extraordinary freedom, and the discernment and contagious power of this freedom which the disciples experienced on Easter. Within the context of the Christian faith, these two elements are inseparable. Van Buren writes:

> The inseparable unity of the freedom of the man Jesus with the fact that first the apostles and then other believers have been set free and have come to participate in his freedom found expression in the doctrine of the inseparable unity of the two "natures." [34]

The Chalcedonian formula also states that both the human and the divine "natures" remained unchanged and unconfused in this union. For van Buren, this expression signifies that the freedom of the believer is not the same as the freedom of Jesus, for one's perspective is not the same as the history on which it is based. History and a perspective based on that history are two completely different realities. Within the context of Christian belief, however, these two components are very closely bound together, both logically and historically, into a unified whole. The transformation or change takes place in the individual, not in the facts of history. No empirical change takes place in the facts; they are simply seen in a totally new way. Thus, the history of Jesus of Nazareth remains a

[32] *Ibid.*, p. 165.

[33] *Ibid.*

[34] *Ibid.*, p. 166.

piece of human history, and the event of Easter and the succeeding occasions of conversion are discernment situations.

Van Buren urges that the Alexandrian or Monophysite tendency to see the human "nature" absorbed into the divine and the inclination to see Jesus as "more than a man" be carefully avoided. He suggests that one follow the Antiochene and the reformed Protestant traditions in their concern for preserving the historical basis of the Christian perspective, lest it be absorbed into the perspective itself.

In summarizing the results of his analytical study thus far, van Buren states that, although no simple correspondence can be found between the patristic interpretation of the New Testament witness to Christ and his own interpretation of that witness, nevertheless one can still discover a logical equivalence between the two. In general, he has tried to place the doctrine of the human "nature" of Christ in the context of language appropriate to the history of a free man, and to place the doctrine of the divine "nature" in the context of language appropriate to a freedom which has been contagious and to the historical perspective which arises from a discernment situation. His own interpretation, he feels, meets the legitimate demands of both the theological "left" and "right" in the contemporary Christological discussion. He concurs with the "right" in insisting that Christology, and not soteriology, be primary, and that theology should make clear the "objective fact" of God's act in Jesus Christ. Christ set men free some nineteen centuries ago. This was an accomplished fact before men came to see it as such, and therefore, in this sense, it is an objective fact. Both the language of history and the language of historical perspective support the "objective" emphasis of conservative theology. On the other hand, he agrees with the insistence of the theological "left" that the Christian faith must be rethought in light of the critique of modern thought. But it is not sufficient, he maintains, to translate the word "God" by such subtly qualified phrases as "transcendent reality" or "the ground and end of all things," as some would suggest. Since contemporary secular attitudes do not allow one to speak of God in analogical terms, modern man finds it impossible to attach a relevant meaning to the existentialist theologian's reference to "experienced non-objective reality." If all his models are taken from the area of human experiences which do not require trans-empirical language, then man is not faced with the difficulty of trying to use circumlocutions.

9. The Implications of a Radical Secular Theology

Christian tradition has always taught, van Buren says, that the relevation of God was situated in Jesus of Nazareth and that God actually is as he is revealed in the history of Jesus. The Christian is forced to admit that it is neither logically nor psychologically necessary that recorded history of Jesus and the Easter event become an occasion of discernment for an individual. But once the believer has adopted the Christian perspective, he is obliged to use his reasoning powers in order to see the full impact of the Gospel message on his own situation. This integration of faith and reason is necessary because the Christian faith is inseparably related to history, and history requires reasoning. Further, this attitude reflects the traditional Christian interpretation that revelation must be logically consistent and that it can never be contrary to right reason. The Christian believes that, although the truths of revelation cannot be discovered by reason alone, reason can still operate upon these truths in an analytic and synthetic way after they have been revealed.

In considering the doctrine of predestination, van Buren feels that a universalist interpretation is most consistent with the historical Christian perspective. Under the influence of men like Barth, modern theology has witnessed a renewed interest in the doctrine of predestination or election. According to the older form of this doctrine, God chose only certain individuals to be numbered among the elect, while others were presumably predestined to damnation. The newer form says that God, in choosing only one man for the sake of all men, has actually chosen all men. The adoption of a markedly different attitude toward what really constitutes the most important characteristic of man is responsible for this universalist interpretation. Following the lead of Catholicism, conservative Protestant theology has tended to distinguish men on the basis of their response to the Gospel, with the result that belief or unbelief is employed as the decisive criterion for distinguishing men. Van Buren is convinced that such theological thinking reflects a conviction that God only loves those who respond to him. Barth's interpretation of this doctrine, on the other hand, tends toward universalism. According to his view, God loves all men regardless of their response to him, since God's love is for man as man. The most important thing about a man is simply his manhood and not his response. This interpretation of the doctrine, van Buren feels, offers many possibilities for the secular-minded Christian of today. It represents a perspective grounded in history and not in the religious experience of the believer. "The two positions are each internally consistent, but their historical bases differ, and this leads to differences in attitude, intention, and action. The Christian historical perspective is more adequately expressed by universalism than by its denial." [35]

In considering the Christian doctrine dealing with creation, van Buren observes that theologians long ago abandoned the claim that the doctrine of creation explains the physical origin of the world and that it is now used to assert that this world—the entire physical universe of matter, energy, and men—is God's handiwork and therefore good. "The doctrine expresses in fact an affirmative view of the world of men and things." [36]

From reflection on the experience of the exodus from Egypt, the focal point of their religious experience, the Israelites came to view themselves as a people brought into national existence by Yahweh "out of nothing." Their faith in Yahweh as the creator of everything else was a corollary of their historical perspective. Likewise, says van Buren, the Christian doctrine of the divine creation of all things "through Jesus Christ" is a corollary of the historical Christian perspective.

Traditional Christianity has always taught that God not only created the world, but directs its course toward an appointed goal. This doctrine of divine providence is a corollary of the doctrine of creation. Today, the misfortunes of the wicked and the prosperity

[35] *Ibid.*, p. 176.
[36] *Ibid.*, p. 177.

of the pious are no longer cited in support of this doctrine. The evidence of history is too ambiguous for this doctrine to be interpreted as a philosophy of history. An assertion compatible with every conceivable set of circumstances is not an empirical assertion. "Taken as the expression of a view of the world, however, the doctrine of providence is significant as an assertion of the strength of the grasp that the Christian's perspective has on him." [37]

Turning to a consideration of sin, justification, and sanctification, van Buren begins by noting that, according to Christian doctrine, man was created good, but he then turned away from the source of his life. Man is now born with a tendency toward "sin," allowing himself to become the key to his historical perspective and seeking his own welfare at the expense of his neighbor. Man is in bondage and in need of freedom. That liberation is proclaimed in the New Testament. Van Buren writes:

> In the New Testament, man is seen in the light of the free man, Jesus of Nazareth, and compared to him, men are not free; they are bound by fear and anxiety, mistrust and self-concern. The word used to describe this condition, when measured by *this* standard, is "sin." The logical structure of this teaching does not depend on the story of the "Fall," or even on a theory of "inherited guilt." The various traditional forms of the doctrine of "original sin" are not empirical observations about man; they are *comparative* statements of man's condition, measured by the historical standard of Jesus of Nazareth.[38]

Because Christ is the ultimate norm by which all men are measured, van Buren continues, one can say that Christ is the final judge, since to use a norm is to compare and to judge. Sin reflects the language of bondage and liberation, and for the Christian the term is meaningful only within the context of the contagious freedom of Jesus. The Christian rejects the Pelagian teaching that man sins solely by his own choice, because this view reflects a naive conception of human freedom and an inadequate appreciation of the Easter event. Traditional Christian theology has also re-

---

[37] *Ibid.*, p. 178.
[38] *Ibid.*, p. 179. Italics in original.

jected the extreme alternative: that sin is "natural" to man. This
definition of man would seem to be taken from man in bondage
and not from the free man, Jesus of Nazareth.

The Gospel teaches man that sin has been conquered by Jesus
and that each man is in a position to receive justification as a gift
of grace, a gift to be received and acknowledged in faith. The doctrine of justification by grace through faith expresses the believer's
conviction that he has been accepted freely, regardless of his
merit, because of Christ. If one tries to understand this doctrine
in empirical terms, van Buren says, it becomes logically meaningless and morally doubtful.

> Understood as the expression of the believer's historical per-
> spective, however, it indicates that his freedom is such that he
> no longer feels the need to "prove" himself to himself or to
> anyone else. He is free to accept himself, convinced that he is
> acceptable, for he has been set free by Jesus of Nazareth.[39]

Van Buren cautions that Bultmann's existentialist interpretation
of justification is liable to misunderstanding because of its emphasis
on *self*-understanding, which could lead to a doctrine of justification by means of faith rather than grace. The Christian must remember that Jesus is the source of the new understanding of
the self. Justification is not something attained by the individual
on his own.

Justification, as Calvin showed, is inseparably connected with
sanctification. The individual is not only set free, but he is oriented
in a specific direction when he adopts the Christian perspective.
Sanctification defines the freedom acquired in the process of justification. Christian freedom consists in being free for one's neighbor,
and therefore sanctification essentially means love for one's neighbor. Furthermore, the verification principle shows that "love for
one's neighbor" means "love for God," since man's love for his
neighbor is a test of his love for God. The Christian is to love his
neighbor after the example of Jesus and by this means he is sanc-
tified.

The Christian believer does not hold his historical perspective
in isolation, van Buren continues, but in the company of others

---

[39] *Ibid.*, p. 181.

within the Christian community. The Christian Church is a community which shares the same contagious freedom of Jesus and which is consciously aware of the source of its freedom. It is a community held together by a shared perspective based on the history of the man who set it free. Initiation into this community is effected through the rite of baptism which has ecclesial as well as individual significance, and for this reason it has traditionally been performed in the midst of the community. In its original form, the immersion in water and the subsequent emergence offered a dramatic representation of what happens when one changes *bliks*. The ritual act of baptism signifies the transition from a state of bondage to a state of liberty.

The sermon preached during communal worship may occasion the renewal and deepening of the hearer's historical perspective, or, if the hearer is not already a Christian, it may become the occasion of discernment which leads him to adopt this perspective. The sermon is primarily a proclamation pointing to the free man Jesus of Nazareth. At times, preaching functions as a way of illustrating various ways in which the hearer can extend the range of his historical perspective so that he may see the whole world as liberated by Jesus and not just believers. Preaching, van Buren continues, may also serve as a secondary form of exhortation. When the preacher tells the congregation that they should act in a certain way "because it is the will of God," he is simply inviting his listeners to see the *logical* implications of the historical Christian perspective.

The preaching of the Word is closely associated with the celebration of the Lord's supper, the memorial of the last meal Jesus had with his disciples. In treating of this memorial, van Buren writes:

The logic of this memorial is revealed in one of the stories of the Easter appearances of Jesus to his disciples, which is set in the context of a meal: in the breaking of bread, "the light dawned" and Jesus was seen in a new way. Similarly, the Lord's Supper is celebrated to provide an opportunity for the believer to "see" more clearly the basis of his "blik" and to be "renewed" in his faith. The invitation to "feed" on Jesus

himself in the sixth chapter of the Gospel of John is a blunt
way of saying that faith has to do with the "flesh" of Jesus,
with Jesus as a concrete historical man. This odd language
underscores the essential role of this history in the Christian
perspective, a role dramatized in the celebration of the Lord's
Supper.[40]

The traditional debates concerning the "real presence" of Christ
are fruitless, he says, because there is no real way of settling these
differences empirically. The term "real presence" has meaning only
when viewed in relation to the language of Easter and the apostles'
assertion that Jesus appeared to them. Participation in the Lord's
supper can become a discernment situation in which the participant
suddenly "sees" that Jesus' freedom was for him. It is *as if* Jesus
were present before him.

Regarding the question of prayer, van Buren notes that a secular
meaning of prayer rules out a "someone" to whom we speak in
prayer. When ancient man prayed to God on behalf of his neighbor, he was doing the most effective thing he knew of to help his
neighbor. Today's Christian will reflect upon his neighbor's needs in
light of the Gospel and estimate the most effective way of aiding
his neighbor. Instead of praying and fasting for days, he will initi-
ate effective action. "The meaning of intercessory prayer is in its
use: it begins in reflection upon the situation in light of the Christian perspective and leads to appropriate action." [41] At times the
Christian will find that he is unable to take efficient action and
will have to remain content with having reflected upon the situation. In other words, his prayers will remain "unanswered." When
prayer is understood as reflection and consequent action, it may
be difficult and time-consuming, but it is a logically clear activity.

Van Buren maintains that the Christian should not be anxious to
go out and convert unbelievers. History shows that, as the Christian Church grew stronger, the world came to be claimed for the
Church rather than for Christ. Furthermore, in the course of time,
the biblical God became more and more otherworldly, so that today man does not even know how to use the word. Man is grad-

[40] *Ibid.*, p. 187.
[41] *Ibid.*, p. 189.

ually learning to stand on his own feet and to help his neighbor without any reference to the "God hypothesis." The Christian should rejoice at this development, remaining content to let the contagious freedom of Christ work its own way into the world without worry about the future of the Church. The mission of the Christian is simply to be a man, as this is defined by Jesus of Nazareth.

In concluding his analysis, van Buren says that he has tried to present a secular meaning of the Gospel and some of the consequences of such an understanding of the Christian faith, neither urging that this path be taken nor denying that there are alternatives. Modern secularism, he suggests, offers a viable philosophy for contemporary man, since it manifests a deep concern for the welfare of man and a firm conviction that life is worth living in a certain way. It demonstrates that it is possible today to be agnostic about otherworldly powers and beings and still place a high valuation on human relationships.

The methodological principles of linguistic analysis, he feels, adequately reflect the empirical attitudes characteristic of contemporary secular thought. Theology ought to be reduced to the human, the historical, and the empirical. The functional definition of meaning provided by linguistic analysis shows it is possible to find a form of Christianity which reflects an appreciation of both the historical Jesus and the Easter event. Although he ends with a reduction of Christianity to its historical, intentional, and ethical dimensions, van Buren is convinced that nothing essential has been left behind. Men should stop peering into the clouds in a vain attempt to find God and start thinking out their existence in terms of man—specifically in terms of the man in whom God has said all that he has to say to man.

10. An Evaluation

Before attempting to evaluate the ideas of van Buren as expressed in the previous sections, it should be noted that he has moved beyond his position in *The Secular Meaning of the Gospel*. A couple of years after the book appeared, van Buren wrote:

My book represents an important step in a personal struggle to overcome my own theological past, and it served to help me over a hump. Since getting to the other side I have been occupied with finding my way about in the realm outside a "theological circle" which was becoming increasingly unreal. I am trying to see the role and nature of theology in the context of the plurality and relativity of contemporary culture.[42]

At the present time, van Buren is engaged in studying religious thought or theology within a cultural rather than an ecclesiastical context. His main concern now is to understand theology as a constructive and critical contribution to thought and cultural development. Having reformulated traditional Christian doctrines in a secular mode, he now devotes all his efforts to discover the role of religion within the context of culture. Man's religious ideas, he argues, form part of the whole study of man. The field of religious studies, therefore, forms a section of the humanities, since it bears a certain affinity to literature, history, philosophy, politics, economics, and so forth. Religious belief was a very important element in man's cultural development, and it is able to serve a useful purpose in the future.

Today, man must come to realize that theology is responsible to society, not to the Church, for its basic orientation is humanistic and not divine. This means that the ultimate norms and criteria of theological reasoning lie in the role that theology plays in society. Therefore, it is not to be judged by whether or not it accords with an inherited standard or ancient text. The religious question today, says van Buren, is not what religious truth might be, but what has religion done for man in the past, and what is it able to do for men in the future. There should be a dynamic and reciprocal interaction between religious belief and culture, with each exerting a mutual influence on the other.

At the very outset of his search for the secular meaning of the Gospel, van Buren clearly outlines his immediate goal and the method to be followed to attain that goal, and his basic principles of operation are systematically and consistently applied throughout. His methodical, rational, and logical approach to the problem recommends itself to the modern mind. One is struck by the

[42] Paul van Buren, "Theology in the Context of Culture," *Christian Century* 82 (April 7, 1965), p. 429.

precision, logical consistency, and inner consistency of the work, qualities upon which the contemporary world puts a very high premium.

According to van Buren's analysis of the present situation, modern man is irretrievably secular in his attitudes and thought. He lives in a world of radical immanence, a world in which the highest values are humanistic and all truth and meaning are essentially empirical. Modern man finds himself to be a man without God, because the existence and nature of a transcendent God are not empirically verifiable. In his evaluation of the present situation, van Buren concludes that the theological "right" is too mythological and that it errs in stubbornly clinging to a theistic interpretation of man and the universe, while the theological "left" is not sufficiently grounded in historical perspective and begs the empiricist's question by employing circumlocutions to speak about God. A rigorous and systematic application of the verification principle, van Buren contends, makes the acceptance of a transcendent, personal God impossible. Despite the atheistic framework of the modern world—a perspective resulting from the disappearance of all transcendental dimensions of reality—today's Christian can remain both a Christian and a secular man. Operating on the conviction that the "meaning is in the use," van Buren has discovered that theological statements do have a meaning and relevance within a given context, one which can be determined by careful analysis of the use of such statements.

Provided one is willing to excise carefully all references to God, the transcendent, and the supernatural, says van Buren, one is still able to profess a form of Christian belief, but a belief centered around the historical man Jesus of Nazareth, who was a man and "in no sense more than a man." He was a man characterized by a rare spirit of independence and an extraordinary freedom and availability for others. His freedom is somehow or other communicated to all men, although only his followers are conscious of the ultimate source of this freedom.

At least two things are debatable in van Buren's presentation of secular Christianity: the contention that modern man is irretrievably secular, and the assertion that linguistic analysis provides the best and only source for determining meaning and truth. It is certainly true that much of contemporary thought is heavily impregnated with secular and positivistic attitudes. This has undoubtedly contributed to the growing unbelief which is currently in evidence. However, it is difficult to measure with accuracy the extent and depth of such an intangible factor. Secondly, the methodology provided by linguistic analysis contributes greatly to a much needed clarification of ideas and concepts, but it cannot be viewed as the sole norm of truth. It cannot, or should not, be expected to supply values. Van Buren's ideas, however, should provoke reflection by Christian thinkers, since he raises two crucial questions: whether the human intellect can reach the transcendent by rational inference, and whether theological predication outside a purely empirical framework can be valid.

For van Buren, Jesus Christ is all there is of "God." For modern man, he says, the term "God" is dead. It is a waste of time to debate theism against atheism, since contemporary man has discovered that he can remain agnostic regarding "otherworldly" matters and still place high value on human interests and commitments. Provided its doctrines are understood in a secular way, Christianity can be taken seriously as a way of life. But in completely rejecting Christianity, the secular humanist, whether atheist or agnostic, seems far more honest and consistent than the proponents of Christian atheism, for, outside of a transcendent framework, what is there to recommend Jesus of Nazareth as the absolute focal point of a total world view? Van Buren bases the centrality of Jesus in his own perspective on the "contagious" freedom of Jesus. But in the final analysis, he is no more successful than Hamilton in showing a real connection between his Christology and his atheism or agnosticism.

One of the weak features of van Buren's presentation is his extreme vagueness about this "contagious" freedom which radiates from Jesus and is communicated to his followers. One would expect greater clarity and precision from a man who holds linguistic analysis in such high esteem. This is a particularly crucial point, since this "contagious" freedom provides the only link between the historical Jesus and the modern believer in van Buren's analysis. Van Buren is certainly correct in stressing the centrality of the historical Jesus of Nazareth as the ultimate ground of the Christian perspective. At times, however, this "contagious" freedom paradoxically seems to assume non-empirical and transcendent dimensions. By avoiding the question of Jesus' physical resurrection and postulating a "contagious" freedom to explain the centrality and dynamism of the Christian perspective, van Buren weakens the Christian foundation of his secular theology.

Van Buren feels that his secular version of Christianity retains all the essential features of Christianity and avoids the deficiencies of the theological "right" and "left." For, although it does away with all reference to a transcendent, personal God, it explains both the relativity and the historical basis of the Christian perspective. This, however, is debatable. Like Hamilton, van Buren has attempted to effect a forced union between secular humanism and a type of Christology, a union which breaks down under close scrutiny. When one analyzes his re-presentation of the key Christian concepts of revelation, sin, justification, prayer, baptism, and so forth, one is immediately struck by the brevity of the treatment accorded each topic and the patent absurdity of retaining Christian labels for these reformulations. If Christian prayer, for instance, is nothing more than thoughtful reflection upon a problem and appropriate consequent action, why not call it precisely *that* and stop suggesting that it be called Christian prayer? The secular humanist is far more honest and consistent, because he does not discuss sin, justification, prayer, revelation, and so forth. He finds no compelling reason why Jesus of Nazareth, more than any other man, should be the focal point of his world view. Although van Buren's understanding of these concepts flows logically from his empirical presuppositions and methodology, nevertheless the complete inversion of meaning which results from the systematic application of the verification principle only underlines the artificiality of his conjunction of secular humanism and Christology.

This becomes even more apparent when one considers his definition of "eschatological" hope as signifying that "one would rather die than abandon it," or his contention that scriptural references to the Holy Spirit indicate that the new freedom and perspective of the believer "are of fundamental importance to him," or his assertion that the New Testament reference to Christ's "eternal" election means that "Yahweh's whole plan and purpose was involved in this choice." [43] Despite van Buren's claim that he main-

[43] Paul van Buren, *The Secular Meaning of the Gospel*, pp. 155, 136, 51.

tains the fundamental intention of patristic and classical Christology, this application of terms appears to be a clear misuse of language. His analysis of classical Christology on its own terms shows that he is familiar with the orthodox interpretation. In fact, this section of the book offers a very good summary of the orthodox position. But his subsequent re-presentation of Christianity in secular terms, a reformulation based on the principle that "fidelity to the intention of the apostolic message demands our willingness to transform the assertions of the apostolic preaching," ends in a clear distortion. Van Buren tries to justify the principle by offering examples which assume its validity.

Besides, his treatment of what he calls "sense-content statements" is deficient and weak. The truth of a statement should be rooted in something more basic than the measured congruence between a verbal expression and subsequent actions felt to be consistent with it. All the deficiencies cited seem to support the judgment that van Buren's book is mainly an exercise in logical construction, a provisional formulation of theological ideas within an ecclesiastical framework and an attempt to see where secular thought-forms will lead. His own remarks about the nature of the book seem to substantiate such a judgment.

Although he is an ordained Episcopal priest, he readily admits that he does not pray or function as a priest and that "if somebody wants to fight about the name, then I guess I would have to admit that I'm just not a Christian." [44] Christian language about God, he feels, is really just a dated way of talking about man.

His book, however, does raise some important theological issues: the relationship between reason and faith, the symbolic knowledge of God, the validity of theological predication, the role and function of theology, the relation of facts to values, and so forth. But the problem of God is not reducible to a logical problem or a semantic difficulty. Nor can it be solved solely by syllogistic reasoning and argumentation. What Christianity may need today is a new hermeneutics rather than linguistic analysis. In the final analysis, van Buren has failed to present a viable *via media* between Christianity and atheism.

[44] Cf. Ved Mehta, "The New Theologian," Part I, *New Yorker* 82 (Nov. 13, 1965), p. 153.

IV
THOMAS J. J. ALTIZER

1. Introduction

One of the leading exponents of the radically new form of Christianity known as Christian atheism is Thomas J. J. Altizer of Emory University, Atlanta, Georgia. Modern man, he argues, is finally coming to accept the event of the death of God and its consequences for man. The traditional and familiar transcendent world view has collapsed, and a wholly immanent world view has replaced the old order. Man has come to realize that the personal, transcendent, "wholly other God" of the Judaeo-Christian tradition is dead. He is not simply hidden or absent; he is dead. At the present time, the radical Christian is the only one who can speak in a meaningful way about the death of God, for he alone sees that the transcendent God has become totally incarnate, totally immersed in flesh, and present in every human hand and face.

Most of Altizer's theological thinking is polarized between a mystical and a dialectical mode of thinking. He attributes most of his theological insights to a study of comparative religion, Oriental mysticism, and the ideas expressed by G. W. F. Hegal, William Blake, and Friedrich Nietzsche, whom he views as radical Christian prophets. The radically new Christian vision which he proposes is a synthetic presentation of theological insights culled from these sources. Drawing upon these resources, Altizer advocates a return to the original, forward-moving, eschatological thrust of authentic Christian faith. Oriental mysticism, he says, attempts to reach the sacred by a retrograde process of negating man's present consciousness and history, and religious or orthodox Christianity uses the same basic method. In fact, a study of comparative religion shows that religion is essentially a dialectical movement which negates the profane in an attempt to reach the sacred, a movement which looks backward to a primordial sacrality. The hallmark of authentic Christianity, on the other hand, is its assertion that the sacred is to be reached only through a strong affirmation of the secular and the profane. Instead of searching for an original primordial sacrality, says Altizer, man should adopt an eschatological understanding of the sacred, looking forward to a new and apocalyptic manifestation of the sacred in this world. All previous forms of the Spirit must be negated so that new forms might emerge. This is in accordance with the intrinsic dynamism of the dialectical process of self-realization. The primordial, wholly other, transcendent, absolute, oppressive, alien, foreign, omnipotent God died in Jesus Christ; the Spirit has become completely immersed in flesh; the transcendent God has annihilated himself by becoming totally immanent in order that a new epiphany of the Spirit might appear under a different form.

The death of God, in Altizer's estimation, provides Christian man's only entrance into the 20th century. This event should be viewed as a redemptive act because it liberates man from servile bondage to an oppressive deity, thereby providing an opportunity for the emergence of a new humanity. Having abandoned all nostalgic and atavistic attachment to the transcendent, today's radical Christian resolutely follows a totally immanent and totally incarnate Christ, a fully incarnate Word of Spirit. The Word is presently operative in the world of men, while expectantly awaiting a new and transformed epiphany of the Spirit in this world.

Altizer is strongly convinced that today's Christian is called upon to proclaim the Gospel, the Good News, of the death of God. He advocates a radically new form of atheism, a form of Christian atheism wherein the definitive self-annihilation of the transcendent God heralds the advent of a new humanity. God is dead, not simply hidden, withdrawn, or absent. In presenting his own version of radical Christianity, Altizer follows Nietzsche in adopting the death-of-God motif; he employs an Hegelian dialectic to relate the sacred to the profane; he uses the mystical insights of Blake to determine the full significance of the death of God for man.

2. Radical Theology

The fundamental thesis of Altizer's version of radical theology is the conviction that only the Christian now can speak of God. Today's Christian is called to proclaim the Gospel of the death of God. The death-of-God motif so prevalent in Altizer's writings conjoins the two basic components of his theological thinking: it combines a mystical and a dialectical understanding of Christianity. In Altizer's evaluation of the present religious crisis, because of the progressive deterioration of traditional Christianity, the modern Christian faces the dilemma of choosing either unfaith or a radically new form of Christian belief. As Altizer sees it, there are only two viable alternatives open to contemporary man: either a complete rejection of Christianity in its entirety or the adoption of a type of Christian atheism.

Altizer says that the modern theologian has recognized for some time that God is no longer operative or visible in the culture, society, and history of a dying Christendom. Nevertheless, he remained persuaded that God is present in an eternal form, in an autonomous Word of faith. As a result of this extreme separation of the sacred and the profane, the theologian was forced into a retreat which ultimately led to the isolation of faith from the present and concrete reality of daily human existence. His religious faith became a haven of refuge and consolation, a psychological support reflecting an attitude of mind completely divorced from the secular framework of today's world.

But a new kind of theologian is coming into prominence today, Altizer says, a theologian who is not so confident of truth or the certainty of faith, who acknowledges the collapse of the transcendental world view in which Christianity is rooted. He realizes that to cling tenaciously to the Christian God in our time is to evade the real human situation. Convinced that faith should be meaningful within the context of the given world and not be something eternally given or wholly autonomous, the new theologian insists on a mutual and reciprocal relation between faith and the world. In concise terms, the radical Christian theologian denies the traditional form of the Word and seeks a wholly incarnate Word, a kenotic form of the Word which signifies the self-annihilation of God and the assumption of a wholly immanent incarnation of the Word. Because he is persuaded that the traditional forms of faith have little or no meaning today, the radical Christian insists that the Christian conception of the incarnate Word must undergo a radical transformation if it is to maintain any congruence with the secular convictions and thought patterns of modern man. In today's world, faith must be wholly and inseparably embedded in the world; it must be thoroughly secular in character. Faith cannot be isolated and autonomous, possessing a reality or a meaning which transcends the immediate actuality of this world.

Christian theology, says Altizer, can no longer be viewed as the continual elucidation of an eternal and unchanging Word. Rather, it must be understood as a thinking response to the Word present on the horizon of secular faith, a horizon which lies in the eschatological future, not in the remote and inert past. Contemporary man must learn to realize that there is no single distilled essence or core of Christian belief; there is no unchanging substratum of belief. The radical Christian is convinced that Christian faith is real only insofar as it undergoes a particular human and historical expression, and only insofar as it is oriented toward an eschatological end rather than a primordial beginning. Christian faith is not confined to primitive and past forms of expression. It is a dynamic, forward-moving, and future-oriented movement, a transfiguring movement which cannot be identified with traditional forms and should not be confused with them.

Despite the anti-Christian tenor of our times, says Altizer, the incarnate Word is still present and operative in the world of men, and the goal of the modern theologian is to unveil the present form of the Word in contemporary culture. Man is gradually coming to realize that what is most authentically human is actually a manifestation of faith. Until the present time, theologians have failed to meet the progressive dominance of atheism in our century, an atheism which is grounded and rooted in the developments of the 19th century. They have been unable to meet the challenge of atheism, offering only empty and meaningless answers until now. Contemporary atheism, Altizer insists, should be met with acceptance and affirmation rather than rejection and negation. This new confrontation with modern atheism by the radical Christian is simultaneously a radical form of Christian faith and a passionate affirmation of the birth of a new humanity.

Altizer believes that the atheistic anti-Christian prophets of the 19th century venerated Jesus but were persuaded that Christian tradition had buried or distorted the message and person of Jesus of Nazareth. In the final analysis, and despite external appearances, George W. F. Hegel, William Blake, Karl Marx, Fyodor Dostoevsky, and Friedrich Nietzsche were in a sense deeply bound to Christianity. Their attacks on Christianity were directed against those theological forms and moral laws which prevent the advent of a new man. Viewed from this perspective, then, men like Hegel, Blake, and Nietzsche represent a revolutionary type of Christian prophet, and their protests against the Christian conception of God provide the radical Christian with a totally new form of faith.

Christianity has been accused of being a flight from life, an evasion of reality, a refusal to accept the human condition as given. Nietzsche's condemnation of Christianity serves as a model for the mood which is beginning to characterize the modern world. He saw the Christian God as the transcendent enemy of the fullness of man's life in the world. Only by the death of God can mankind be liberated from this tyranny and the dawn of a new age of humanity appear on the horizon. Altizer writes:

> Unlike the far weaker contemporary attacks of a Lawrence or a Camus, Nietzsche's protest against Christianity, like Blake's and Hegel's, is most fundamentally directed against the Christian God. It is God himself who is the transcendent enemy of the fullness and the passion of man's life in the world, and only through God's death can humanity be liberated from that repression which is the real ruler of history. Standing upon the threshold of what he believed to be a new age of humanity, the nineteenth-century prophet identified the God of Christianity as the deepest obstacle to liberty and joy. Blake gradually came to the realization that the true name of the Christian God is Satan, just as Hegel conceived of the "false infinite" or the impassive and unmoving Absolute as the ultimate source of alienation, and Nietzsche disclosed God to be the very embodiment of an infinitude of man's self-hatred and guilt. Thus the triumphant Blake could say in *The Everlasting Gospel*: "Thou art a Man; God is no more." [1]

[1] Thomas J. J. Altizer, *The Gospel of Christian Atheism* (Philadelphia: Westminster Press, 1966), p. 22.

An acceptance of the death of God, the transcendent Christian God, is the starting point for a radical theology. But it is only a starting point, for the faith of the radical Christian is bipolar. The negative aspect of this faith, the death of God, is balanced and complemented by a positive element based on the conviction that the totally incarnate and eschatological Word is currently operative in the world. An acceptance of the death of God provides the only clear entrance to the 20th century. Thus, the radical Christian sees that authentic Christianity is inseparable from an attack on God. True faith requires the abolition and dissolution of God. The Christian alone can proclaim the death of God in meaningful terms because the actuality of the death of God is perceived only by the man of faith. The faith of the radical Christian is founded upon a realization of the kenotic self-annihilation of God manifested in Christ. Today, all residual traces of transcendence are gradually being dissolved, while a radical immanence is becoming more and more prominent. But while it is true that a new and transformed humanity can emerge only after the death of God, the disappearance of the absolute or the transcendent need not lead to nihilism. Contemporary Christianity need not be a flight from this world to a transcendent world beyond. A viable alternative solution, Altizer suggests, lies in the adoption of a form of atheism, a radically new form of Christian belief based on the passionate affirmation of the death of God.

Altizer's proposal of Christian atheism is fundamentally a theological synthesis based on what he considers to be the prophetic Christian visions of Hegel, Blake, and Nietzsche. The actual history of the development of radical Christianity, he maintains, is difficult to reconstruct, mainly because Church historians have been delinquent in their work. Fundamentally, one can say that radical Christianity is a search for total redemption, a search for a total union with the spiritual Jesus or the incarnate Word. It resolutely repudiates the God who is sovereign Creator and transcendent Lord, while firmly believing in the third and apocalyptic age of the Spirit. It seeks to return to the original Word of faith, rejecting a literal interpretation of the bible, while demanding instead a pneumatic or spiritual understanding of the Word. Radical Christianity recognizes the reality of the process of history and the forward-movement of the Word or Spirit; it seeks a renewal of the original Jesus in the spiritual or universal form demanded by the final or apocalyptic age of the Spirit. The radical Christian does not desire a return to the Word and person of the historical Jesus. Rather, he looks for a total transformation and rebirth of the Christian Word because the present form of Christianity is demonic and repressive. Altizer points out that, although some Christian thinkers such as Paul, John, Augustine, Luther, and Kierkegaard have effected some degree of transformation, this new transformation is wholly unique. Today's radical Christian finds that the language for a new form of faith is provided by the atheistic Christian revolutionaries of the 19th century.

Revelation, for the radical Christian, is not a closed affair limited to the confines of the canonical bible. Following the prophetic belief that revelation continues in history, the radical Christian inherits the eschatological belief that we are living in the third and final age of the Spirit. He believes that today a new revelation is being disclosed which transcends the earlier revelation of the Old and New Testaments. This new revelation indicates a definitive age of the Spirit. In passing beyond the limits of the canonical bible, this revelation demands a totally new transformation of faith. The radical Christian refuses to bind himself to a now empty and lifeless form of the Word, and therefore he looks for a new and eschatological form of the Christian Word. Altizer notes that the discontinuity between the old and new revelation should not lead one to reject the new form of the Word which is currently appearing, for this new revelation offers the basis for a radically new form of Christian faith.

In the final analysis, then, only two possible alternatives are available for the modern Christian who has discovered that the established form of faith is unreal. He is confronted with the choice of total unbelief or a radically new form of Christian belief founded on the premise of the death of God.

3. The Uniqueness of Christianity

The idea of "religionless" Christianity is being widely discussed today. Dietrich Bonhoeffer's suggestive use of the term has turned it into a currently popular shibboleth. To be meaningful today, it is claimed, Christianity must be relevant and religionless. Altizer is in full sympathy with the prevailing mood which demands that contemporary Christianity should be religionless, and he offers his own reasons why. Studies in comparative religion, he observes, indicate that religion is essentially a dialectical process, a negative, backward-moving process oriented toward a primeval sacrality. The sacred is reached in a religious way by negating the profane and moving backward through history and consciousness until the primordial nature of the sacred is attained. Altizer is persuaded that a comparison between Christianity and the higher forms of non-Christian religion reveals that there is a unique and distinctive difference between Christianity and all other forms of religious belief. This radical difference provides justification for the claim that true Christianity is religionless. Christianity transcends and negates religion.

The Oriental mystic reaches the sacred by way of radical world-negation. In its highest forms, Oriental mysticism transcends the mythical and ritual forms of communal and cultic religion and culminates in an interior epiphany of the primordial totality, symbolically known as Brahman-Atman, Nirvana, Tao, or Sunyata. By means of a complete and total negation of the fallen forms of the world, it reaches the original identity of an unfallen cosmos. Altizer says that, although there are real differences among the Oriental systems and although each system employs different techniques to attain the sacred, nevertheless a certain common denominator is shared by all of them: total redemption is attained by a radical negation of the reality present to the individual and isolated consciousness.

All religions, says Altizer, in some measure share in such a dialectical movement of negation. Christianity, however, differs from the higher forms of Oriental mysticism because its basic thrust is forward, not backward. While Oriental mysticism is essentially a return to a paradisical beginning, authentic Christianity is oriented toward an eschatological end. By reversing ordinary consciousness and history, Oriental mysticism returns to a primordial totality through a process of involution. All forms of Oriental mysticism terminate in an inactive and quiescent totality, a timeless eternity, a nothing, or a void, where the annulment of spatial location and temporal duration results in the epiphany of a pre-cosmic and pre-temporal totality. On the other hand, in the Christian vision of reality we find the prophetic faith of the Old Testament and the primitive faith of Christianity to be forward-moving and oriented toward an eschatological end. But Oriental mysticism is not the only religion which looks backward, since all expressions of religion share this movement of negation. Both Judaism and Christianity have their cultic forms of *anamnesis,* a solemn recalling of a past event. But the radical Christian sees that the basic thrust of authentic Christianity is eschatological and future-oriented.

Insofar as it speaks of the sacred by inverting the meaning of the profane, the language of Oriental mysticism is dialectical. The mystical process consists of a reversal, a negation of immediately present being, culminating in silence and eventually doing away with symbols. Silence seems the most appropriate attitude for man to adopt at this point. The terminal point in this process is an eternal, inactive, quiescent totality. In describing this terminal point, the Oriental mystic talks about "non-being" and "nothingness," categories of thought which are foreign to Western man when used in this context. Western man would be inclined to identify this point with Being itself.

But it should be noted, says Altizer, that this process is not one of simple negation. An initial opposition is posited and then removed. The negation of the profane results in an epiphany, a renewal, a repetition of the totality of the beginning. Dialectically speaking, an absolute negation of the profane is identical with an absolute affirmation of the sacred. There is, therefore, in Oriental mysticism a *coincidentia oppositorum,* a coincidence of the opposites. This *coincidentia* does not signify simply a harmony or a unity. It must ultimately mean a non-dialectical "identity," because the polar or dialectical opposition between the profane and the sacred is abolished by the absolute negation of the profane. Once the sacred returns to its previous form of absolute quiescence, all opposition ceases. Thus, a transcendence of religion, a transcendence of the movement of dialectical negation, is the ultimate goal of the Oriental mystic.

Altizer believes that an understanding of Oriental mysticism offers an insight into the historical forms of Christianity and also provides an indication of the uniqueness of authentic Christianity. He writes:

> Surely it gives us insight into the presence of universal religious forms within the historical body of Christianity: a nostalgia for a lost paradise, a quest for an original innocence, a cultic re-presentation or recollection of a sacred history of the past, a conception of faith as contemporaneity with an ancient or long distant epiphany of Christ, a belief in a primordial God whose very sacrality annuls or negates the existence of the profane, and a longing for an eschatological End that will be a repetition of the primordial Beginning. At all these points and others we find religious forms within Christianity that belie its claim to uniqueness. Assuming that the true center of Christianity nevertheless remains unique, what is the relation of that center to these universal religious forms? Can it fully appear or become truly manifest apart from a negation or transcendence of these forms? The call for a "religionless Christianity" can mean no less than this, nor can it have real meaning apart from a resolution to abandon the whole religious body of Christianity, even if that body should prove to comprehend very nearly everything which Christianity once knew as faith. Above all, a reborn and radical Christian faith must renounce every temptation to return to an original or primordial sacred, or to follow a backward path leading to an earlier and presumably purer form of the Word, or to seek a total silence in which both Word and world will have disappeared.[2]

Religion then knows the sacred as an original, immobile, and impassive reality. The Christian Word, on the other hand, appears neither in a primordial nor an eternal form. The radical Christian confesses an incarnate Word which is real only to the extent that it becomes one with human flesh and identifies itself with the existential human condition. The uniqueness of Christianity centers around its proclamation of the incarnation as a dynamic, active, and forward-moving process, a process in which Spirit becomes entirely immersed in flesh by emptying itself completely. It is an anti-Christian temptation, Altizer contends,

[2] *Ibid.*, pp. 39–40.

to view the Word as an eternal, abstract, non-human, and non-historical form because such an approach is regressive and does not do justice to the forward-moving character of the Christian Word. Thus, the distinctive feature of Christianity is found in the fact that it is fundamentally a witness to an incarnation in which Spirit becomes flesh in such a manner as to continue to exist and to act as flesh. It is only the religious or orthodox form of Christianity which follows the retrograde process of moving backward to a transcendent, sovereign, and impassive God. Radical Christianity completely rejects the idea of God as an eternal and unmoving Being, the conception of God as found in Greek metaphysics and later adopted by orthodox Christianity. Altizer writes:

> Christian theology has never thought through the full meaning of the Incarnation if only because it has remained bound to an eternal and primordial form of the Spirit. When Spirit is apprehended in this religious form, it obviously can never be known as becoming fully incarnate, and thus the Christian doctrine of the Incarnation has thus far only been able to posit a Word that is partially flesh and partially Spirit. Despite the Nicene formula, the Word cannot be fully God and fully man if, on the one hand, it continues to exist in an eternal form and, on the other, it is unable to move into the present and the full reality of history.[3]

Thus radical Christianity follows the forward-moving tendency of the incarnational process precisely because of its religionless thrust. Only in the radical understanding of Christianity does one find the total fulfillment of the incarnate movement. God cannot exist in an eternal form and still move in the full reality of history. A primordial deity who remains completely unaffected by the process of time and history cannot appear in his uniquely Christian form as the kenotic Christ. Thus, the task facing theology today is adequately to formulate a kenotic Christology which acknowledges the incompatibility between the primordial, transcendent Christian God and the revelation of the incarnate Christ. To be meaningful, the incarnation must effect a real change in God himself; it must signify the complete self-annihila-

---

[3] *Ibid.,* pp. 41–42.

tion of God himself. God, if fully incarnate, must cease to exist in his primordial form.

Religion, Altizer maintains, finds its most repressive form in the Christian view of a wholly other, transcendent God. No other religious tradition, he says, has so isolated humanity and deity. Radical Christianity, on the other hand, understands the human reality of history as an epiphany of the Word. The epiphany of the incarnate Word in the concrete history of man and the world gives Christianity its historical character. The radical Christian views the Word as an evolving, forward-moving process, and he looks forward to the eschatological goal of the absolute reversal of flesh and Spirit. Christian theology, says Altizer, has never examined the real meaning of an apocalyptic understanding of *coincidentia oppositorum*. An apocalyptic interpretation does not abolish the opposition between the sacred and the profane by annihilating the reality of the flesh, as is done in Oriental mysticism. In an eschatological understanding of *coincidentia oppositorum,* the sacred and the profane are understood as dialectical opposites whose mutual negation culminates in a metamorphosis of each into its respective other. Each moves dialectically into its own other: Spirit moves kenotically and historically into flesh, and flesh is subsequently transformed into a new and final form of Spirit. Thus, an apocalyptic or an eschatological understanding of *coincidentia oppositorum* differs from that held by Oriental mysticism.

By emphasizing the myth of the fall, religious Christianity resists the forward movement of the incarnate Word. No other religious tradition, Altizer says, puts such an emphasis on a primeval fall. Radical Christianity, however, has consciously and deliberately abandoned the religious quest for an unfallen sacred, repudiating the God who alone is God, and firmly renouncing all attachment to the past. The intrinsic dynamism of authentic Christianity is revealed in the attempt to transcend the universal movement of religion and in the effort to reverse the direction of the religious search for the sacred. The radical Christian confesses a fall, but for him this fall signifies the incarnational introduction of Spirit into the world. It indicates that the Word has died in its original and sacred form and is now manifest only at the center of the radically profane. Historical revelation discloses the sacred as fallen, and therefore religious Christianity errs in fleeing to the primordial God of an unfallen beginning. The radical Christian confesses the actual metamorphosis of the sacred into the profane, a transformation which takes place within the confines of human history. This fall of the sacred is a total and irreversible process.

> To speak of the totality of the Fall is to recognize that no way lies present in history to an unfallen innocence or a primordial Word. Once history has become truly manifest in its fully profane form, both an original paradise and a primordial sacred have been forever lost. Confronted with the advent of a totally profane world, faith has an inevitable temptation to flee the past. Yet radical Christianity points the way to a new epiphany of the Word—a Word that has died in its original and sacred form, and is now manifest only at the center of the radically profane.[4]

The idea of death is closely connected with the concept of a fall. Death, Altizer says, is a universal motif in the history of religions, but only the Christian is invited to participate so fully in the ultimate reality of death and to share in the transfiguration and rebirth of the sacred. Altizer criticizes orthodox Christianity for retreating from the factuality and finality of death. He writes:

> Once again, however, we must note that the historical forms of Christianity have thus far failed to embody the full and radical consequences of the Christian Word. Not only did unchristian ideas of immortality creep into the body of Christianity, but the very religious form of traditional Christianity has foreclosed the possibility of its acceptance of the finality of death. A belief in the resurrection of Jesus in the form of an eternal and primordial God must necessarily annul the reality of his death, either reducing it to a mere transition to a higher state or retrogressively conceiving it as an abolition of his human condition. Unlike the doctrinal expressions of orthodox Christianity, Christian meditation upon the passion of Christ has grasped his death as an ultimate and human event, a concrete but decisive event that has transformed the primordial relation between man and God. Despite its claim of being a

[4] *Ibid.,* pp. 50–51.

historical faith, orthodox Christianity tenaciously clings to the primordial Creator, an eternal and unchanging Lord. Thus it is closed to the presence in Christ's passion of God himself. Trinitarian forms of Christianity have inevitably dissolved the actual and the historical reality of the Crucifixion and the Incarnation, because in identifying Christ with an eternal Word they have eliminated the possibility of either actual death or real movement. Therewith, too, they have retreated from the factuality and finality of death, for death cannot be real in the presence of an eternal and primordial Word.[5]

In order for death to become fully actualized in this world, says Altizer, it must penetrate the realm of the sacred. For an incarnate Word to truly enter the profane, it must not only appear in a fallen form, but it must also pass through the ultimate reality of death, thereby completely emptying itself of its original condition. In the crucifixion, the incarnate Word died in its original form, underlining the kenotic process whereby Spirit became fully flesh. Thus, religious Christianity has erred in understanding the Word as an eternal reality. But today Christians are coming to realize that the incarnation is an actual reality only when it effects the death of the original sacred, the death of God himself. "If God has truly died in our history, then he must be negated by the Word of faith. It is the Christian who must murder God, or, rather, it is the Christian who must bury the decomposing God who continues to haunt our memory of things past."[6]

4. The Kenotic Christ

But why should there be an absolute claim in the name of Jesus? Is Jesus present to man today? In response to such questions, Altizer points out that radical Christian prophets such as Hegel, Blake and Nietzsche claim to have uncovered the real significance of the name of Jesus. These men reject the Jesus of the Christian tradition on the grounds that he is lifeless and alien, a distortion and an inversion of the original Jesus. Jesus, for these

[5] *Ibid.*, pp. 51–52.
[6] Thomas J. J. Altizer, "Word and History," *Radical Theology and the Death of God,* Thomas J. J. Altizer and William Hamilton (Indianapolis, Ind.: Bobbs-Merrill Company, 1966), p. 135.

men, is no mere symbol of a higher man. Rather, he represents a universal process of redemption, a transformation, a kenotic process which remains hidden from the adherents of the traditional interpretation of Jesus. To reach the living Jesus, says Altizer, modern man must transcend all forms of orthodox Christianity. Today's radical Christian, he says, looks to Hegel, Blake, and Nietzsche for inspiration. For Nietzsche, Jesus is the free spirit who abolished religion, thereby making possible the emergence of a new humanity free of guilt and resentment. For Hegel, Jesus represents the kenotic Word, that pure negativity that is the source of all life and movement. For Blake, Jesus represents a universal humanity, and thus he urges men to accept the goal of becoming identical with Jesus. The radical Christian of today, following the lead of these Christian prophets, insists that the real Jesus is fully present and manifest now and refuses to identify Jesus with a particular or isolated person or event of the past. The uniquely Christian Jesus is a contingent, not an eternal Jesus.

Since the ideas of Hegel, Blake, and Nietzsche are central to the vision of radical Christianity, Altizer tries to indicate at length their full significance concerning Jesus of Nazareth. He begins by accepting Nietzsche's new Zarathustra as a radical Christian image of Jesus. As understood by Nietzsche, the original Jesus abolished or reversed religion, thereby annulling the search for a primordial beginning. When viewed from this perspective, Jesus himself cannot appear in a moment of lost time, but must be present in the fullness of time itself as a forward-moving, transfiguring Word. Thus, the radical Christian witnesses to the immediate presence of Jesus, firmly convinced that the only way to the true Jesus is through a total transcendence of the orthodox tradition. By opening himself to the immediate actuality of the moment present before him, the radical Christian gradually comes to know Jesus as being actually present in the fullness of time, even if that time should prove to be a negation or reversal of the past event of Jesus of Nazareth.

At the present time, therefore, the radical Christian devotes all of his energies to a search for the God who *is* Jesus, seeking union with the Word made flesh and rejecting the wholly other God of the Judaeo-Christian tradition, because a transcendent, wholly other, eternal God is isolated and divorced from the world and interests of men. This lifeless and static conception of God reaches its zenith, says Altizer, in the Scholastic conception of God as *actus purus* (pure act), a distant and non-redemptive God who is aseitic, i.e., self-derivative. At the same time that the Scholastic view was being formulated, a contrary vision of God began to appear in the realm of Christian mysticism, a vision based on the individual's experience of God in the innermost depths of the soul where God is believed to generate each individual soul as the eternal Son of God. Thus, the radical Christian mystic came to know himself as the generated Son of God. This idea is conveyed by the use of a term coined by Meister Eckhart, *"istigkeit,"* which is perhaps best translated as *"is-ness."* Within the context of radical Christian mysticism, God's "is-ness" is identical with that of the individual. Altizer notes that this mystical conception of God was suppressed by ecclesiastical authorities, but it continued to exist in an underground way in some quarters, finally reappearing with renewed strength in the thought of Jakob Böhme and his circle of friends. They provided the germinal or seminal source for Hegel's conceptual vision of the incarnate or kenotic movement of God.

Hegel, Altizer says, inverts the Western ontological tradition by reversing the idea of the aseity of Being, conceiving Being as a process of becoming its own other. The center of Hegel's dialectical thinking is the idea of absolute or pure negativity. Within this framework, negativity is the process of self-realization, the self-mediation of Absolute Spirit. Spirit is the kenotic or emptying process of negativity which constitutes the true actuality of the world. In a religious context, the kenotic process of negativity must be interpreted as the self-sacrifice, the self-annihilation of the divine Being. Thus, it is only in Hegel that one finds an idea of God or Spirit or Being which provides a viable formulation of the theological understanding of the incarnation. In Altizer's estimation, Hegel's dialectical system cannot be divorced from its Christian ground.

For Hegel, Spirit alone is the ultimate reality. This contention should not be understood as traditional monistic pantheism, Altizer cautions. According to Hegel's dialectical understanding of

Spirit, Spirit alone is the ultimate reality and yet is fully identical with itself when it exists as the world or "otherness." Thus, Spirit is defined by Hegel in terms of a forward movement of self-negation or self-redemption. This dialectical process can be concisely described in the following manner: Spirit-in-itself (*an sich*) negates itself, thereby becoming Spirit-for-itself (*für sich*); and by the negation of negation, Spirit-for-itself transcends itself and once more becomes Spirit-in-itself; yet this final form of Spirit is far richer and fuller than its initial beginning. Spirit, therefore, can best be defined in Hegelian terms as Being which is in the process of retaining identity with itself in its otherness. While existing in its kenotic form, Spirit can never be known and apprehended as pure Spirit and must instead be known as the opposite of Spirit.

Following this dialectical conceptualization of Spirit, the radical Christian rejects the wholly other, self-sufficient, transcendent, self-enclosed God of the orthodox Christian tradition. He confesses the God who has totally negated himself in becoming flesh, the God who has died in Jesus Christ. In his incarnate epiphany, God is revealed as a self-giving and self-negating Being, as a God who no longer exists in his primordial form. Reversing the primitive orthodox confessional statement, "Jesus is God," the radical Christian proclaims: "God is Jesus." God has ceased to exist in his primordial and transcendent mode, and in totally negating himself by becoming flesh, he presents himself to man under the form of love. Thus, the epiphany of the Word in the form of flesh reveals a truly kenotic movement of God. Altizer writes:

> God *is* Jesus, proclaims the radical Christian, and by this he means that the Incarnation is a total and all-consuming act: as Spirit becomes the Word that empties the Speaker of himself, the whole reality of Spirit becomes incarnate in its opposite. Only the radical Christian witnesses to the full reality of Jesus or the Incarnate Word, because he alone responds to the totally kenotic movement of God. If Spirit truly empties itself in entering the world, then its own essential or original Being must be left behind in an empty and lifeless form. Now, Spirit can exist and be real only in a kenotic or incarnate mode that is the very opposite of its original Being. Hegel

and the radical Christian would teach us that finally Spirit is this eternal movement of absolute negation. Apart from what Hegel called the process of absolute negativity, there lies no way of apprehending the ontological reality of the Incarnation, and unless the Incarnation is known as effecting an absolute negation of the primordial or essential Being of God, there can be no knowledge that God *is* love. A Christian proclamation of the love of God is a proclamation that God has negated himself in becoming flesh, his Word is now the opposite or the intrinsic otherness of his primordial Being, and God himself has ceased to exist in his original mode as transcendent or disincarnate Spirit: God *is* Jesus.[7]

In Altizer's opinion, Blake and Hegel share a common vision of Jesus. For Blake, the incarnate Word is both the source and the substance of life. He firmly believed that Jesus is the body of humanity and that he is somehow present in every human hand and face. When viewed from this perspective, the incarnate Word is not confined to the particular individual, Jesus of Nazareth, and the death of God is not confined to the particular death of Jesus. The epiphany of Jesus, Blake believed, represents the full coming together of God and man. With the appearance of Jesus, humanity is freed from the oppressive presence of the primordial, transcendent, wholly other Being, from the oppressive power of every alien reality. Thus, a new humanity is created by the death of God. Altizer comments:

Once again we see the theological implications of a radical Christian affirmation of the Incarnation: in dying to his primordial and transcendent form, God himself becomes fully incarnate in the "Word" or "Body" of Jesus, and thus he ceases to be present or real as the God who alone is God. Or we could also express this truth of radical faith in Blakean terms by saying that the death of God in Jesus effects a transition from Innocence to Experience: humanity is banished from the original paradise of Eden—which Blake calls *"beulah"*—the timelessness of that paradise is now at best a momentary release from the burden of time, for Innocence is forbidden the Christian who has been initiated by Jesus into the actuality of Experience. We might even say that Jesus is

[7] Thomas J. J. Altizer, *The Gospel of Christian Atheism, op. cit.,* pp. 68–69. Italics in original.

the Christian name of the totality of Experience, a new actuality created by the abolition of the primordial Being, whose death inaugurates a new humanity liberated from all transcendent norms and meaning. But with this new actuality there also comes a terrible darkness resulting from the obliteration of all inherited and established forms of judgment and understanding. So revolutionary was this actuality that it was not until after eighteen centuries that it penetrated the historical body of Christendom, first appearing in an anti-Christian form, and then finally eroding the foundations of the whole Western historical tradition. Yet the very darkness brought on by the historical actualization of the death of God makes possible the movement of the Incarnate Word into the universal body of humanity.[8]

The transcendent realm must be completely emptied and darkened before Jesus can appear as universal humanity. Modern man, Altizer feels, is finally beginning to see the intrinsic meaning and value of a fully actualized process of concrete and historical time, a process which reveals the kenotic transformation of the transcendent God. The God who *is* Jesus is becoming ever more deeply incarnate in the vast body of humanity, losing every vestige of his former appearance and now appearing wherever there is energy and life.

5. Dialectical Theology

In order to survive in the modern world, Altizer maintains, theology must pass through the death of God. Accordingly, today's radical Christian rejects the finality of biblical revelation and seeks contemporary expressions of faith. This new development should be viewed as a chance for rebirth, says Altizer, and not as a capitulation to dissolution, for only by abandoning a religious form of faith and archaic categories of thought can theology reflect the forward motion of the incarnational process. The incarnate Word is embodied in the historical process in such a way as continually to negate its original and earlier forms. In its insistence upon using abstract and formal terms, orthodox theology has betrayed the historical reality of the incarnation. The radical

[8] *Ibid.,* pp. 72–73.

Christian, however, sees that theology can capture the dialectical meaning of the incarnational process only by the adoption of a dialectical mode of thinking. Theological language must undergo a continual transformation if it is to reflect the kenotic metamorphosis understood as the death of God.

Altizer points out that a dialectical way of thinking entered Christian theological thought in Augustine's understanding of nature and grace and in Luther's understanding of law and Gospel. Neither one, however, was able to accept the full implications of the movement of dialectical negation because of a dualism inherent in both their systems. He also points out that the thinking of some contemporary theologians like Paul Tillich and Rudolph Bultmann is not sufficiently dialectical. He comments:

> Yet it is of fundamental importance that neither Bultmann nor Tillich is dialectical enough to rise to an acceptance of Nietzsche's vision of Eternal Recurrence. Both believe that human existence apart from "grace" can only culminate in despair, and thus both have developed a fundamentally hostile attitude toward the modern consciousness. Neither Tillich nor Bultmann will follow Kierkegaard in his negation of Christendom, for both are closed to Nietzsche's proclamation of the death of God. Clinging to the vanishing symbols of a now fallen Christendom, they stand on the "knife-edge" between *Angst* and faith. But it is increasingly apparent that the dialectical theologian is standing on thin air, the cloud is lifting, and now we are beginning to see the illusory nature of a stance that would exist "half-way" in the radical immanence of modern man and "half-way" in the transcendence of Christian faith. Finally, neither Tillich's nor Bultmann's method is fully dialectical. We find here neither the radical faith of Kierkegaard nor the radical doubt of Nietzsche. Yet their methods are partially dialectical, and we may hope that their dialectical methods have saved theology from the temptation of the "positivism of revelation" (Bonhoeffer's words) of the Barth of the *Church Dogmatics*. Indeed, the source of the success of Tillich's and Bultmann's work lies in the dialectical method which they both employ. The time has now come for theology to *deepen* and *extend* that method.[9]

[9] Thomas J. J. Altizer, "Theology and the Death of God," *Radical Theology and the Death of God,* p. 109. Italics in original.

The radical Christian adopts a thoroughly apocalyptic and dialectical way of thinking. As long as the Christian binds himself to the abstract and static cagetories of Western thought, he cannot be open to the dialectical movement of the incarnational process, for a theology that is rooted in the logical laws of identity and contradiction cannot apprehend a forward-moving, self-transfiguring Word. Further, a theology that posits an absolute distinction between God and man is closed to the total presence of the incarnate Word. Thus, rejecting any dualistic mode of thought which posits an ultimate distinction between two realms of reality or meaning, the radical Christian adopts a dialectical manner of thinking in which opposites move dialectically into one another. Within this framework, all separation between God and man is annulled and all opposition between the sacred and the profane is abolished. The radical Christian finds that the Hegelian dialectic provides him with a very useful paradigm for his interpretation of the intrinsic significance of the incarnation.

For Hegel, contradiction or opposition is the root of all movement and life. When viewed against this background, dialectical understanding transcends or negates the logical laws of understanding. Following the fundamental insights of Hegel about the nature of Spirit, the radical Christian sees that a primordial religious diety is the antithesis of life and history and he adopts a dialectical mode of thinking. If theology is to reflect the kenotic and historical metamorphosis of the Word, says Altizer, it has no choice but to adopt a dialectical mode of thought. Any temptation to regression, any temptation to assume a religious form of faith, is the supreme enemy of the Christian faith. The incarnation is a forward-moving process, a kenotic movement wherein the Word moves from God through the historical Jesus to the universal body of humanity. Thus Christian theology must learn to negate every past form of the Word in order to remain open to further manifestations of the Spirit.

Rejecting the eternal and primordial God who remains bound to his initial identity, the radical Christian conceives of God as a forward-moving process of self-negation or self-annihilation. He resolutely refuses to adopt the priestly or religious form of Christianity, with its postulate of a static, eternal, transcendent, autonomous God, because traditional Christianity has failed to understand the real meaning of the self-transformation of God himself.

Christian revelation, says Altizer, is a movement from beginning to end. It is dialectical and apocalyptic, revealing the God who has become fully and totally incarnate in Jesus Christ—a wholly immanent God who progressively becomes real and actualized in history. It is the transcendent, wholly other God of the Old Testament who kenotically reveals himself in Jesus of Nazareth, a God who undergoes a continuous transformation and moves forward by negating present and previous forms. In presenting the radical Christian conception of God, Altizer insistently maintains that one ought to speak of God as a dialectical process rather than as an existing individual Being. The God who acts in the world and in history is revealed as a God who negates himself. One finds a movement from beginning to end, a movement whereby transcendence becomes immanence and Spirit becomes flesh. God becomes the kenotic Christ. The same God who was once real and manifest to man as Creator and Lord became Christ, thereby ceasing to exist in his transcendent mode, ceasing to be the wholly other, autonomous Being of the orthodox Christian tradition.

According to Altizer, Blake saw that the God of deism and the God of orthodoxy are identical, since both conceptions banish the redemptive God from the existential world of men, conceiving him as either the impassive, utterly detached source of cosmic order or as the tyrannical despot of history. Both deism and orthodoxy share a common conception of a distant, remote, and alien God. Religious Christianity has only deepened the chasm between creature and Creator and widened the gulf between Creator and Redeemer. The radical Christian, on the other hand, has found a way to bridge that gulf by understanding God as a self-negating, self-emptying, self-annihilating process—a process in which all opposition eventually ceases and the transcendent realm of Spirit undergoes a complete metamorphosis to become wholly immanent.

The fundamental principle of dialectical theology, says Altizer, is the firm conviction that God is a forward-moving process of kenotic transformation who remains himself even while passing through a movement of absolute self-negation. Non-dialectical expressions of Christianity are unable to comprehend the full reality of God. Regarding such non-dialectical expressions of Christianity, Altizer observes:

> Both natural and revealed theology refuse the full reality of God: the one conceiving a primordial or eternal nature of God that is incapable of either forward movement or redemptive action, and the other positing a sovereign Lord who is infinitely removed from the immediate or historical reality of his creation. Yet, most damning of all, both the dogmatic expressions of revealed theology and the established forms of philosophical theology isolate God from Christ, establishing an unbridgeable chasm between the Creator and the Redeemer, or the primordial and the consequent natures of God, thus finally regressing to pagan or religious forms of Christianity.[10]

Both Blake and Nietzsche saw the God of orthodox Christianity as essentially foreign and alien. The Christian God, for Nietzsche, was the deepest embodiment of man's self-hatred and resentment, a God who was actually an instrument of man's self-torture. He saw the Christian God as infinitely distant and remote, the deification of nothingness, a projection of the absolute polarity posited between God and the world. To Nietzsche, such a God represented the very contradiction of life, and therefore he spoke of him as the God of the sick, a spider, a God who crushes the very life of man, a totally alien, oppressive power annulling the energy and movement of humanity.

Only orthodox Christianity, says Altizer, views God as the *mysterium tremendum et fascinans,* as absolute majesty engendering guilt and dread on the part of man. The radical Christian follows Nietzsche in deliberately rejecting such a God. He also follows Blake in his rejection of the Christian God. Both Blake and Nietzsche understood the chaos lying on the horizon as a nothingness evolving out of the death of God. Modern man is just beginning to realize the full import of the death of God, a realization which brings him a new liberation. Despite the present chaos and darkness, the radical Christian remains confident that new and more

---

[10] Thomas J. J. Altizer, *The Gospel of Christian Atheism, op cit.,* p. 91.

meaningful manifestations of the Spirit will appear in the world.

Ultimately, Blake came to view the Christian God as Satan, arguing that man's redemption can be actualized or realized only after the transcendent and numinous God has undergone a cosmic and historical epiphany as Satan. As Satan, the Christian God represents the ultimate ground of alienation and repression, the derivative source of the bondage of humanity. It was probably in its original Persian expression, Altizer suggests, that apocalyptic religion first evolved a belief in a Satan or an anti-Christ, a cosmic and historical power of evil and nothingness, the polar opposite of a beneficent Creator. Today, the radical Christian follows Blake in proclaiming the liberating message that God is Satan. The "kingdom" announced by Jesus reverses the values and institutions of history, signaling an end to all tyrannical and repressive power and marking the end of the wholly other, transcendent God because Jesus proclaimed the fall of Satan, the source of evil and nothingness. Thus, man is liberated from all previous subordination to an oppressive deity. Altizer writes:

> By coming to know the total presence of God in the Incarnation, Blake and every radical Christian is liberated from the God who is wholly other than man, and likewise liberated from the authority of a heteronomous law and an autonomous Creator. To the spiritual or radical Christian, the very name of Jesus not only symbolizes but also makes actually present the total union of God and man, and for that reason it likewise gives witness to a concrete reversal of history and a dawning apocalyptic transfiguration of the cosmos. The name of Jesus embodies the promise of these final things, while simultaneously calling for a "self-annihilation" that issues in a total identification with our neighbor. Truly to pronounce his name is to give oneself to Jesus as he is manifest in the weak and broken ones about us, and as he is present in the darkness, the anonymity, and the choas of a fallen history. Consequently, Blake reveals that a fully Christian repetition of the name of Jesus annuls those empty spaces separating man from man, and man from God.[11]

[11] Thomas J. J. Altizer, "William Blake and the Role of Myth in the Radical Christian Vision," *Radical Theology and the Death of God,* pp. 181–182.

6. The Death of God

The radical Christian maintains that the traditional Christian conception of God effects a complete reversal of the forward thrust of the divine kenotic process of self-annihilation. Rejecting this distorted image of God, he embraces the full reality of the death of God with all its consequences, even willing the death of God to experience its liberating effects. Symbolically conceived by Blake as self-annihilation and by Hegel as the negation of negation, the death of God provides the basis for the radical Christian vision of God and his relation to the world. Only the radical Christian, Altizer contends, can grasp the full significance of the death of God, since neither the religious believer nor the non-dialectical thinker can fully understand a self-negating God. In analyzing the ultimate meaning of the death of God for men, Altizer concludes:

> To confess the death of God is to speak of an actual and real event, not perhaps an event occurring in a single moment of time or history, but notwithstanding this reservation an event that has actually happened both in a cosmic and in a historical sense. There should be no confusion deriving from the mistaken assumption that such a confession refers to an eclipse of God or a withdrawal of God from either history or the creation. Rather, an authentic language speaking about the death of God must inevitably be speaking about the death of God himself. The radical Christian proclaims that God has actually died in Christ, that this death is both a historical and a cosmic event, and, as such, it is a final and irrevocable event, which cannot be reversed by a subsequent religious or cosmic movement. True, a religious reversal of the death of God has indeed occurred in history, is present in the religious expressions of Christianity, and is now receding into the mist of an archaic, if not soon to be forgotten, past. But such a religious reversal cannot annul the event of the death of God; it cannot recover the living God of the old covenant, nor can it reverse or bring to an end the progressive descent of Spirit into flesh. Religious Christians may know a resurrected Lord of the Ascension, just as they may be bound to an almighty and distant Creator and Judge. Yet such a flight from the finality of the Incarnation cannot dissolve the event of the Incarnation itself even if it must finally impel the Christian to seek the presence and the reality of Christ in a world that is

totally estranged from Christianity's established vision of the sacred.[12]

In delineating his ideas on the death of God, Altizer distinguishes between the original or primal death of God in Christ and the actual or historical realization of the whole movement of human experience. The incarnation and the crucifixion, he says, ought to be viewed as primary expressions of a forward-moving and eschatological process which eventually terminates in the total self-annihilation of the primordial, transcendent deity. For the Oriental mystic, the sacred totality completely annihilates or transfigures the profane. For the radical Christian mystic, on the other hand, the incarnational process manifests the descent of the sacred into the profane. God dies to the extent that he becomes immersed in the world. He actualizes himself by negating his original and previous expressions, and no part of his Being is immune to this dialectical process of self-annihilation.

Having become aware of the true nature of this divine transformation, the radical Christian repudiates the classical and orthodox forms of Christian faith. Because of his present historical conditioning, he views the New Testament and early Christianity as alien forms of belief. He finds that history has revealed a God totally different from the one frozen in the orthodox tradition. Traditional Christianity fails to reflect the forward motion of the incarnational process, a transformation understood today as the death of God. In the final analysis, the radical Christian understands the kingdom of God to mean the final consummation of the dynamic process by which the transcendent becomes immanent. In this context, Altizer observes that neither Paul nor the early Church was able to overcome bondage to a transcendent and primordial God.

The radical Christian turns away from orthodox Christianity and refuses to look for an historical Christ because he views such a search as a religious tendency toward regression. Instead, he adopts an apocalyptic and dialectical mode of thought which provides him with an understanding of the inner significance of the death of God and with a vision of its ultimate meaning for humanity. Today's Christian Gospel announces the Good News of

[12] Thomas J. J. Altizer, *The Gospel of Christian Atheism, op. cit.,* p. 103.

the death of God. Such a proclamation, far from casting man into the empty abyss of darkness and despair, liberates man from all restrictive forces, ultimately pointing to a final union of God and man. The spiritual emptiness of the present era underlines the actuality of the death of God. But instead of fearing the darkness caused by the death of God, the radical Christian joyfully proclaims it because it signals man's complete liberation.

The original death of God in Christ inaugurated the kenotic movement of God into the whole body of humanity. It is a final and irrevocable event. The incarnational process is an irreversible transformation. The metamorphosis of the Word into flesh is continuous and forward-moving, a process which is gradually and progressively realized in the evolution of human history. Actually, by its progressive banishment of the dead body of God to an ever more transcendent and inaccessible realm, Altizer observes that traditional Christianity helped to prepare the way for a more comprehensive historical realization of the death of God, for in the course of its development it has evolved the most alien, most remote, and most oppressive deity in the history of man. In the final analysis, the Christian God gradually recedes into an empty and vacuous nothingness. But now that the transcendent, autonomous, oppressive deity has annihilated itself, Altizer continues, modern man can no longer evade the fact and the responsibility of an autonomous human condition. No longer can he atavistically cling to an original innocence or nostalgically yearn for a pre-incarnate Spirit. Furthermore, the radical Christian realizes, by his own participation in the forward movement of the body of Christ, the ultimate victory of the self-negation of the Spirit. Every man today is aware of the absence of God, but only the radical Christian knows that God is dead and not simply withdrawn, absent, eclipsed, or hidden. Since he lives in the incarnate body of Christ, he does not fear the darkness caused by the death of God because he is consciously aware of his own participation in it.

According to Altizer's radical Christian vision, therefore, the religious understanding of deity culminates in a transcendent beyond, while the rational and non-dialectical apprehension of the deity results in an impassive, unmoving, and self-enclosed God. Only the radical, profane, and fully dialectical apprehension of deity terminates in a meaningful conception of a self-annihilating God.

Orthodox Christianity has always associated two ideas with the theological centrality of the death of Christ: the doctrine of atonement and the doctrine of the forgiveness of sin. The radical Christian, of course, completely rejects the traditional interpretation of these doctrines, but in his own apprehension of the inner meaning of the Christian message he discovers a new and deeper significance relating these ideas to the death of God in Christ. He finds that God is not only the author and the agent of atonement and reconciliation, but the subject as well, for once God has died in Christ, his transcendent epiphany of absolute sovereignty recedes into a completely alien form which is eventually seen as the ultimate matrix of all repression. In other words, God is seen as Satan, for the kenotic movement of the incarnational process reveals a God who empties himself of his original power and glory and gradually becomes manifest as an oppressive and alien nothingness. The whole movement is essentially an atoning process, since this appearance of God as Satan weakens the power of evil. This epiphany of God under the form of Satan also highlights the regression inherent in any religious attempt to return to the emptiness of the primordial sacrality of God.

The incarnation and the crucifixion, Altizer points out, should not be viewed as forms of a simple negation, but rather as forms of dialectical negation, as a negation of a negation, as the self-annihilation of the ultimate source of evil. In this process, transcendence is transformed into immanence, thereby abolishing the ground of every alien other. But if the victory over alienation and estrangement is to be more than illusory, the very root of alienation must be destroyed. The reversal effected by this kenotic process must be extended to every alien sphere before atonement can be consummated. The original sacrality of God was reversed in the crucifixion of Jesus of Nazareth, but the movement of atonement will not be completed until this self-negated sacrality has entered into the full range of human experience.

Before this atonement is consummated, Satan must become totally present and undergo a kenotic transformation in the eschatological epiphany of Christ. God is annihilated under the form of Satan. Altizer writes:

> So long as Christianity knows the Crucifixion as a vicarious sacrifice for a totally guilty humanity, as the innocent sacrifice of the eternal Son of God to a just but merciful Father, it can never celebrate the definitive victory of the Crucifixion; for such a redeemed humanity remains in bondage to the transcendent Judge, and must continue to be submissive to his distant and alien authority, ever pleading for mercy when it falls away from his absolute command. If the Crucifixion does not express and embody a decisive self-transformation of God, then at most it can only give a guilty humanity a temporary respite from the sovereign power of the transcendent Creator, while at worst it can seal a fallen humanity in its abject state of powerlessness and self-abasement, totally repressing every tendency to movement and life. The radical Christian, who is in quest of a total redemption, must repudiate every religious promise resting upon a perpetuation of man's fallen state, and recognize in the orthodox image of the crucified Christ an image of the victory of that Satan who would bind man to a broken and shrunken condition. Not until the Christian recognizes the Crucifixion as enacting and embodying the self-negation of the sovereign and transcendent Creator can he celebrate an atonement which is the source of the abolition of all confinement and repression.[13]

Altizer claims that Hegel's philosophical method complements Blake's poetic vision of the atoning death of God in Christ. Radical Christianity, as understood by Hegel, interprets the atoning death of God in Christ as the manifestation of the transition of Spirit from its alienated epiphany as transcendent Being to its final appearance as incarnate Spirit. Furthermore, Altizer says, the radical Christian sees that the present darkness caused by the death of God must be transformed into light. Understanding the advent of total darkness as the reign of the anti-Christ, he views this chaos as the darkness before the dawn, confident that the darkness will eventually be transfigured into light. Against this background, therefore, he adopts the imagery of the descent into hell as being most symbolic of the essential message of Christianity, rejecting the traditional imagery of the resurrection and the ascension. Christ represents

---

[13] *Ibid.*, pp. 116–117.

the God who descends ever more fully into darkness and flesh, a God whose final appearance in man's history is in a totally alien and lifeless form. The radical Christian sees that the transcendent matrix of evil and nothingness is abolished by the epiphany of the anti-Christ. This epiphany is redemptive, because in unveiling the full reality of repression and alienation it prepares the way for their ultimate and eventual reversal. Thus, today's Christian is called upon to accept the anti-Christ, the totality of the dead body of God, as a final kenotic epiphany of Christ.

Traditional Christianity has always connected the death of Christ and the concept of atonement with the notion of the forgiveness of sin. But the radical Christian finds that orthodox Christianity has not reached a proper understanding of the forgiveness of sin. Its conception of sin has been based, for the most part, either on a postulated natural and universal moral law or on the absolute duality of creature and Creator, thereby separating sin from grace. But he joins the greatest reformers of the Christian faith, Altizer observes, in discovering that the forgiveness of sin must culminate in the abolition of the very memory of sin. All traces of sin must be permanently obliterated. He supports his claim by appealing to such scriptural passages as Jer. 31: 31-34 in the Old Testament and 2 Cor. 3: 12-18 in the New Testament. This complete abolition of sin is effected by the kenotic and redemptive movement of the Godhead.

Along with Kierkegaard, the radical Christian sees sin as being opposed to faith and not to virtue. Within the framework of radical theology, sin is understood as a state of solitude and guilt as the product of self-alienation. This alienation is cosmic as well as individual. Viewed from this perspective, man is seen as being sealed within the isolation of his own selfhood and requiring a total and cosmic regeneration. In this context, the forgiveness of sin is understood as a cosmic process of "self-annihilation," a universal and apocalyptic process of redemption. The self-annihilation of God effects the forgiveness of sin by bringing about the complete reversal of all solitary selfhood, by inaugurating a union of God and man in which both transcendence and solitary selfhood are abolished. Altizer follows Blake in asserting that, once man is delivered from his selfhood, once his solitary and autonomous ego is abolished, good and evil cease to be. Furthermore, once God has ceased to exist as the omnipotent and numinous Lord, all transcendent moral imperatives cease and humanity is freed from obedience to an eternal authority.

In its fallen state, selfhood isolates man from man and man from God. With the death of God in Jesus, however, the transcendent source of guilt and alienation is annihilated, thus bringing about an apocalyptic and total union of God and man. A new *coincidentia oppositorum* is reached. Transcendence becomes immanence, and solitary selfhood is dissolved into a new totality of "Love." In Blakean terms, one finds an ecstatic union of Satan (God) and Jerusalem (the liberty of man) as Albion (universal but fallen humanity) experiences the final epiphany of Jesus. Regarding Blake's radical Christian vision, Altizer comments:

> Blake was the first of the great modern seers. Through Blake we can sense the theological significance of a poetic reversal of our mythical traditions, and become open to the possibility that the uniquely modern metamorphosis of the sacred into the profane is the culmination of a redemptive and kenotic movement of the Godhead. The Blake who proclaimed that God must eternally die for man, that a primordial Totality must pass through "Self-Annihilation," was the Blake who envisioned a uniquely contemporary Christ, a Christ whc becomes Antichrist before he is resurrected as Jerusalem.[14]

7. The Element of Risk

Because the radical Christian believes in a present and a contemporary Christ, he launches a violent attack on the traditional conception of God, convinced that the Church has betrayed the present kenotic Christ by reversing the forward thrust of the incarnation. As interpreted by radical theology, the original heresy within the Church was the identification of the Church with the body of Christ, for by positing this identity the Church created a chasm between Christ and a very large segment of humanity. The Christian Church, Altizer contends, has sought to bring the world

[14] Thomas J. J. Altizer, "William Blake and the Role of Myth in the Radical Christian Vision," *loc. cit.*, p. 191.

into submission to the inhuman authority and power of an infinitely remote Creator, Lord, and Judge. The Church's conception of Christ is a reversal of the incarnate Christ because it betrays the present and kenotic reality of Christ. Radical Christian theology, on the other hand, indicates the path to a fully incarnate Christ, a Christ who epitomizes the kenotic metamorphosis of the Godhead, a Christ who is present and operative in the contemporary world. Radical Christian theology repudiates the traditional conception of Christ as sovereign and transcendent Lord because such a conception cannot express the present reality of Christ in the world. Recognizing the antithesis between the primordial and transcendent reality of God, on the one hand, and the immediate and kenotic reality of Christ, on the other, the radical Christian resolutely puts his faith in the kenotic epiphany of Christ. He is firmly convinced that the finality of the incarnation prohibits any attempt to return to a primordial, transcendent, wholly other God.

Further, if theology is to reflect the inner dynamism of the incarnational process, it must transcend archaic and outmoded expressions of faith. It must continually negate all previous forms of expression, precisely because the incarnational process itself is a forward movement of continual negation and self-annihilation —a metamorphosis which has now become manifest in every human hand and face. The contemporary Christian, Altizer observes, must therefore accept and even will the death of God, since a persistent belief in a transcendent realm blinds one to the present kenotic reality of Christ. Altizer admits that the bible, the Church, its liturgies, its creeds, and its confessions may very well embody an epiphany of Christ, but such an epiphany, he argues, is utterly foreign to contemporary man.

The exigencies of the present situation demand a new form of faith, and any form of faith involves the element of risk if it is to be authentic faith. Both the orthodox and the radical Christian risk something, Altizer says, in their different faith commitments. The orthodox Christian wagers that Christ is the same yesterday, today, and tomorrow, and that there is one single epiphany of Jesus. In making such a wager, he faces the loss of a Christ who is now present in his full actuality. The radical Christian, on the other hand, makes the opposite wager, trusting in a totally incarnate Christ whose immanent presence in the contemporary world negates all previous epiphanies. Both make their choice with full awareness of the ultimate risk involved in such a decision.

> Either risks losing both the true reality of Christ and all that life evolving from the presence of Christ. Both are genuine expressions of faith because each enacts a genuine wager, and they are united in repudiating any form of faith that does not demand an ultimate wager. The radical Christian who chooses a fully contemporary Christ not only must be willing to abandon the Christ of our Christian past but he must accept the fact that no clear path lies present to the Christ whom he has chosen, and no final authority exists to direct him upon his quest. Moreover, the Christian who wagers upon a totally incarnate Christ must negate every form and image of transcendence, regardless of that area of consciousness or experience in which it may appear. Thus he must forswear every transcendent ground of judgment, and be banished from every hope in a transcendent life or power. He has chosen a darkness issuing from the death of every image and symbol of transcendence, and he must bet that the darkness of his destiny is the present form and actuality of a totally incarnate body of Christ.[15]

Altizer observes that the Church can no longer speak to man about hell and damnation because today's Christian is liberated from fear of damnation through his faith in Christ. For the radical Christian, guilt is the consequence of a retreat from life. Altizer notes that Nietzsche and Kierkegaard both concur in identifying existence as guilt. Since human consciousness and experience are grounded in repression, guilt is to be understood as a conscious realization of the fallen condition of humanity. This sense of guilt is actualized in the individual when he reaches an awareness of his own bondage to repression. Because man can only bear so much reality, he therefore tries to escape his painful situation by reversing or denying the actuality of existence. Altizer refers to this refusal to accept the reality of human existence as resentment. As understood by Nietzsche, resentment is fundamentally a rebellion against the brute reality of human existence, a form of non-dialectical negation, a form of No-saying which rebels against

[15] Thomas J. J. Altizer, *The Gospel of Christian Atheism, op. cit.*, pp. 138–139.

life itself—a rebellion arising from the inability or the refusal to accept the harsh actuality of human existence. Resentment is therefore an evasion of the human condition. It hardens guilt and confines human existence to ever-narrowing spheres, terminating ultimately in a passive submission to the brokenness of the human condition. It indicates an adamant refusal of every promise of forgiveness.

To the extent that a repressed and guilty humanity is conscious of its guilt, it must submit to the alien authority of an imperative, an opposing other. The Christian message, however, is a proclamation of the forgiveness of sin, an announcement of the release of the sinner from the bondage of law and judgment. Insofar as the Christian exists in faith, he is freed from the bondage of the law. Faith alone uncovers the true nature and meaning of human guilt and repression. Nietzsche's understanding of sin and guilt, Altizer asserts, is not unique. It reflects a long tradition of a radical Christian interpretation of sin, a tradition rooted in Paul and found in Augustine, Luther, Pascal, Kierkegaard, and Dostoevsky.

A man judges others by imposing a moral judgment on them only when he exists in a state of alienation and guilt. To the extent that he himself is forgiven, however, he becomes incapable of judging others. As a Christian, he knows that he has been forgiven and that he must refrain from judging others. By virtue of his life in Christ, the Christian is liberated from the alien power of a moral imperative, and he becomes aware of a moral imperative only insofar as he is estranged from Christ.

The radical Christian wagers that God is dead, believing that, with the death of God in Christ, the ultimate ground of guilt and resentment was dissolved, thus freeing man from every terror of the transcendent beyond. Such a wager certainly entails an ultimate risk. Altizer writes:

The contemporary Christian who bets that God is dead must do so with a full realization that he may very well be embracing a life-destroying nihilism; or, worse yet, he may simply be submitting to the darker currents of our history, passively allowing himself to be the victim of an all too human horror. No honest contemporary seeker can ever lose sight of the very real possibility that the willing of the death of God is the way to madness, dehumanization, and even to the most totalitarian form of society yet realized in history. Who can doubt that a real passage through the death of God must issue in either an abolition of man or in the birth of a new and transfigured humanity? [16]

Whether he likes it or not, says Altizer, today's Christian is forced to make a choice between traditional Christianity and a radically new form of contemporary faith. Modern man, he contends, must come to realize that his only hope for the future lies in acceptance and affirmation of the radical immanence of the contemporary world. He must learn to realize that all forms of No-saying which take refuge from the radically profane by positing an ultimate transcendent ground of reality only lead to the further enslavement of man to the tyranny of the transcendent. What is most needed today is a new dialectical form of Yes-saying, a strong affirmation of absolute immanence. By discovering a new way to the sacred through the labyrinth of profane darkness, the radical Christian prophets have uncovered a new form of Yes-saying. By employing non-Christian and even anti-Christian symbols and motifs, and by inverting the sacred langue of the mystics, these radical Christian prophets offer man a new vision of reality, a vision which enables man to understand pain and darkness as necessary consequences of the death of God.

Altizer feels that Nietzsche's vision of eternal recurrence graphically describes the thinking and experience of modern man in face of the onslaught of the radically profane. This vision is actually a corollary of his proclamation of the death of God. It is not intended to convey a metaphysical or a cosmological idea but is rather a symbol of the deepest affirmation of existence. Having jettisoned every fixed source of meaning and value, Nietzsche gradually came to the realization that the very foundations of Western history had collapsed. He saw the dissolution of all previous forms and structures within that history. With the disappearance of the very center and direction of that historical process, there emerges a new chaos of nothingness and meaninglessness. But it is only by passing through such chaos, he argues, that man is able to discover new forms and structures. By consciously reversing the forms of inherited consciousness and experience, man

[16] *Ibid.*, p. 146.

opens himself to the possibilities of a new freedom and a new life.

The two world epochs of history are symbolically described by Nietzsche in terms of Zarathustra. The Persian Zarathustra, he believed, created a moral and religious vision which later became the foundation of Western history. To describe the new world epoch, Nietzsche created a new Zarathustra whose prophetic vision embodies the final disintegration of Western history. For Nietzsche, all things eternally recur. The world has fallen away from its center, and all that remains now is a perpetual and meaningless flux, without beginning or end, without purpose or direction. Sheer chaos now prevails. Against this background, the new Zarathustra offers a new form of Yes-saying for man, a new form of faith which enables man to embrace and affirm a radically profane nothingness because it provides an insight into the kenotic movement known as the death of God. With the death of God in Christ, all forms of oppression and transcendence were abolished, and man is now confronted with a new and absolute immanence which appears as the final kenotic transformation of Spirit into flesh. The new Zarathustra provides a means of accepting and affirming the radical immanence of the contemporary world. With the death of God in Christ, man was liberated from all forms of No-saying and presented with the opportunity for participating in the forward movement of the incarnational process. Altizer writes:

> We must observe that Eternal Recurrence is a dialectical inversion of the biblical category of the Kingdom of God. Jesus' proclamation of the Kingdom of God makes incarnate a transcendent Wholly Other, a Wholly Other that radically reverses the believer's existence in both the being and the values of the Old Aeon of history and makes possible even now a participation in the New Aeon of grace. So likewise the "existential" truth of Eternal Recurrence shatters the power of the old order of history, transforming transcendence into immanence, and thereby making eternity incarnate in every Now. Eternal Recurrence is the dialectical antithesis of the Christian God. The Creature becomes the Creator when the Center is everywhere. Hence Zarathustra, the proclaimer of Eternal Recurrence, is the first "immoralist," and his proclamation is a product of the "second innocence" of atheism. The atheistic Nietzsche was the enemy of God and Christ. But Nietzsche was a dialectical thinker. His opposition to Christ was directed against the Christ of Christianity,

against religion itself, rather than against the actual figure of Jesus. Again and again, in *The Antichrist,* Nietzsche portrays Jesus as a kind of naive forerunner of Zarathustra. For Jesus is incapable of resentment (non-dialectical negation), is liberated from "history," and is himself the exact opposite of Christianity.[17]

In the final analysis, Altizer feels that the radical Christian insights offered by Hegel, Blake, and Nietzsche provide modern man with a new form of contemporary faith. Freed from all tyrannical bondage to the transcendent, humanity is now free to explore the myriad possibilities of absolute immanence. Against this background, the radical Christian rejects every temptation to seek the sacred by trying to reach a primordial sacrality. Instead, he strongly affirms the radical immanence of the contemporary world, confessing a fully incarnate, totally profane, and forward-moving Christ.

8. An Evaluation

Thomas J. J. Altizer's God is a process deity who has annihilated himself in a truly kenotic way so that man might be liberated from all oppressive servitude. Only the Christian can speak of the death of God as a joyous and liberating event, because he alone participates in the death of God. He confesses a wholly immanent and totally incarnate Word, a fully kenotic Word that is currently operative in the world of men. To be truly meaningful, says Altizer, the incarnation must effect a change in God himself, resulting in the complete self-annihilation of God. With the death of God in Christ, the ultimate and transcendent source of all human repression and alienation has been completely abolished. The result is that man is now free to pursue full human integrity, maturity, and autonomy within the framework of a wholly radical immanence, in union with a totally immanent God who is now present in every human hand and face.

Unlike Oriental mysticism and orthodox Christianity, authentic or radical Christianity moves forward toward an eschatological end

---

[17] Thomas J. J. Altizer, "Theology and the Death of God," *loc. cit.,* p. 99.

and the final epiphany of Spirit in this world, rather than backward toward a primordial beginning that is static and eternal. In presenting his version of Christian atheism, Altizer claims to have discovered the true significance of such authentically Christian concepts as the incarnation, atonement, redemption, the forgiveness of sin, and so forth, and he attempts to convey this radical Christian vision in philosophical, mystical, and poetic terms. According to his analysis of the present religious crisis facing man, one is compelled to choose between a complete and final rejection of Christianity and an acceptance of the tenets of radical Christianity, between total unbelief and Christian atheism.

Is Altizer's evaluation of the present situation accurate? Is man currently faced with the two alternatives that he proposes? Who is this God who has died in Jesus Christ, annihilating himself so that the chasm between God and man might disappear? In what sense is Jesus the incarnate Word of God? Does authentic Christian faith demand an attack upon God? Has the history of man unfolded a new and discontinuous revelation of God as Satan? Is the sacred to be reached only through a strong affirmation of the profane? Did God have to die so that a new humanity might emerge?

Altizer takes great care to describe very carefully the God who has died in the collapse of the transcendental world view. It is the eternal, wholly other, transcendent, self-sufficient, self-derivative, immutable, omnipotent, and absolute God of the Judaeo-Christian tradition. The static, immobile, aseitic, impassive, transcendent source of human alienation and repression had to be abolished in order for a new humanity to emerge. God had to die, to annihilate himself completely, in order that man might fully live. With the appearance of Christ, one finds a wholly kenotic epiphany of Spirit in a totally profane form under the aspect of love, a completely profane manifestation of the God who is now present in every human hand and face, having traversed the abyss that separated man and God.

The Hegelian conception of the negation of Absolute Spirit provides Altizer with a philosophical framework within which to delineate his ideas concerning the death of God. The mystical poetry of Blake provides him with an insight into the full significance of this event for man. But despite his extended treatment of this theme, it is very difficult at times to determine with any degree of certainty whether he is referring to a person or to a process when speaking of the event of the death of God. If he is referring to a person, then it would seem that the very notion of an eternal, immutable, aseitic, and absolute God would preclude any possibility of deterioration or death; if he is referring to a process or a principle, then it would appear to be a superfluous and unnecessary projection. Secular humanism is fully capable of presenting a concise, logically consistent, and fully coherent view of the world without finding it necessary to superimpose a type of process-deity on the evolutionary transformation of man and the world.

Altizer's dialectical and mystical understanding of God and man exhibits certain pantheistic overtones. He bases his interpretation of God on mystical and dialectical criteria, bypassing the traditional norms of religious truth. His vision of Christianity is not rooted or grounded in the apostolic account of the teaching of Jesus or in the corporate faith of the believing Christian community, but rather in the philosophical and mystical insights of Hegel, Blake, and Nietzsche. Thus questions immediately arise: Who is the most qualified interpreter of the true meaning of Christianity? Who is the ultimate judge of religious truth? What are the criteria of religious orthodoxy?

During the present religious crisis, Altizer suggests that the modern Christian follow the path chosen by radical Christian theology and adopt a thoroughly mystical and dialectical approach to belief. Recognizing fully the ultimate risk involved in such a choice, he urges the Christian of today to accept the vision of the new Zarathustra, while confessing a wholly immanent God who has annihilated himself for the sake of man. The modern Christian, he suggests, should adopt a form of "religionless" Christianity, resolutely rejecting any attempt to move backward in search of a primordial beginning, since authentic Christianity transcends religion and repudiates the retrograde motion of orthodox religious belief. But in describing orthodox Christianity as a regressive movement toward a primordial beginning and radical Christianity as a progressive movement toward an eschatological end, Altizer is guilty of gross exaggeration and oversimplification because he completely neglects the eschatological aspect of orthodox Christianity. His rejection of the traditional Christian interpretation of the incarnation is somewhat hasty and uncritical. In his effort to present a Jesus who is currently operative in the world of men, he overlooks the fact that orthodox Christianity also confesses a Jesus who is operative here and now in the world of men, a Jesus who will eventually appear as the apocalyptic Son of Man.

Furthermore, there is a blurring of the Christological focus in Altizer's vision of radical Christianity which weakens the Christian foundations of his atheism. Altizer is consistent in maintaining that, according to a dialectical understanding of Spirit, all previous manifestations of the sacred must be continually negated, including that epiphany found in Jesus of Nazareth. However, this insistence upon continual negation tends to destroy the historical grounding of the Christian perspective. The historical anchor of the orthodox Christian perspective is not found in Altizer's Christian atheism. The radical Christian, he says, should not look backward to the historical Jesus, but should attempt to find Jesus in the world about him. As a result of this insistence, the Jesus presented by Altizer becomes a very elusive and ambiguous figure. This aspect of Altizer's version of Christian atheism, therefore, only serves to reinforce the judgment that modern secular man finds unqualified secular humanism far more satisfying, intellectually speaking, than the hybrid proposal of Christian atheism. Altizer's presentation of Christian atheism is attractive from a poetic and mystical point of view, but it is fundamentally a compromise. His perspective is not radical enough. If the orthodox Christian view is false, then the only viable alternative is secular humanism.

Thus, in the final analysis, the two alternatives proposed by Altizer appear to be the wrong ones. The option now facing the modern Christian is not the choice between total unbelief and radical Christianity; rather, the ultimate choice is between orthodox Christianity and secular humanism. Altizer's ingenious union of pantheism, radical humanism, and a mystical form of Christology remains essentially unconvincing both to the believing orthodox Christian and the contemporary secular humanist. The hybrid proposal of Christian atheism is not a viable mode of belief for modern man, religious or secular.

V
EPILOGUE

Aristotle noted that all men have a natural desire to know. Man is engaged in a never-ending search for truth, and modern man is no exception. Today, amid the tension and the crisis and the uncertainty of the modern world, reflective individuals are making a concerted effort to fathom the ultimate meaning of human existence, thereby continuing man's perennial search for truth and meaningful answers. Closely allied to the root problem of man and the meaning of human existence is the problem of God. During the present era of confusion, questioning, and doubt, contemporary man, like all his predecessors, is groping for a satisfactory answer to the problem of God.

Analysis reveals that there are presently two rather clearly defined foci—atheistic or secular humanism and Christian theism—both claiming to offer a final solution to the problem of God. The current American phenomenon of Christian atheism is reductively an attempt to find a suitable *via media* between these two fundamental alternatives. The proposal of Christian atheism on the part of some radical Christian theologians represents a serious but ultimately unsuccessful attempt to present a viable mode of Christian belief for the secular man of the 20th century. In the final analysis, the hybrid proposal of Christian atheism is essentially unsatisfactory both to the secular humanist and the Christian theist, for the secular humanist finds this kind of synthetic proposal superfluous and anachronistic, while the orthodox Christian believer finds it completely untenable. The committed secular humanist might respect the example and ideals of Jesus of Nazareth; yet he would find no compelling reason to adopt a Christocentric humanism. There are many *contemporary* models available for the secular humanist in his effort to structure his humanism. From the Christian perspective, the ultimate choice facing the modern believer is not the choice between orthodox and radical Christianity, but the more basic and ultimate choice between secular humanism and Christian theism.

While it is completely unacceptable to the believing Christian theist, the current formulation of Christian atheism serves the useful function of forcing the reflective Christian to refine and clarify his religious thinking. He must re-examine such cardinal issues as the nature of God, the nature and destiny of man, the role of the kenotic Christ in the salvation of man, and the nature of authentic religious belief. The ideas expressed by men like Hamilton, van Buren, and Altizer call attention to some of the major problems which confront today's Christian theologian, problems centering around such issues as the conceptualization of God, the secularization of Christianity, Christology, theological predication and so forth.

The Christian is aware of his inability to conceptualize God and to verbalize his beliefs about God's nature in a wholly adequate manner. Human language about God is extremely weak and deficient, but it is the only means available to man, and therefore he must make use of it to the best of his ability. Of necessity, man's conceptualization of God is anthropomorphic in character, but this does not mean that man's idea of God is simply an anthropocentric projection. The serious Christian thinker is conscious of the fact that the reality of God cannot be circumscribed by limited human concepts. While it is true that man's understanding of God is to a very great extent culturally determined, the reality of God is independent of the cultural framework within which it is grasped. The Christian God remains wholly other. Realizing this, the Christian must constantly strive to abandon all false conceptions of God, all pseudo-gods, and all idolatrous and shallow surrogates for God.

Ultimately, all authentic concepts of God must be based upon the religious experience of God, both personal and corporate. The Christian believer is more than just a theist. He is a particular kind of theist. He believes in the God revealed in Jesus of Nazareth. For the orthodox Christian, this revelation is the ultimate criterion for determining what constitutes an authentic concept of God. Because he is a reasoning human being, the Christian must strive to attain a balanced integration of faith and reason, avoiding the extremes of fideism and rationalism. While it is true that there can be no strict equivalence between the reality of God and man's concept of God, man can still acquire an analogous knowledge of God, a knowledge which is admittedly deficient but nonetheless real. The creative tension occasioned by polarized forces of belief and unbelief provides an opportunity for the modern Christian to refine his thinking on the nature of analogous reasoning and analogous predication. Because of its concreteness and its immediate relevance, the current death-of-God controversy compels the orthodox Christian to think through his ideas about the precise relationship of faith and reason. It forces him, for example, to reconsider such important questions as the ability of the human intellect to reach a trans-empirical reality through logical inference, and the knowability of God in contemporary terms.

Radical theology in general, and the death-of-God movement in particular, offers a challenge to orthodox Christianity because it calls attention to the increasing demand for a new theological formulation of the role and function of true secularity in the authentic religious commitment of man. Since modern Western man now lives in an urbanized, industrial, and technological society, the basic truths of the Judaeo-Christian revelation regarding the sphere of man's involvement with the world around him must be reformulated within the framework of the thought forms of modern man. The perennial task facing the theologian is the need to interpret the reality of God in contemporary terms. Modern man is asking: What does it mean to be a Christian in the 20th century? What does it mean to be a Christian in the secular city? The Christian theologian of today must therefore attempt to show the nature of man's religious commitment to God within the context of the secular city, within the context of the city of man, since true secularity is an essential component both of authentic human existence and authentic Christian belief. Christian theology must address itself to the needs and aspirations, the hopes and desires of modern man. Its formulations must be relevant to the present human situation.

Relevance has become a shibboleth in current discussion of religious questions. The truth of Christianity, it is asserted, must be
made relevant, meaningful, and wholly contemporary. While it is
certainly true that Christianity must be relevant and meaningful
within the context of man's present situation, yet the excessive demand for relevance has made relevance an end in itself. The result
is that pragmatic truth has sometimes replaced religious truth.

Besides provoking serious thought about problems like the conceptualization of God and the secularization of Christianity, the
death-of-God controversy also compels the orthodox theologian to
delineate a modern Christology, a Christology which makes the
incarnation particularly meaningful for contemporary man. From
the orthodox Christian perspective, the weakest features of the
death-of-God proposal are the Christological considerations which
underlie this strange amalgam. Although the death-of-God advocates are correct in trying to find a concrete and presently active
Christ operative in the world and affairs of man, they err seriously
in their neglect of the centrality of the resurrection in the early
Christian kerygma. Hamilton and Altizer neglect the issue entirely,
while van Buren circumvents the difficulty by speaking simply of
the "Easter event." Yet the truth or falsity of the Christian claim
rests squarely on the question of the resurrection. As St. Paul says:

If Christ has not been raised, your faith is futile and you
are still in your sins. Then those who have fallen asleep in
Christ have perished. If for this life only we have hoped
in Christ, we are of all men the most to be pitied. (1 Cor.
15: 16-19)

A further challenge to orthodox Christianity on the part of the
death-of-God movement is found on the level of theological predication and verification. The Christian theologian must examine
carefully the structure and method of theological thought, and he
must think through the relationship between philosophy and theology. He must distinguish carefully between the reality of God
and man's finite attempt to comprehend that reality. Van Buren's
analysis of the question of theological predication provides an indication of the magnitude and complexity of the problem facing

the Christian theologian, particularly when the theologian is dealing with non-empirical realities.

Modern man has gradually arrived at a more profound awareness and appreciation of the social or functional aspect of language. Human language about God is always anthropomorphic,
provisional, and culturally determined. Even the manner in which
man grasps the reality of God is culturally determined to a great
degree. Yet the Judaeo-Christian religious consciousness understands God as a reality which ultimately transcends all cultural de-
terminations. Only an approximation of the reality of God can be
grasped and expressed in language which follows culturally determined patterns. Man's knowledge of God is indirect, symbolic, and
analogous. The death-of-God theologians err in denying all symbolic and analogous knowledge of God.

In summary, therefore, it can be said that the death-of-God controversy provides a serious Christian thinker with an opportunity
for refinement and clarification in his own religious thought. In itself, however, Christian atheism does not afford a viable mode of
belief for either the secular humanist or the Christian theist. From
the viewpoint of secular humanism, the proposal asserts too much,
and from the perspective of orthodox Christianity it says far too
little. In the final analysis, the hybrid proposal of Christian atheism remains essentially unconvincing both to the Christian and the
atheist.

BASIC BIBLIOGRAPHY

Altizer, Thomas J. J. *Oriental Mysticism and Biblical Eschatology*. Philadelphia: The Westminster Press, 1961.

_____ *Mircea Eliade and the Dialectic of the Sacred*. Philadelphia: The Westminster Press, 1963.

_____ *The Gospel of Christian Atheism*. Philadelphia: The Westminster Press, 1966.

_____ and William Hamilton. *Radical Theology and the Death of God*. Indianapolis, Ind.: Bobbs-Merrill Company, 1966.

_____ "Theology and the Death of God," *The Centennial Review*, VIII (Spring, 1964), pp. 129-146.

_____ "Creative Negation in Theology," *Christian Century* (July 7, 1965), pp. 864-867.

_____ "Word and History," *Theology Today* 22 (October, 1965), pp. 380-394.

_____ "William Blake and the Role of Myth in the Radical Christian Vision," *The Centennial Review* 9 (Fall, 1965).

Hamilton, William. *The Christian Man*. Philadelphia: The Westminster Press, 1961.

_____ *The New Essence of Christianity*. New York: Association Press, 1961.

_____ and Altizer. *Radical Theology and the Death of God*. Indianapolis, Ind.: Bobbs-Merrill Company, 1966.

_____ "Banished from the Land of Unity," *Journal of Religion* 39 (October, 1959), pp. 245-262.

_____ "Thursday's Child: The Theologian Today and Tomorrow," *Theology Today* 20 (January, 1964), pp. 487-495.

_____ "Dietrich Bonhoeffer," *Nation*, April 19, 1965.

————— "The Death of God Theology," *Christian Scholar* 48 (Spring, 1965), pp. 27-48.

————— "The Shape of a Radical Theology," *Christian Century* 82 (October 6, 1965), pp. 1219-1222.

————— "Radicalism and the Death of God," *Christianity and Crisis* 25 (December 13, 1965)

————— "The Death of God," *Playboy* 13 (August, 1966)

Vahanian, Gabriel. *The Death of God*. New York: George Braziller, 1961.

————— *Wait without Idols*. New York: George Braziller, 1964.

————— *No Other God*. New York: George Braziller, 1966.

————— "The Lost Iconoclasm of Christianity," *The Nation* 192 (April 22, 1961), pp. 354-357.

————— "Beyond the Death of God," *Dialog* 1 (Autumn, 1962), pp. 18-21.

————— "The Future of Christianity in a Post-Christian Era," *The Centennial Review* 8 (Spring, 1964), pp. 160-173.

————— "Swallowed Up by Godlessness," *Christian Century* 82 (December 8, 1965), pp. 1505-1507.

Van Buren, Paul. *The Secular Meaning of the Gospel*. New York: Macmillan, 1963.

————— "Linguistic Analysis in Christian Education," *Religious Education* 60 (Jan.-Feb., 1965).

————— "Theology in the Context of Culture," *Christian Century* 82 (April 7, 1965), pp. 428-430.

————— "The Dissolution of the Absolute," *Religion in Life* 34 (Summer, 1965), pp. 335-342.

INDEX